The Light & the Rod

Volume 1

Why Biblical Governance Works

If you purchased this book without a cover you should be aware that this book is stolen property. It was reported as "unsold and destroyed" to the publisher and neither the author nor the publisher has received any payment for this "stripped book."

The Light & the Rod, Volume 1

Copyright © 2020 Dan Wolf. All rights reserved, including the right to reproduce this book or portions thereof, in any form. No part of this text may be reproduced, transmitted, downloaded, decompiled, reverse engineered, or stored in or introduced into any information storage and retrieval system in any form or by any means, whether electronic or mechanical without the express written permission of the author. The scanning, uploading, and distribution of this book via the Internet or via any other means is illegal and punishable by law. Please purchase only authorized electronic editions and do not participate in or encourage electronic piracy of copyrighted materials.

Printed by Kindle Direct Publishing

Other books by the author:
Collectivism and Charity
A War for God
A Handbook of Natural Rights

Visit the author website:
http://www.livingrightly.net

Other articles by the author can be found at:
http://www.vachristian.org

ISBN: 978-0-9987567-8-3 (eBook)
ISBN: 978-0-9987567-6-9 (Paperback)

Version: 2019.11.28

Table of Contents

Introduction	i
Chapter 1 – Tribal (State) Religions	1
Chapter 2 – The Need for Virtue	23
Chapter 3 – Reason and Faith	49
Chapter 4 – The Two Cities	87
Chapter 5 – The Scholastic Master	141
Chapter 6 – The Biblical Principles Model	193
Appendix A – Timeline of Events and Persons	211
Notes	213

The Light & the Rod

Volume 1

Introduction

The Light & the Rod is an update of *Do You Want to Be Free*, first written about seven years ago. This revision expands on previous topics, reorganizes material, and adds new content that presents a fuller picture of the main concepts and their implications. Based on the discourse we hear from the media, politicians, and academics today, these volumes are needed more than ever to present an honest discussion of our choices rather than relying on others to tell us what to think. Instead, let us think for ourselves.

The Light & the Rod examines the two threads of thought Man has used to govern himself since the beginning of recorded history. These threads result in two distinct, contradictory, and incompatible governance models. One model is based upon God's principles for how to live, the other upon pagan principles centered on Man. These models have profound implications for our rights, freedom, justice, virtue, morality, and how order is brought about within society. The choice could not be more stark or important.

Volume 1 uses the writings of five men to build the case for each model: Plato, Aristotle, Clement of Alexandria, Augustine, and Thomas Aquinas. Those wanting an overview need only read Chapters 1, 2, and 6. Volume 2 traces the presence of these two models through history, starting with the Roman Empire's fall. It leverages the changes in ideas presented by writers such as Machiavelli, Spinoza, Hobbes, Locke, and Rousseau. It also looks at a few of the most significant relevant documents written during this same period. All this serves to express Man's thoughts for how he should govern himself. Finally, two pagan responses to a *Biblical Principles* model are developed, one based upon ideas underlying the French Revolution and the second based on Islam's tenets.

I think we would find general agreement that whatever governance form we choose, it should support Man fulfilling his purpose. Some of the connections between the present work and previous books by the author is outlined below, providing background for why this material is relevant to the task at hand.

From a Biblical perspective, our actions are to order society. The end result of those actions is charity—voluntarily supporting the common good. A model of charity is developed using some of Clement's, Augustine's, and Thomas's writings in *Collectivism and Charity: The Great Deception*. The ideas underlying pagan and biblical charity are compared, and the writings of Jonathan Edwards and John Locke used to develop both approaches.

We see there are actually two types of charity, one based upon ideas centered on God and the other on Man. As a people, we've largely forgotten the difference. While many do good works today, they fail to do *powerful* works because they've forgotten what charity really is. The result is many do not benefit from what they receive as charity. In fact, more often they become dependent and thus enslaved. Man's charity leads to dependence. God's charity provides the opportunity to develop independence, and therein lies the difference.

A Handbook of Natural Rights examines at a high level the rights we've received from God. These rights are inherent in our equal nature. We all share them, and they cannot be taken away by Man. However, we can refuse to accept them through the choices we make. This book outlines the differences between natural and human rights; negative and positive ones; and rights and laws. These differences are critical. It also presents the case for why accepting natural rights comes with corresponding moral duties. Nothing is free, although it may be freely given.

We possess natural rights in the areas of *being*, *action*, and *dominion*. These rights are supported by scripture. Scripture brings out in more detail each right as well as its corresponding duty. This matters because our natural rights are almost exclusively negative: They inform us about what we are *not* to do. The rest is up to us. The implications from this one simple idea are far-reaching within society. Without understanding this basic idea, it is unlikely any society will be successful for long.

The final two books examine different Judeo-Christian covenant corruptions. *A War for God* examines Islam from a Christian perspective. It lets Islam speak for itself by using original source documents where possible. There are many good books already out there on the subject, but most focus on only one or two areas. *A War for God* is more comprehensive and reviews Islam from the perspectives of its documents and their development, Mohammad's life, doctrine development, concepts, history, attitudes, and beliefs. Where appropriate, subject areas are compared with their Christian counterparts.

Coexist examines the interfaith movement. It specifically uses some local interfaith events to show how this movement's original intent has been corrupted, primarily because it was founded upon Man's ideas rather than God's.

As in all my work, the only answers worth finding are the ones you arrive at yourself. I do not want to lead you one way or the other. I simply try to present you with the facts, using original source documents wherever possible. I believe the choices are very clear, but it is up each one of us to make them. It is both our right and our duty, and we are each accountable for our choices in the end. But making good choices requires knowledge—education—and today we are no longer taught what is important to truly succeed. Once we have knowledge, we have an obligation to act. These are the *knowing* and *doing* Christ spoke of in the Gospels.

It takes the effort of each one of us. The material isn't the easiest to understand, but nothing ever truly worthwhile is easy. Are you up for the challenge?

I pray whatever your choice, your journey is a good and fulfilling one.

Chapter 1
Tribal (State) Religions

I have a proposition for you. We will see that all forms of governance break down into one of four models based on ideas and principles. The first two models are developed in this volume, and the final two in the next. We will also see those final two are simply variations of the first one presented in this volume. Underlying all four models are two different and incompatible sets of ideas.

Ideas matter. They determine what alternatives we consider. Those alternatives shape and influence our actions. Those actions determine our character—they shape who we choose to become. *But it all begins with ideas*. This first chapter develops support for a model based on state religion societies. These are the societies we all studied in our history classes: for example, Egypt, Assyria, Babylonia, Greece, and Rome, as well as others such as the Aztecs, Mayans, and Incas. This model serves as a baseline for the rest of the discussion.

We'll begin by defining some terms used throughout our discussion in order to develop an initial shared understanding. This matters today as some ideologies exercise a type of word pollution: the meanings of words are corrupted in order to achieve specific goals. This corruption is necessary because, as we will see later, the promoted ideas are always the same and have always failed, so each time these ideas are presented they need to be repackaged in order to be resold.

Next we will look at religion and governance development within these societies, finding they are much more alike than different. We'll also go into the philosophy they each developed, but don't worry. It won't be very deep—just enough to draw out some important ideas on which these societies were built. We will see the promoted ideas influence some of society's most fundamental aspects. Every society's specific views of rights, virtue, justice, law, and freedom are all derived from these basic ideas.

There is a second matter to keep in mind, particularly in the second volume. The models developed there take the state religion societies to be Man's baseline, his beginning. They ignore the biblical view of where Man began. As such, they have problems explaining some of Man's most basic abilities, such as language.

We are each free to make our own decisions, but we should make them in the full light of facts and understanding. All I request is you consider what is presented and ask yourself what is true. Discerning the true from the false is integral to achieving our purpose. It only comes about by wrestling with problems and cases that stretch our minds and develop our abilities.

Definitions

Democracy
A true democracy would entail each citizen having a vote on each and every issue a society wants to address. This is not feasible except in relatively small geographic areas, like the Greek city-states. We often refer to our American government as a democracy, but, in fact, it is a representative republic. Citizens within a republic elect representatives, granting them the right to take certain actions on their behalf while barring them from taking other actions. These arrangements are generally defined within a social contract such as a constitution. When using the term *democracy* in this book, we will be referring to the type of government just described and existing within the United States.

Freedom
Freedom means many things to many people. In this book, we will use a definition provided by M. Stanton Evans: Freedom "means the absence of coercion—to the extent that this is feasible in organized society. It means that ability of human beings to act in voluntary fashion, rather than being pushed around and forced to do things."[1]

This definition has the advantage of saying that people can decide things for themselves, without saying what those things are. We can therefore evaluate freedom itself, separate from other things. There is an important caveat to this definition. The freedom to act on one's own behalf cannot infringe upon another's freedom. Freedom without moral direction becomes a license to do whatever one wants and becomes simply power. Equal liberty (see below) for all citizens must exist in order to prevent an individual or group, whether minority or majority, from becoming repressive.

Preventing an individual or group from using coercion against others requires a mechanism ensuring equal liberty is maintained. This mechanism is government, and it primarily exists to protect freedom and rights. Checks and balances are applied against government within a self-governing society to prevent it from becoming oppressive. A social contract between the governed and government is normally used to state the terms for governing, with the governed determining the rights and powers to be granted to, or barred from, the government. Within a self-governing society, power originates from the people, and some portion is delegated to the government. *There is separation between power and its sovereign exercise. This is a fundamental difference between biblical principle societies and all others.*

Liberty
In this book, liberty will refer to the freedom from oppression, tyranny, or domination by a government. In short, it is political independence.

Rights
In this book, rights refer to specific capabilities, which are derived from just or moral principles. Virtue is moral righteousness. All rights are grounded in virtue—they are righteous. Of particular importance in this discussion is the virtue of justice. Justice is simply each person receiving what they are due based upon their actions. It is about accountability. There is a close relationship between virtues, rights, freedom, and justice that we will explore later.[2]

Providence
For a definition of providence, we will look to Thomas Aquinas (Thomas) who said,

> We have to declare that God has providence. He creates every goodness in things.... This good order existing in created things is itself part of God's creation. Since he is the cause of things through his mind, and, as we have already made clear, the idea of each and every effect must pre-exist in him, the divine mind must preconceive the whole pattern of things moving to their end. This exemplar of things ordained to their purpose is exactly what Providence is.[3]

When providence is referred to in this book, it will mean our creator's providence unless otherwise noted.

Religion

Two definitions for religion will be used. Definition 1 is provided by Rodney Stark, and is consistent with the *State Religion Society* model: "Religion consists of explanations of existence (or ultimate meaning) based on supernatural assumptions and including statements about the nature of the supernatural, which may specify methods or procedures for exchanging with the supernatural."[4] Further, the supernatural is defined as "somewhat mysterious forces or entities that are above, beyond, or outside nature and which can control, suspend, alter, or ignore natural order."[5]

Definition 1 has several advantages. First it allows for the inclusion of godless religions such as Buddhism and some other Eastern religions, as well as some tribal religions, which only recognize a divine essence. Second, it allows for religion based on more than one god defined as "supernatural beings having consciousness and intentions."[6] Third, it separates religion from magic as magic is an effort to "manipulate the supernatural to obtain desired outcomes, without reference to a god or gods and without general statements about existence or ultimate meaning."[7]

Definition 2 comes from a dictionary, according to which religion is a set of beliefs held by Man concerning some supreme deity, nature, being, essence, or will. I am going to make one small change to this definition: *Religion concerns the relationship between Man and some supreme deity, nature, being, essence, or will.* This definition forms the basis for a *Biblical Principles* model in Chapter 6.

Definition 2 has at least two advantages. First, it excludes all of the godless and tribal religions included in the first definition. Second, the definition differs in its creation story. Within state religions, creation often comes down to one of two stories: Either two gods fight one another, one is killed, and from that act the land, seas, heavens, etc. are formed, or a creator god and a female counterpart together make the rest of creation. *These are stories of transformation because creation alone is viewed as eternal and the gods a part of creation.* The monotheistic religions of Judaism, Christianity, and Islam view creation as God creating something out of nothing—that is, ex nihilo. *Only God is eternal; God created and is separate from nature.*

Definition 2 also makes a clear distinction between religion and ideology.

Ideology
Religion according to the second definition above is about a relationship that begins with Man and extends into the heavens. It is between God and Man. Ideology is complementary. It concerns how Man orders interactions with his fellow human beings, particularly how he chooses to govern himself. It is earthbound. Religion and ideology are not the same. This difference will become more important in building the final two models as both attempt to substitute ideology for religion.

Theology
Theology is usually defined as the study of religion or the synthesis between religion and philosophy. We will use a more specific definition for theology within in this book, again provided by Stark:

> Theology involves formal reasoning about God. The emphasis is on discovering God's nature, intentions, and demands, and on understanding how these define the relationship between human beings and God. The gods of polytheism cannot sustain theology because they are far too inconsequential. Theology necessitates an image of God as a conscious, rational, supernatural being of unlimited power and scope who cares about humans and imposes moral codes and responsibilities upon them, thereby generating serious intellectual questions.[8]

This definition is also consistent with Definition 2 for religion. Philosophy is more closely related to ideology and Definition 1.

Finally, Eastern religions either have a single, remote, impersonal, supernatural essence lacking consciousness, or many small gods. While one can contemplate on such a divine essence, it is not reasonable to ask the "big questions" as this essence is either not rational or lacks consciousness. In short, these divine essences are not gods by our definition. Christianity, Islam, and Judaism are the only religions which developed theology according to the above definition as they all center on a single, conscious, all-powerful God.

A list of relevant intellectual questions considered in this book is developed at the end of Chapter 2.

The Assumption
There is only one beginning assumption used in this book: There is a God, and He is the creator of everything that has ever been created. Otherwise, there would be absolutely no purpose in writing it. We will get into the effects of excluding God as the beginning point for existence later. But for now, let it suffice there is no logical basis on which to build if Man is his own beginning point. Indeed, as we will see shortly, the evidence would instead suggest it is more likely we all began having some knowledge about our creator and over time fell away from that knowledge.

There are a few conventions followed when using the word *god* throughout this book. First, when referring to the creator god of the three monotheistic religions (Judaism, Christianity, and Islam), we will use the word God with a capital *G*. When referring to any other god(s), we will use the word *god* with a lowercase *g*. This usage is consistent with the definitions of religion and theology just laid out. Generally, when talking from a theological perspective, the term *Creator* will be used. This will allow for a broader discussion of who God is, what He created, whether a relationship exists between Creator and created, and, if so, its nature. However, there will be an exception: Direct quotes will use the terms, as well as the original spelling and punctuation, as they are found within those texts.

Later, we will use the term *Allah* when reviewing Islamic tenets while using *God* elsewhere. There are some significant differences between Islam and Judeo-Christian principles. Those differences affect some of the questions posed within this book, so using the two terms will help clarify which set of beliefs is being discussed.

Tribal Religions
This book's purpose is to, as best we can, trace the evolution and state of religion up to the development of Judeo-Christian values, values chosen by America's Founders as the basis for our governance. The information we have on tribal religions is, at best, very fragmented and incomplete. In addition, much of the tribal religion literature assumes that gods are created by Man and focus on various human conditions that might have caused them to be created. Therefore, they are either very limited or of no use for this work. Finally, an objective look at the evidence demonstrates that much of this literature is incorrect.

However, there are some exceptions and excellent field studies from the last several centuries from which some knowledge can be obtained. Stark, in his book *Discovering God,* provides an overview of this prior work and proposes a theory relevant to the topic at hand. The following content is summarized from his book.[9] While I could have rebuilt the wheel by also going to the sources he cites, there is no reason to do that. Additional readings are included at the end of this chapter for those interested in exploring this topic further. Stark's book also contains an extensive bibliography citing additional resources.

Most of the early tribal religion literature was derived from ethnographic sources and focused on the attributes of various tribal religions. They focused on the *what* about religion and not *why* it existed in the first place.

Much of these writings were based upon conjecture, generally taking one of two forms. According to the first, cultural diffusion was a greater driver of human progress than individual innovation, and certain cultures were more isolated and therefore unable to keep pace with the rest of humanity. Using this conjecture, a case is made for surviving primitive cultures being an adequate representation of the past.

According to the second, humans until recently lacked sufficient intelligence or consciousness to be able to entertain notions such as religion. This conjecture is based upon (1) the slow rate of progress and change in culture during Man's early years and (2) biology, but appears to present some inconsistencies. Consider that the gap today between our modern and archaic cultures is as great as the gap between these same modern cultures and those of the Neanderthals. While the Homo sapiens of today differ biologically from yesterday's Neanderthals, that is no longer relevant today. The biological difference has disappeared, but the cultural difference remains.

There are two points upon which there is consensus within this ethnographic literature. First, religion is a universal attribute of human culture. Second, primitive religions were very crude. We will see that this second point is not always true. Culture may be primitive, but its religion does not necessarily have to be primitive. However, both of these points still address the *what* about religion and not *why* it exists at all.

Using the cultural conjectures above, Stark applies a basic economic argument to culture: New elements are generally adopted and integrated if humans evaluate the new element as useful. He posits that "Humans will tend to adopt and retain those elements of culture that appear to produce 'better' results, while those elements of culture that appear to be less rewarding will tend to be discarded."[10]

Therefore, if humans have religion, they must derive some benefit from it. What does Man finds useful? Much of the literature attributes the existence of religion to primitive humans' fear of nature. However, Paul Radin's ethnographic literature study concluded primitive people are "afraid of one thing, of the uncertainties of the struggle of life ... of the battle for existence under the difficult conditions that prevail in primitive societies."[11] In short, they take direct action to address the things they can control. They turn to the supernatural for things they cannot control such as rain for crops, success in hunting, victory over an enemy, and the like. In doing this, they acknowledge "the supernatural is the only plausible source of many things that human beings desire."[12]

If human culture adopts gods, then one would expect those gods provide something useful over the supernatural. It was noted above that religion is a universal attribute of human culture —and gods do exist in many primitive cultures. The supernatural consists of those things outside of Man's ability to control, comprehend, and understand. As noted earlier, divine essences are not gods; they are merely supernatural. Gods are "supernatural beings having consciousness and intentions. When given the choice, humans prefer Gods."[13] If true, cultures must prefer the rational and conscious over the irrational and unconscious.

If humans prefer gods, then what type of gods do they seek? According to Stark, "Humans will tend to adopt and retain images of God(s) that appear to provide greater satisfactions, both subjective and material."[14] He proposes a hierarchy from lower to higher preferences in gods should exist as follows:

1. Human images of a god or gods will tend to progress from those having smaller to those having greater scope (high gods).
2. These high gods tend toward "a conception of god(s) of infinite scope and absolute power."
3. Finally, people will prefer "a conception of a god as a loving, conscious, rational being of unlimited scope, who created and rules over the entire universe."[15]

Why Does Religion Exist?
So back to *why* does religion exist? From the above, religion and the concept of a high god or gods provide a means to ask great existential questions that Man is unable to answer by himself—which can explain existence and ultimate meaning—questions such as "Why are we here?" "What can we hope for?" "Can we hope?" and "Is death the end?" Man is unable to answer such questions on his own. Religion is found almost everywhere because we all share the same basic existential questions.

Much of the ethnographic literature derived a consensus that groups in the earliest stages of cultural development had no gods and belief "in a moral Supreme Being is a very late result of evolution."[16] In short, gods were created and evolved over time as culture evolved. This is consistent with the notion that gods were created by Man.

However, Andrew Lang in the late 1800s performed a thorough review of the most reliable ethnographic accounts of religion in surviving primitive societies. In his book *Myth, Ritual, and Religion*, he turned existing wisdom on its head when he wrote that primitive groups, scattered in different parts of the world, believed in the existence of high gods who are "moral, all-seeing, directors of things and of men ... eternal beings who made the world, and watch over morality."[17] Further, since they were so prevalent among the primitive tribes, he asserted religions with high gods must represent the earliest form of religion and other forms such as naturism, animism, etc. represent a devolving of religion within primitive societies. This was not monotheism, but an early form of polytheism.

Lang was initially discredited, but eventually after his death his research findings were vindicated. Radin wrote of Lang's work that he "has been abundantly corroborated.... That many primitive peoples have a belief in a Supreme Creator no one today seriously denies."[18] Another finding from this later literature is that there are two types of high gods. One type is an active, concerned high god and the other an inactive, withdrawn high god.

The Jesuit scholar Wilhelm Schmidt took Lang's arguments to their ultimate conclusion. The Bible states that we are all descended from Noah's sons after the flood. Schmidt declared that the existence of high gods in so many primitive tribes indicated that "The Supreme Being of the primitive culture is really the God of monotheism." Further, the similarities in religions around the world were evidence of a "universal revelation" that occurred in the earliest of times, and the variations actually represented the insertion of human inventions into religion. From this he demonstrated how the earlier ethnographic literature supported the Bible's account of creation and Man's fall within the book of Genesis.

A Test

To test these ideas, Stark took a data set consisting of 563 past and present cultures. One of the variables in this study looked at whether a high god existed and if so whether it was active or inactive. From the original data set, 136 cultures were removed due to incomplete information. Another 127 cultures were excluded because they did not qualify as being primitive. These included the Romans, Greeks, Egyptians, and Hebrews, among others. There were three developmental stages within the remaining primitive cultures: (1) nomadic groups, (2) slash-and-burn agriculture groups, and (3) gathering groups.

If Lang and Radin's positions were correct, then the data should reflect a higher percentage of high gods within the nomadic groups with a greater number of active high gods in that group. The gatherer groups should reflect a greater number of cultures without a high god, and those with a high god should have relatively more inactive high gods. The results of his analysis are presented in the table below.

Believe in:	Nomadic	Agriculture	Gatherers
An active high god	42%	23%	16%
An inactive high god	22%	44%	27%
No high god	36%	33%	57%
	100%	100%	100%
Number of Cases	36	144	120

These results support the ideas expressed by Lang, Radin, and Stark, among others. So if cultures devolved from ones generally having high gods to ones having no high gods, why did this occur? Also, what form(s) of religion replaced those containing high gods? These are the next section's topics.

State Religions

The results indicate the focus on high gods decreases as cultures increase in complexity. Where high gods are present, they are viewed as withdrawn or replaced by many gods smaller in scope and stature. But this appears to contradict the hierarchy presented in the previous section of belief in which there is evolution from many smaller gods to one all-powerful creator god. Lang provided a resolution for this apparent contradiction. His studies indicate "People are more comfortable with Gods who are less awe-inspiring and human, less demanding and more permissive: Gods who are easily propitiated with sacrifices."[19] People found it useful to have gods more like them and less demanding, reflecting human faults that could be appealed to by ritual. After all, if true, then what reason exists for Man to change except in ways he desires rather than what God asks?

More emphasis was placed on idols and less on the creator gods over time. Stark states that there was "something very reassuring and attractive about very tangible, very 'human' Gods; in contrast, monotheism is a very demanding discipline, difficult to achieve and hard to sustain."[20] Denis Baly adds,

> Belief in only one God does not, it would seem, come easily to the human mind, for it is attended by serious intellectual problems, notably the problem of evil, and one of the most marked characteristics of a monotheistic God is his tendency to retreat into the distance, and there to be completely lost to sight.[21]

Temple Gods

The new gods were normally conceived of as ordinary human beings. They were usually immortal. They had some supernatural powers, but also many human desires. They were more like us. Initially there were large numbers of gods, but the numbers would decrease over time. They at times resided within idols, which were considered to be living beings.

Another change in culture occurred when moving from nomadic to agriculture and gathering groups: They became larger communities that were better able to support themselves economically. As the number of people within a culture grew larger, specialization developed. As Stark puts it, "As groups become larger and their culture more complex, specialization appears, and seemingly the first two specialties involve leadership and religion, eventuating in the appearance of full-time rulers and priests."[22] This could take several forms. The ruler and priest could be one and the same person, or in some cases the ruler could be a god. At times, these two roles were filled by different people who often were blood relatives. The interesting point here is "that there usually is not separation of church and state. Rather ... most ancient civilizations had state 'churches.'"[23]

The Temples and Priests

State churches are not the church institutions we know today. Worship occurred in a temple not generally open to the public. A temple was served by priests who in turn served clients. Clients did not belong to the temple; they simply went to the temple. There was no community, no sense of congregation within a temple. Priests were the intermediaries between their clients and the temple god. Each god generally had its own temple. These were not competing faiths. The gods were all part of a single cosmology. In this respect, they were more like parishes within a particular denomination.

The priesthood itself was exclusive and the position often hereditary. Priests themselves often came from a culture's wealthy families. Their role was serving an idol by conducting rituals. These rituals were often complex events spanning multiple days. It was thought that by performing the correct ritual the god could be brought from his cosmic dwelling place into the idol and a request or appeal could be made. There were rituals for feeding, bathing, clothing, and repairing the idols, in addition to many others. These rituals were shrouded with mystery, creating a heavy investment by the priests in their knowledge. All that mattered was performing them correctly. There was therefore no room for innovation in religion. Innovation was synonymous with error. Little incentive for change existed within these state religions.

Rituals
Many of these rituals required providing large amounts of livestock, foodstuffs, or wealth to the priests. As already noted, the priests' clients were often very wealthy. But this was not a temple's only source of wealth. Temples were normally subsidized by the state, often being granted large herds and flocks. Finally, lands around a temple were normally divided. About a third went to commoners who used those properties for their own existence, about a third was rented to the more affluent, and the remaining third was set aside for the temple god. Commoners were often required to provide a certain number of work days each year for the benefit of the land set aside for the god. The production from this land also supported a temple and its priests.

Early cultures often buried their dead beneath their houses. It was thought the dead were still present in family life. The same was true for temple gods. A temple site was chosen by its god, and each locality had its own patron god. These temples were often on an acropolis that normally contained both the temple and palace, thereby solidifying a state–church relationship. As a temple site was considered consecrated, a temple was not moved. Instead when a temple needed to be replaced, the old temple was leveled and a new one built on the same site. As a result, temple sites grew to be higher and higher over time.

Rulers

Early culture rulers did not necessarily consider themselves divine. Instead, a ruler was chosen by the gods, and they aided the ruler. In early Samaria, for example, rule was considered a gift to humans given by the gods. A text from their early history confirms this:

> They [the Gods] had not yet set up a king for the beclouded people
> No headband and crown had been fastened ...
> No scepter had been studded with lapis lazuli ...
> [Then] kingship descended from heaven.[24]

They were mortals chosen by the gods to carry a divine burden. Later rulers increasingly came to assert they were divine themselves, as demonstrated by the monumental burial structures they had built for themselves.

Commoners

Commoners were considered to be the subjects of the god and ruler. There was a sense of collective morality within these cultures. Deviation by individuals or groups from the collective moral code brought disaster on the entire community. The priests performed rituals to avert disaster from occurring.

What Do We Know?

So how do we know about these early state religions? Some cultures have left us with extensive writings on their history and their culture. We know a great deal about Samaria from the clay tablets and monuments this civilization left behind. Egypt also left a fair amount of information from its monuments. We know a great deal about the Aztecs and Mayans from their temples and buildings. We know less about the religions of Greece and Rome where much of that information was put on mediums which did not survive.

What we do know paints a consistent picture. This is not as surprising in the area around the Mediterranean Sea. Through cultural diffusion, one would expect the spread of similar religious concepts from Samaria to Egypt, Israel, Greece, and Rome.

However, many of the gods of Egypt and Greece cannot be traced back to Samaria. In addition, cultural diffusion cannot be used to explain similarities between the Mediterranean region and the Aztec, Mayan, and American Indian cultures.

So what are some of these similarities? They include the existence of a high god removed from daily life, who, with a female counterpart, created all of the other gods. This god was called An in Samaria, Ra (Re) in Egypt, Cronus in Greece, Ometechuhtli by the Aztecs, and Hunab Ku by the Mayans. An afterlife was a part of the religions of these same cultures, though the Aztecs and Mayans viewed the departed as becoming deified or grafted onto the celestial divine substance. Common "myths" were told, like the story of the great flood in the Bible. Similar myths exist not only in Samaria and the Aztec culture, but also within the *Epic of Gilgamesh*, as well as the tales of the Maori of New Zealand and the North American Indians. This story also has the same moral: Even if everyone sins, we have a personal moral responsibility to god for our own choices. This moral is very similar to the parables told by Jesus in the New Testament.

Other commonalities include the concept of a cycle of creation and destruction. Blood sacrifice was required to avert this destruction. In some cultures, this sacrifice was provided by livestock; however, the Aztec culture required human sacrifices—a variation accounted for by this culture's narrative around the creation of the fifth world and the gods born of their creator god. Finally, other similarities include the existence of a professional class of priests performing these rites; the priest's role within culture; the relationship between religious and political power; the temple and palace's positioning; and the nature, number, and type of gods themselves.

Some Greek Philosophical Truths
Consistent with these state religion societies, Greek philosophers generally viewed the universe as being uncreated and eternal. Further, history was an endless series of cycles of progress and decay. As such, knowledge was not new, just endlessly repeated. Aristotle wrote in *On the Heavens* that "the same ideas ... recur in men's minds not once or twice but again and again."[25] He reiterated this point in his *Politics*, saying that everything has "been invented several times over in the course of ages, or rather times without

number."[26] Parmenides believed the perception of change was only an illusion, that the universe was already in a static state of perfection and it was "uncreated and indestructible; for it is complete, immovable, and without end."[27] In addition, Greek philosophers generally believed the heavenly bodies were in fact living things. These bodies acted by their own will, a view consistent with the various state religion gods discussed earlier.

Aristotle and Plato both professed to believe many things today we would not believe to be true. The following passages from Aristotle's *Politics* outline some of his views on governance and the relationship between the people and their leader. Similar passages can be found in Plato's writings.

> When a whole family, or some individual happens to be so pre-eminent in excellence (virtue) as to surpass all others, then it is just that they should be the royal family and supreme over all, or that this one citizen should be the king ... the only alternative is that he should have the supreme power; and that mankind should obey him, not in turn, but always.[28]

Further, "that some should rule and others be ruled is not only necessary, but expedient; from the hour of their birth, some are marked out for subjection, others for rule."[29] Differences in Man's nature exist. This notion provides the basis for different classes and their role within state religion societies.

"It is clear ... that some men are by nature free, and other slaves, and that for these latter slavery is both expedient and right."[30] "The art of war is a natural art of acquisition ... an art we should practice against wild beasts, and against men who, though intended by nature to be governed, will not submit; for war of such a kind is naturally just."[31] "We cannot consider all those to be citizens who are necessary to the existence of the state.... The best form of state will not admit them to citizenship ... nor to every free man as such, but only to those who are freed from necessary services ... for no man can practice excellence (virtue) who is living the life of a mechanic or laborer."[32] "The good of the state and not the individual is the proper subject of political thought and speculation."[33] Therefore,

"The citizen should be moulded to suit the form of government under which he lives.... Neither must we suppose that any of the citizens belongs to himself, for they all belong to the state."[34]

Aristotle believed: (1) the state is the lowest level of existence which matters; (2) rule should be by those possessing a superior ability; (3) therefore, all are not equal—there is an elite class or set of classes; (4) the practice of good is the province of the elite (educated); (5) freedom is not a right for all citizens; (6) slavery is not only acceptable but just; (7) citizens should be molded to fit the needs of their government; (8) all people are the property of the state; and (9) war is justified against those who are inferior and do not submit. As for the practice of commerce, Aristotle "condemned commercial trade as unnatural, unnecessary, and inconsistent with 'human virtue.'"[35]

Plato's views were even darker. In the *Republic* he wrote,

> You are forgetting again that it isn't the law's concern to make any one class in the city outstandingly happy but to contrive to spread happiness throughout the city by bringing the citizens into harmony with each other through persuasion or compulsion and by making them share with each other the benefits that each class can confer on the community. The law produces such people in the city, not in order to allow them to turn in whatever direction they want, but to make use of them to bind the city together.[36]

This view is based on an equality of outcomes—outcomes determined by the state and the class one is in, and not Man's inherent natural equality.

Here we have another difference in ideas. Within state religion societies, social order is brought about by governance—that is, law. We will see that, according to the second model, society is ordered by our individual decision-making. However, the same pagan ideas expressed by Aristotle and Plato exist today. We hear them in the cries of those within the "progressive movement" striving for "social justice" based upon outcome equality rather than our shared human nature. Much more will be said about this view later.

Further passages from Plato's *Republic* suggest the following in regards to a citizen's place:

> If a city is to achieve the height of good government, wives must be in common, children and all their education must be in common, their way of life, whether in peace or war, must be in common, and their kings must be those among them who have proved to be best, both in philosophy and in warfare.[37]

Regarding the ruler, "Then you, as their lawgiver, will select women just as you did men, with natures as similar to theirs as possible, and hand them over to the men. And since they have common dwellings and meals, rather than private ones, and live together and mix together both in physical training and in the rest of their upbringing, they will, I suppose, be driven by innate necessity to have sex with one another."[38] Further,

> The best men must have sex with the best women as frequently as possible, while the opposite is true of the most inferior men and women, and ... that if our herd is to be of the highest possible quality, the former's offspring must be reared but not the latter's. And this must all be brought about without being noticed by anyone except the rulers, so that our herd of guardians remains as free from dissension as possible ... there'll have to be some sophisticated lotteries introduced, so that at each marriage the inferior people we mentioned, will blame luck rather than the rulers when they aren't chosen.[39]

Intercourse outside of the limits set by the government is promiscuity, and

> promiscuity is impious in a city of happy people, and the rulers won't allow it. No, for it isn't right. Then it's clear that our next task must be to make marriage as sacred as possible. And the sacred marriages will be those that are most beneficial.[40]

The above are some of the ways in which the state should mold its citizens to fit its needs. Plato advocated (1) the sharing of women,

(2) state-controlled selective breeding, (3) marriages controlled by the state, (4) infanticide, (5) abortion,[41] and (6) the use of lies and deceit in order to promote the state's goals. This last is Aristotle's idea of the noble lie: All good ends cannot be achieved by good means. In those cases, the means matter less than the ends themselves because the ends must be achieved at all costs.

These are only some of the natural political ends inherent in Greek philosophy. They are also some of the ultimate ends of all the "isms" (such as communism, socialism, fascism, and progressivism), which will be taken up again in the second volume.

The State Religion Society Model
From the state religion material, we can build the first model.

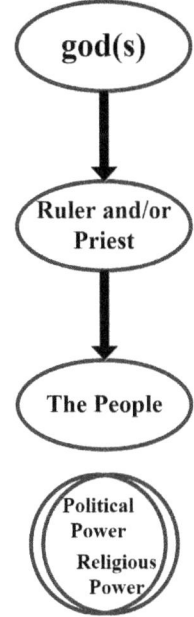

These societies have one or more gods. They have a ruler and/or priest. The people belong to their god and ruler. The ruler or elite are the lowest level within society that matters, because people exist to serve their state to ensure it is successful. That success entails perpetuating its existing social classes. Change within such societies is usually viewed as a threat to be eliminated. Finally, political and religious power are not the same, but there is a very close relationship between them.

Summary

Ethnographic literature suggests religion is a universal attribute of Man and exists because it provides something useful to him: an explanation for the things that Man himself cannot control. When taken to their logical conclusion, the similarities in tribal religions around the world suggest that initially Man believed in an active high god and over time fell away from that belief. Over time, the belief in that high god was replaced by many gods smaller in scope and stature—the idols worshipped within the temples of the ancient world. In those ancient world societies, a deep connection existed between religion and governance, along with a belief in a collective societal morality. Individuals became the property of the state; their needs were secondary to the state's.

Additional Readings on Tribal Religion:

1. Lang, Andrew, *The Making of Religion,* London: Longmans, Green, and Co., 1898.

2. Lang, Andrew, *Myth, Ritual, and Religion,* London: Longmans, Green, and Co., 1887.

3. Radin, Paul, *Monotheism among Primitive Peoples,* London: George Allen & Unwin, 1924.

4. Radin, Paul, *Primitive Man as Philosopher,* New York: A. Appleton & Co., 1957.

5. Radin, Paul, *Primitive Religion: Its nature and Origin,* New York: Dover Publications, 1957.

6. Schmidt, Wilhelm, *The Origin and Growth of Religion: Facts and Theories,* London: Methuen and Co., 1931.

7. Tyler, Edward Burnett, *Limits of Savage Religion,* Journal of the Anthropological Institute 21, 1891, pp. 283-301.

8. Tyler, Edward Burnett, *Primitive Culture,* New York: Harper and Row, 1958.

9. Tyler, Edward Burnett, *Religion in Primitive Culture,* New York: Harper and Row, 1958.

Chapter 2

The Need for Virtue

This chapter opens by looking at an influential source of ideas differing from those presented in the last chapter: the Hebrew Tanakh. This second set of ideas forms the basis for the second model presented at the end of this volume. What this source is, its development, and its influence on the Greek philosophy presented in the last chapter will all be discussed. This information is used to determine philosophy's purpose and its connection to education. These latter points will be developed by some early church fathers and America's Founders.

The Hebrew Tanakh
As noted earlier, state religions were usually entrenched. A professional priest class with strong incentives to stifle change was in place. So how did monotheism rise again among the Jewish people? What we know of their history comes from their Tanakh. It consists of (1) the Torah (first five books of the Bible), (2) the Nevi'im (books of the Prophets), and (3) the literary books of the Kethuvim (Psalms, Proverbs, Song of Solomon, etc.). These last were likely once oral as they are largely written as poetry. Christians recognize these documents as the Old Testament. The Tanakh's writings differ from other religions of that period. *They chronicle who God is, the relationship between God and Israel, and the Jewish people's history.*

These writings are remarkably accurate in many ways. The kings mentioned are confirmed by other historical sources as are the wars, captivities, and geographies. Many of the other gods worshiped during this period, often by the Israelites themselves, are also mentioned. While mentioned, these other gods were meant to be off-limits to the Jewish people. Their inclusion in the Tanakh often refers to instances where the Israelites strayed from the commands they had received.

There were insertions and additions made to the Tanakh, most likely sometime during the middle of the sixth century BC by a group called the Deuteronomists. The books of Exodus, Leviticus, Deuteronomy, Joshua, Judges, 1 and 2 Samuel, and 1 and 2 Kings were most affected. The Book of the Law mentioned in the Old Testament, found during the Jewish temple's reconstruction in the seventh century BC, is thought to have contributed to what became Deuteronomy. Several older documents appear to contribute to this book's contents. Also, an individual known only as Second Isaiah wrote Chapters 40–55 of that book during this time, and another known only as Third Isaiah added the remaining chapters 56–66. These changes coincide with Israel's Babylonian exile. Although insertions were made to scripture at this time, *it should be noted again that the source documents supporting those changes were likely far older.*

These changes do not mean the scriptures have been corrupted. It is likely that by the sixth century when the insertions were made their "human recipients were better able to understand God's words. Keep in mind that all revelations are limited by the capacity of humans to comprehend. It was on that basis that John Calvin dismissed Genesis as an account of Creation told in 'baby talk' in order to penetrate the ignorance of Israel."[1] This view is supported by Augustine of Hippo (Augustine), who wrote,

> Therefore, while every man tries to understand in Holy Scripture what the author understood therein, what wrong is there if anyone understand what you, O light of all truthful minds, reveal to him as true, even if the author he reads did not understand this, since he also understood a truth, though not this truth?[2]

Much more will be said about this later when philosophy is discussed.

Therefore, if the belief in an active high god devolved into polytheism, how did monotheism come back into existence?

Specifically, how did the monotheistic Judaism we know today develop? Stark asserts that, "All new religions are founded by gifted individuals ... significant religious innovations are the work of people who are in some important ways *outsiders*—even when they are members of the elite."[3] As the priests of the established temple religions had a strong incentive to prevent change, these innovators had to

> attract sufficient support to withstand the substantial opposition they invariably arouse—they must create effective social movements.... [E]ven attractive and very plausible ideas win out only when they are persuasively advocated or are imposed by force. Therefore, to explain how the Israelites became monotheists, it is necessary to search for an organized faction of devoted monotheists and to examine the means by which they won out.[4]

Stark states that this organized faction had to be a "Yahweh-only" sect. A sect is defined as a "religious group that sustains a relatively intense level of religious commitment, thereby maintaining a substantial degree of tension with its cultural environment." In any society, there will be variance in "religious tastes and preferences. Sects are formed by and appeal to, those *persons who desire a relatively intense form of religion* ... sect formation also is shaped by the social situation."[5]

Unlike most societies in that part of the world, "for much of its history Israel lacked a state, and even while they reigned, the Israelite kings were relatively weak. Eventually, of course, Israel was ruled by cultural outsiders who usually took little or no interest in its religious controversies. As a result, Israel enjoyed a relatively unregulated religious economy." A result of this environment was that sects were frequently present throughout Israel's history. Furthermore, sects were generally not lower-class movements, but instead movements among the privileged: "Those who form and sustain sects may not hold the reins of power, but they often are the wealthy sons and daughters of those who do, and their grievances stem from the failure of power and privilege to satisfy spiritual concerns."[6]

Several papers discuss the existence of this Yahweh-only sect. It is thought this sect existed prior to the Israelite kingdom's establishment. The prophet Samuel was likely one of its leaders. A case is also made that Elijah and Jeremiah were leaders within this sect. The references to Elijah's followers, the sons of the prophets, is said to be a reference to a Yahweh-only sect.

When the Babylonians defeated Israel, Nebuchadnezzar took many political, military, and religious leaders prisoner. Once the Israelites were in Babylonia, he made efforts to assimilate them. Many Israelites integrated into Babylonian society, but some did not. The group that did not most likely consisted of members from the Yahweh-only sect. These included the prophet Ezekiel and the person known as Second Isaiah. Before Israel's defeat, the prophets' messages were of doom for Israel for the sins it had committed. But after their exile, Ezekiel began to make prophecies about hope and deliverance if Israel would make an exclusive commitment to Yahweh.

So while the group of exiles who were sent to Babylonia included members who worshipped gods other than Yahweh, the group returning to Israel likely consisted primarily of Yahweh-only sect members. This group not only believed that Yahweh was the one God of Israel, but He was the universal one God of all. This group was very wealthy when it returned. They also reclaimed the status they had when initially exiled. The wealth and power of this group, coupled with the weakness of the new nation's rulers, allowed for both the growth of additional sects and influence of the Yahweh-only sect over time.

Some Greek Philosophy Inconsistencies
Contrary to the ideas presented in the previous chapter, another set of ideas also appear within Greek philosophy. We'll look at some of these inconsistencies first, then explore why they might be present.

It should be noted that Alexandria played a pivotal role in the collection and dissemination of philosophical learning. It was a place where the Tanakh was translated from Hebrew into Greek. An active and highly regarded community of Jewish scholars resided there. Finally, it was the location of the famed ancient library. Many ancient scholars came to Alexandria to study.

The quotes below all come from Clement's *Stromata* and represent only a few examples.

> Thus the truth-loving Plato says, as if divinely inspired, "Since I am such as to obey nothing but the word, which after reflection, appears to me the best."[7]

> But that of which Socrates speaks in Plato. "For there are (as they say) in the mysteries many bearers of the thyrsus, but few bacchanals'; meaning, 'that many are called, but few chosen." He accordingly plainly adds: "These, in my opinion, are none else than those who have philosophized right; to belong to whose number, I myself have left nothing undone in life, as far as I could, but have endeavoured in every way. Whether we have endeavoured rightly and achieved aught, we shall know when we have gone there, if God will, a little afterwards."[8]

> Heraclitus of Ephesus says, "If a man hope not, he will not find that which is not hoped for, seeing it is inscrutable and inaccessible."

> Plato the philosopher, also, in *The Laws,* says, "that he who would be blessed and happy, must be straight from the beginning a partaker of the truth, so as to live true for as long a period as possible; for he is a man of faith. But the unbeliever is one to whom voluntary falsehood is agreeable; and the man to whom involuntary falsehood is agreeable is senseless; neither of which is desirable. For he who is devoid of friendliness, is faithless and ignorant."[9]

> Now Plato, teaching that the virtuous man shall have this likeness accompanied with humility, explains the following: "He that humbleth himself shall be exalted." He says, accordingly, in *The Laws*: "God indeed, as the ancient saying has it, occupying the beginning, the middle, and the end of all things, goes straight through while He goes round the circumference. And He is always attended by Justice, the avenger of those who revolt from the divine law."[10]

> And Pythagoras seems to me, to have derived his mildness towards irrational creatures from the law. For instance, he

interdicted the immediate use of the young in the flocks of sheep, and goats, and herds of cattle, on the instant of their birth; not even on the pretext of sacrifice allowing it, both on account of the young ones and of the mothers; training man to gentleness by what is beneath him, by means of the irrational creatures. "Resign accordingly," he says, "the young one to its dam for even the first seven days."[11]

From the above passages, we have the following beliefs also expressed within Greek philosophy. First is obedience to 'the word.' Second, at some point we will go before God and will know then if we have lived rightly. Further, happiness is achieved by living in the truth, growing in faith, and developing hope—the last two being cardinal virtues orienting us toward God. Finally, God is a being who both occupies a beginning, middle, and end, and yet is also all around them. He administers justice to those who do not obey His laws. How is it these ideas also appear within Greek philosopher's writings?

There seem to be two streams of ideas present. One stream on the existence of and obedience to the needs of the state, and a second comprises the existence of God and obedience to His divine laws to do what is good. How do we reconcile these two disparate notions?

What is Philosophy's Purpose?
Clement believed that philosophy contributed to understanding divine truth. He said,

> As many men drawing down the ship, cannot be called many causes, but one cause consisting of many;— for each individual by himself is not the cause of the ship being drawn, but along with the rest;—so also philosophy, being the search for truth, contributes to the comprehension of truth; not as being the cause of comprehension, but a cause along with other things, and co-operator; perhaps also a joint cause ... so while truth is one, many things contribute to its investigation ... if philosophy contributes remotely to the discovery of truth ... it aids him who aims at grasping it ... to apprehend knowledge ... then we shall avow it to be a preparatory training for the enlightened man.... [I]t is the mind which is the appropriate faculty for knowing it.[12]

Philosophy is the search for truth. That search takes place only in the mind. In order to find its truth, we must examine Greek philosophy's sources.

Greek Philosophy's Development

Augustine outlines two schools of philosophy. The first is the Italian and the second the Ionian.

> Pythagoras of Samos is said to be the founder of the Italian school and also the originator of the word philosophy. Before his time, any person of outstanding achievement was called a sage....
>
> Thales of Miletus, who initiated the Ionian school, was one of the celebrated Seven Wise Men.... Thales took up the study of nature and committed the results of his researches to writing.... His main theory was that the primary stuff of all things is water, and that from this principle originated the elements, the cosmos and everything which the world produced. As far as he was concerned, nothing of all this universe, so marvelous to gaze upon, was directed by divine intelligence.[13]
>
> To Socrates goes the credit of being the first one to channel the whole of philosophy into an ethical system for the reformation and regulation of morals. His predecessors without exception had applied themselves particularly to physics and the natural science.[14]
>
> Socrates realized that his predecessors had been seeking the origin of all things, but he believed that these first and highest causes could be found only in the will of the single and supreme Divinity and, therefore, could be comprehended only by a mind purified from passion. Hence his conclusion, that he must apply himself to the acquisition of virtue.[15]
>
> Of the pupils of Socrates, Plato was so remarkable for his brilliance that he has deservedly outshone all the rest ... he traveled far and wide to wherever there was any hope of gaining some valuable addition to knowledge. Thus, in Egypt he mastered the lore which was there esteemed. From

there he went to lower Italy, famous for the Pythagorean School, and there successfully imbibed from eminent teachers all that was then in vogue in Italian philosophy.[16]

Now, the pursuit of wisdom follows two avenues – action and contemplation.... The former deals with the conduct of life.... Contemplative philosophy considers natural causality and truth as such. Socrates excelled in practical wisdom; Pythagoras favored contemplation.[17]

It is to Plato's praise that he combined both in a more perfect philosophy, and then divided the whole into three parts: first, moral philosophy which pertains to action; second, natural philosophy whose purpose is contemplation; third, rational philosophy which discriminates truth and error. Although this last is necessary for both action and contemplation, it is contemplation especially which claims to reach a vision of the truth. Hence, this threefold division in no way invalidates the distinction whereby action and contemplation are considered the constituent elements of the whole of philosophy.[18]

Perhaps this may be said of the best disciples of Plato—of those who followed most closely and understood most clearly the teachings of a master rightly esteemed above all other pagan philosophers—that they have perceived, at least, these truths about God: that in Him is to be found the cause of all being, the reason of all thinking, the rule of all living. The first of these truths belongs to natural, the second to rational, the third to moral philosophy.[19]

Greek Philosophy's Roots

Clement not only calls "the Greeks pilferers of the Barbarian philosophy"[20] but also claims "they have plagiarized and falsified (our writings being, as we have shown, older) the chief dogmas they hold, both on faith and knowledge and science, and hope and love, and also on repentance and temperance and the fear of God,—a whole swarm, verily, of the virtues of truth."[21] He goes further when quoting Numenius, the Pythagorean philosopher, who writes, "For what is Plato, but Moses speaking Attic Greek?"[22] He also cites Aristobulus (Ptolemy VI) who wrote the following into a book he addressed to Philometor: "And Plato followed the laws given to us, and had manifestly studied all that is said in them."[23] Clement then goes on to build a case for the roots of most Greek philosophy coming from either Indian or Egyptian thought (the Barbarians) or the Hebrew Tanakh.

As noted earlier, the Tanakh was put into its current form during the Jewish exile in Babylon during the middle of the sixth century BC. This is roughly during the life of Pythagoras, and at least a century before the lives of Herodotus, Euripides, and Socrates. Its final form was put together from much older documents, and Clement considered its re-creation a divinely-inspired event. He states, "Since the Scriptures having perished in the captivity of Nabuchodonosor, Esdras the Levite, the priest, in the time of Artaxerxes king of the Persians, having become inspired in the exercise of prophecy restored again the whole of the ancient Scriptures."[24]

Clement discusses the translation of the Scriptures from the "dialect of the Hebrews into the Greek language in the reign of Ptolemy the son of Lagos,"[25] the writing of the Septuagint in Alexandria. He also notes several additional translations of the Hebrew texts into Greek in the following:

> Before Demetrius there had been translated by another, previous to the dominion of Alexander and of the Persians, the account of the departure of our countrymen the Hebrews from Egypt, and the fame of all that happened to them ... also Pythagoras, who transferred many things from our books to his own system of doctrines.[26]

Clement builds his case with Moses. He goes through various chronologies using information from the Old Testament, Greek, and Egyptian histories to show that Moses lived considerably earlier than Thales, the first of the seven great sages within Greek philosophy. Clement's conclusion "has been discussed with accuracy by Tatian in his book *To the Greeks*, and by Cassian in the first book of his *Exegetics*."[27] Although some of his dates appear off, such as Inachus founder of Argos being a contemporary of Moses and the Trojan War occurring during the reign of Solomon, his overall conclusion appears to be accurate. Moses preceded Thales, the first of the Greek seven sages who in turn preceded Pythagoras by about nine hundred years. Moses was more likely a contemporary of Triopas of Greece, Cecrops founder of Athens, and Scamander founder of Troy, and lived during the settlement of Italy by the descendants of Pelasgus, all well before Greek philosophy's founding.

Having established the age of the Tanakh relative to Greek philosophy, Clement refers to the use of symbols, enigmas, allegories, etc. in both Egyptian and Hebrew writing, particularly when referring to the first principles of things.[28] He connects some of the sayings of Pythagoras, a passage from Homer, and other Greek philosophers with the earlier writings of Moses and the use of symbols in their philosophy, especially when referring to first principles.

Clement then adds that many great philosophers were not even Greek. Examples presented include Pythagoras as a Tuscan or Tyrian who learned from the Egyptians, Chaldeans, and Magi; Orpheus as an Odrysian or Thracian; Homer an Egyptian; and Thales as a Phoenician by birth influenced by the Egyptians. Two specific examples of Greek philosophers drawing on "barbarian" knowledge are also cited by Clement.

Some Examples
The first is Plato of whom he says,

> Plato does not deny that he procured all that is most excellent in philosophy from the barbarians; and admits that he came into Egypt. Whence, writing in the Phoedo that the philosopher can receive aid from all sides, he said: "Great indeed is Greece, O Cebes, in which everywhere there are good men, and many are the races of the barbarians." ... and in the Symposium, Plato, lauding the barbarians as practicing philosophy with conspicuous excellence, truly says: "And in many other instances both among Greeks and barbarians, whose temples reared for such sons are already numerous." And it is clear that the barbarians signally honoured their lawgivers and teachers, designating them gods ... and it appears to me, it was in consequence of perceiving the great benefit which is conferred through wise

men, that the men themselves were honoured and philosophy cultivated publicly by all the Brahmins, and the Odrysi, and the Getae.[29]

He further cites Democritus who wrote, "I have roamed over the most ground of any man of my time, investigating the most remote parts. Have seen the most skies and lands, and I have heard of learned men in very great numbers. And in composition no one has surpassed me; in demonstration, not even those among the Egyptians ... with all of whom I lived in exile up to eighty years."[30] From these examples, Clement concludes

> Thus philosophy, a thing of the highest utility, flourished in antiquity among the barbarians, shedding its light over the nations. And afterwards it came to Greece. First in its ranks were the prophets of the Egyptians; and the Chaldeans among the Assyrians; and the Druid among the Gauls; and the Samanaeans among the Bactrians; and the philosophers of the Celts; and the Magi of the Persians ... The Indian gymnosophists are also in the number, and the other barbarian philosophers. And of these there are two classes, some of them called Sarmanae, and others Brahmins.[31]

Clement also notes that philosophy is not the only art originating among the barbarians, but in fact was quite common, citing the Egyptian and Chaldean origination of astrology, the Estruscan and Phrygian invention of certain musical instruments, the origination of copper-working and iron-making among the Norici, and the creation of linen among the Assyrians.

In *Stromata* Book VI, Clement adds to his case an entire chapter (II) of Greek plagiarisms from one another. These borrowings were not limited to philosophy, but include the works of Homer, Orpheus, Euripides, Antigone, Hipponos, Hesiod, and Theognis among others in the areas of history, poetry, literature, and rhetoric.

Last, he adds some plagiarisms from Hebrew writings. He cites the Old Testament translations from Hebrew into Greek noted earlier, and states that Plato is an imitator of Moses in framing the laws:

> Plato the philosopher, aided in legislation by the books of Moses, censured the polity of Minos, and that of Lycurgus

> ... while he praised as more seemly the polity which expresses some one thing, and directs according to one precept.... Accordingly, therefore, he interprets what is in the law, enjoining us to look to one God and to do justly. Of politics, there are two kinds: the department of law, and that of politics, strictly so called.
>
> And he refers to the Creator, as the Statesman (o politikos) by way of eminence ... and those who lead an active and just life, combined with contemplation, he calls statesmen (politiko) ... that department of politics which is called "law," he divides into administrative magnanimity and private good order ... the department of law founded on generation, that of politics on friendship and consent ... he consequently joined to the "polity" (or "republic"). Then in my opinion, the end both of the statesman, and of him who lives according to the law, is contemplation.... For he who is wise will live concentrating all his energies on knowledge, directing his life by good deeds,... and following the pursuits which contribute to truth. And the law is not what is decided by law, nor every opinion. But law is the opinion which is good, and what is good is that which is true, and what is true is that which finds "true being" and attains to it.... In accordance with which, namely, good opinion, some have called law, right reason, which enjoins what is to be done and forbids what is not to be done.[32]

The end of law is good, is truth rooted in "true being." This is natural law, as we shall see in a moment.

At another point, Clement states Mosaic law is the source of all ethics, including that contained within Greek philosophy: "It is clear also that all the other virtues, delineated in Moses, supplied the Greeks with the rudiments of the whole department of morals. I mean valour, and temperance, and wisdom, and justice, and endurance, and patience, and decorum, and self-restraint, and in addition to these, piety."[33]

There is an entire chapter on Greek plagiarisms of the Old Testament and another chapter on plagiarisms of the knowledge of God. In regard to virtue being God-given, Plato says, "From this argument then, O Meno, virtue is shown to come to those, in whom it is found, by divine providence.... If, then in this whole treatise we have investigated well, it results that virtue is neither by nature, nor is it taught, but is produced by divine providence, not without intelligence, in those in whom it is found."[34]

And in a misunderstanding of the term *Sons of God*, Plato says, "But to speak of the other demons and to know their birth, is too much for us. But we must credit those who have formerly spoken, they being the offspring of the gods, as they said, and knowing well their progenitors, although they speak without probable and necessary proofs."[35] Clement asserts that Plato is talking about belief without proof: More than mere trust, Plato is again referring to faith.

Plato also taught about creation: "Whether was it that the world had no beginning of its existence, or derived its beginning from some beginning? For being visible, it is tangible; and being tangible, it has a body.... It is a difficult task to find the maker and Father of the universe."[36] This is contrary to the prevailing thought at this time of an uncreated always existing universe, including the Earth.

In relation to the seventh day being sacred, we have the following: "Hesiod says ... 'And on the seventh the sun's resplendent orb.' And Homer: 'And on the seventh then came the sacred day.' ... Callimachus the poet also writes: 'It was the seventh morn, and they had all things done.'"[37]

In reference to the good, Socrates says in Phoedrus, "that it has not been ordained that the bad should be a friend to the bad, nor the good be not a friend to the good."[38] Plato further adds, "For every good man is like every other good man; and so being like to God, he is liked by every good man and God."[39] This appears to be both an emphasis on goodness being best and a misunderstanding of equality among Man, the latter being contrary to the prevailing view of the state being foremost in importance, with the individual's importance being secondary to the state's needs.

Conclusions
The above are just a few of pieces of evidence Clement presents to support his case. I have not even mentioned anything from the chapter in Book VI presenting the biblical miracle plagiarisms by Greek philosophers. But this is more than enough to make the point.

To summarize, Greek philosophy in large part was derived from both barbarian (pagan) and Hebrew sources. Clement makes several more claims within the *Stromata* in relation to these plagiarisms. First, the Greek philosophers are the "thieves and robbers" referred to in John 10:8. He later relates this theft of Hebrew knowledge to passages in Isaiah 29:14 ("The wisdom of the wise will perish") and 1 Corinthians 1:19 ("I will destroy the wisdom of the wise"). Second, he stresses that all sects of philosophy contain at least a germ of truth. Third, while some truth exists within Greek philosophy, it is not the full truth. Finally, the incorporation of Hebrew knowledge into Greek philosophy was an act of divine providence. Each of these points will be briefly laid out before concluding this section.

In regards to the first point above, Clement closes his analysis by stating that

> There is then in philosophy ... a slender spark, capable of being fanned into flame, a trace of wisdom and an impulse from God. Well, be it so that the "thieves and robbers" are the philosophers among the Greeks, who from the Hebrew prophets ... received fragments of the truth, not with full knowledge, and claimed these as their own teachings, disguising some points, treating others sophistically by their ingenuity, and discovering other things, for perchance they had "the spirit of perception."[40]

Towards all sects of philosophy containing some germ of truth, Clement writes,

> Since, therefore, truth is one (for falsehood has ten thousand by-paths) ... so the sects both of barbarian and Hellenic philosophy have done with truth, and each vaunts as the whole truth the portion which has fallen to its lot. But all, in my opinion, are illuminated by the dawn of Light. Let all, therefore, both Greeks and barbarians, who have aspired after the truth,—both those who possess not a little, and those who have any portion produce whatever they have of the word of truth.[41]

In regards to Greek philosophy presenting incomplete truth, Clement says,

> The Greek preparatory culture, therefore, with philosophy itself, is shown to have come down from God to men, not with a definite direction but in the way in which showers fall down on the good land, and on the dunghill, and on the houses. And similarly, both the grass and the wheat sprout; and the figs and any other reckless trees grow on sepulchers. And things that grow, appear as a type of truths. For they enjoy the same influence of the rain. But they have not the same grace as those which spring up in rich soil, inasmuch as they are withered or plucked up.[42]

He speaks of Greek philosophy receiving some truth and Greek culture as preparatory, but preparatory for what? In the following, Clement states that there are two types of truth. The Greeks have the first, and it is preparation for the second.

> One speaks in one way of the truth, in another way the truth interprets itself. The guessing at truth is one thing, and truth itself is another. Resemblance is one thing, the thing itself is another. And the one results from learning and practice, the other from power and faith. For the teaching of piety is a gift, but faith is grace.[43]

He completes the point in the following passage: "Philosophy was necessary to the Greeks for righteousness. And now it becomes conducive to piety; being a kind of preparatory training to those who attain to faith through demonstration."[44]

Toward the final point, Clement adds,

> But among the lies, the false prophets also told some true things.... Nothing withstands God; nothing opposes Him; seeing He is Lord and omnipotent. Further for the counsels and activities of those who have rebelled ... but are guided by universal Providence to a salutary issue.... It is accordingly the greatest achievement of divine Providence, not to allow the evil, which has sprung from voluntary apostasy, to remain useless, and for no good, and not to become in all respects injurious. For it is the work of the divine wisdom, and excellence and power, not alone to do good ... but especially to ensure that what happens through

the evils hatched by any, may come to a good and useful issue.[45]

Finally, "One righteous man, then differs not, as righteous, from another righteous man, whether he be of the Law or a Greek. For God is not only Lord of the Jews, but of all men, and more nearly the Father of those who know Him."[46]

Here is a summary of this chapter so far: Greek philosophy obtained much of its knowledge from pagan and Hebrew sources. The ideas coming from each source were very different. Pagan sources reflected life within societies where state religions existed. These included concepts such as (1) the city-state is the lowest significant level within society, (2) all citizens belong to the state, (3) rule by an elite, and (4) freedom is not for everyone. Hebrew knowledge from the Tanakh was very different and included (1) God's importance over all Man, (2) all men are made in God's image, (3) obedience first to God's law, and (4) God rules His people. Mingling these ideas left the Greeks with only partial truth.

Before we end this chapter, we'll take a look at philosophy and history's influence on education. This will serve to guide the rest of our discussion.

History and Philosophy's Influence on Education
History and philosophy provide classical education's foundation. This view is supported by America's Founders. Classical education had a very specific goal. The "stated purpose of most classical literature, including works of history, (has) always been to inculcate morality."[47] John Adams emphasized this point in writing the following to his son John Quincy: "In company with Sallust, Cicero, Tacitus, and Livy, you will learn Wisdom and Virtue. You will see them represented with all the Charms which Language and Imagination can exhibit, and Vice and Folly painted in all their Deformity and Horror."[48] Students also encountered classical models in popular modern histories of that era. Of particular note was the work of Charles Rollins who wrote *Ancient History*. Rollin's "chief message was the same as that of the ancient Roman historians he cited: defeat lurks within victory, since the wealth and power which result from success lead to corruption and, hence, to ultimate ruin."[49]

The Founders encountered many different models of virtue in their classical studies. Their heroes included characters taken or derived from the works of Homer, Hesiod, Virgil, Ovid, Polybius, Tacitus, Livy, Sallust, Herodotus, Thucydides, Xenophon, and Plutarch, among others. They not only found examples of virtuous individuals, but examples of societal and governmental models of virtue as well. Of particular interest were the Greek republics of the fifth and fourth centuries BC and the early Roman Republic from the sixth to first centuries BC. However, they not only found models of virtue within the classics, they also found anti-models. These were "ancient individuals, societies, and government forms whose vices they wished to avoid"[50] that played just as significant a role in their education. They found many examples of anti-models among the Roman emperors.

Studies of the classics were a way of teaching virtue, and their studies placed within the Founders an understanding of the need for virtue within society. Our Founders believed "the purpose of history was the prevention of tyranny"[51]—prevention of the excesses that came with the wealth and power of success. Without virtue, a society was not likely to long endure or prosper.

History was considered to represent experience. When "seeing virtue represented in present and past examples, children instinctively recognized its inherent beauty and sought to reproduce it. Conversely, children who rarely experience virtuous behavior could not develop their moral sense to its full potential."[52] The following statement by Livy supports this notion:

> What chiefly makes the study of history wholesome and profitable is this, that you behold the reasons for every kind of experience set forth as on a conspicuous monument: from these you may choose for yourself and for your own state to imitate, from these marks for avoidance what is shameful in the conception and shameful in the result.[53]

But experience is not enough. Intuition needs to be developed within students, and intuition cannot be awakened "without the aid of *reason and experience.*"[54] While history examines the past, both its behaviors and outcomes, philosophy exercises the mind using reason to determine what is good and true from what is bad and false. As such, it develops the mind for future decision-making.

According to Clement, philosophy provides a means of training in reason as it is "characterized by investigation into truth and the nature of things."[55] Further, "philosophy came into existence, not on its own account, but for the advantages reaped by us from knowledge, we receiving a firm persuasion of true perception, through the knowledge of things comprehended by the mind."[56] The writings of the Greek philosophers contributed much to the Founder's views on human nature and the theory of law needed to govern society. But these theories were based upon the "rights of the people" and not the individual rights we construe today. That level of individualism came much later in our history and will be covered at the appropriate time.

Natural Law
The Stoics contributed much to the Founder's concepts of human nature. The Stoic branch of philosophy developed from the teachings of Zeno of Citium. They possessed an optimistic conception of human nature and contributed to the theory of natural law. The Stoics assumed a middle position between the philosophical writings of Plato and Aristotle "concerning the mechanics of human nature."[57] And that natural law was "imbedded in human nature through a sort of intuition ... that it (natural law) could be accessed only with the help of reason acting upon sensory information."[58] The beginnings of thought around natural law can be found Plato's writings:

> Meno: You are probably right, Socrates, and no one wants what is bad.
>
> Socrates: Were you not saying just now that virtue is to desire good things and have the power to secure them?
>
> Meno: Yes, I was.
>
> Socrates: The desiring part of this statement is common to everybody, and one man is no better than another in this?
>
> Meno: So it appears.[59]

Cleanthes taught that virtue lay in "living agreeably to nature in the exercise of right reason." In his work *Hymn to Zeus*, Cleanthes believed that "humans were distinct from other species in possessing a reason of their own, though it was connected to the divine reason."[60] Finally, but by no means the only other place where natural law is discussed, Epictetus (in Discourses, I.22.I) believed that humans were born with two common preconceptions: (1) righteousness is good, and (2) that good is a more profitable and worthy choice than evil.[61]

Natural law "arises from the very existence of rational, social, and political animals."[62] "Natural law comprises many commands ranged in various degrees of closeness to the fundamental imperative that men should seek good."[63] Natural law is only one category of law mentioned by Thomas Aquinas in his *Summa Theologicae*. Other categories included Eternal, Divine, Positive, and Human. We will defer Positive Law for now. He defines Eternal Law as transcending and sustaining "every created manifestation of intelligence and will commanding activity for the common good."[64] Eternal Law is supreme. Divine Law covers all of the commands received through divine revelation. It is broader than natural law as it more broadly represents God's will. Human law is complementary to natural law. It is created for the safety and well-being of the community. Human law is "right because commanded, not commanded because right."[65]

Sir Edward Coke viewed English law as natural law. Tradition was the basis for English law and also the product of natural law. This reliance on tradition was viewed as being "much more reasonable than reliance on unaided reason."[66] He viewed English law as a thing refined by trial and error, with the good being kept and the bad being discarded. Natural law both had the capacity to change over time to changing needs, and also improve—but again a strong moral foundation within society was required for this improvement to occur. Later, the Huguenots summarized the natural law as life, liberty, and property. More will be said about natural law later when discussing both philosophy and America's Declaration of Independence (Declaration). From our discussions so far, it is clear that the need for virtue within individuals was not only important, but also doesn't just happen; it needs to be cultivated. More will be said about natural law and its relation to rights, justice, freedom, and virtue when the biblical model is developed in Chapter 6.

The Founder's and Classical Education
Our Founding Fathers were a diverse lot in many respects. They came from varied backgrounds and social means. Of the fifty-six signers of the Declaration, almost half had worked within the legal profession as judges, lawyers, or officers of the law. Other Founders included merchants, farmers, doctors, educators, surveyors, theologians, and an iron master. Some, such as Charles Carroll, Richard Henry Lee, Benjamin Rush, Edward Rutledge, James Wilson, and John Witherspoon, received their education in Europe, but most were educated in America. Some were either self-taught, such as Benjamin Franklin, or were like George Wythe, taught the classical languages by his mother who was fluent in both Latin and Greek. In all, thirty of the signers of the Declaration had a college degree and, in addition, another twenty-two had received some type of private education. One thing they all had in common was their views and beliefs were shaped by the classical education just described.

Colonists derived their classical education curricula and pedagogical methods from the English educational system, which, like the other European systems, had originated in the Middle Ages.

> This curricula focused on the medieval "trivium" (rhetoric, logic, and grammar) and 'quadrivium' (arithmetic, music, geometry, and astronomy) ... Jesuit schoolmasters thoroughly grounded their students in theology, philosophy, Latin, Greek, and the ancient historians Herodotus, Xenophon, Plutarch, Livy, Sallust, Quintus Curtius, and Cornelius Nepos. Their method emphasized the usual rote memorization.... The Protestant nations of Germany, England, and especially Scotland equaled the Jesuits in the rigors of their classical training. The same ancient Romans—Cicero, Horace, Virgil, and Ovid—held sway throughout Europe. Far from abolishing the standard classical studies, the Protestant Reformation had only added programs designed to promote literacy in the vernacular

languages. Roughly the same hours, strict discipline, declamations and competitions existed in each nation.[67]

Long hours of study were the norm: "Classical training frequently began at age eight, whether under the direction of public grammar schoolmasters or private tutors. Grammar school students commonly studied the classics every morning from eight to eleven and every afternoon from one until dark."[68] Studies would include the learning and memorization of grammatical rules and translation of works written in the classical languages to English. This translation would generally first be done orally and then later the student would be required to write out his translation. Often a third step would then be to translate the written translation back into Greek or Latin, but in a different tense. This process was not only applied to the works of those such as Cicero, Homer, Virgil, Xenophon, Aristotle, and Plato, but also to the Greek New Testament as well.

Teachers impressed upon their students the need for a classical education if they wanted to be successful. The Reverend James Maury, whose students included Thomas Jefferson, stated "an acquaintance with the Languages antiently [sic] spoken in Greece and Italy, is necessary, absolutely necessary, for those who wish to make any reputable Figure in Divinity, Medicine, or Law."[69] Many of these schoolmasters were extremely skillful. James Madison studied the classics first under Donald Robertson. He returned home in 1767 for two years of further study under the Reverend Thomas Martin. He arrived at the College of New Jersey in 1769 just two weeks before final examinations. He sat and passed the examinations in Greek, Latin, English, the New Testament, and mathematics. Not all schoolmasters were as skilled. However, the socialization within the classical education process was so complete that "even bad teachers, employing the most brutal and unimaginative pedagogical techniques, often instilled a love of the literature in their students."[70]

In addition to their studies, many students kept "commonplace books" where they copied passages from classical works and transcribed them into English. John Adams commonplace book included extensive tracts from Sallust's *Catiline's War*. James

Madison's contained passages from Plato and Aristotle, both of whom influenced his essay *A Brief System of Logick*. Alexander Hamilton not only kept a commonplace book during his studies, but converted his pay book during the Revolutionary War into a commonplace book, copying lines from Demosthenes' orations. Thomas Jefferson kept two commonplace books well after the completion of his formal education.

Reason Alone Is Not Enough
America's Founders received a classical education whose primary purpose was developing morality within its students. They learned reasoning skills from their studies of the ancient languages and subjects such as history and philosophy. They derived models and anti-models of virtue from the study of those works, many of which contained traces of Old Testament knowledge. In addition, they studied the New Testament, acquiring additional models of virtuous behavior there as well, including truth, goodness, and happiness, all of which lead to wisdom. And virtue coupled with wisdom leads to faith, because they create a truth which is strong enough to withstand the assault of falsehoods, something sorely needed in American society today.

This is the same premise put forward by Clement almost two thousand years ago. Concerning knowledge and reason, he writes,

> Those who are wise in mind have a certain attribute of nature peculiar to themselves; and they who have shown themselves capable, receive ... of perception a double measure.... Those also that are occupied in instruction, train the sensibility.... For those who practice the common arts, are in what pertains to the senses highly gifted.... For sensibility finds and invents.... And practice will increase the application which has knowledge for its end. With reason ...—by art, by knowledge, by faith, by prophecy—for our benefit.[71]

In discussing philosophy, Clement claims the benefit of the "discourse which consists of demonstrations, implants in the spirit of him who follows it, clear faith; so that he cannot conceive of that which is demonstrated being different; and so it does not allow us to succumb to those who assail us by fraud."[72] Faith is the end of knowledge, and faith is necessary to prevent being led astray. Clement further adds that "it is impossible for a man without learning to comprehend the things which are declared in the faith. But to adopt what is well said, and not to adopt the reverse, is caused not simply by faith, but by faith combined with knowledge."[73] In short, "neither is knowledge without faith, nor faith without knowledge."[74] True wisdom requires both.

Knowledge attained from the Tanakh underlies much of what the Founders studied, and was supplemented by New Testament studies. It is important to understand their ideas and their effect on governance in order to understand the Founder's intention when writing America's Declaration and Constitution. It is also clear from the expressions used in the Declaration that this course of knowledge had an influence on that document in its use of terms such as Creator, Laws of Nature, Nature's God, Opinions of Mankind, Truths, Life, Liberty, Happiness, Principles, Mankind, and Evils. In order to understand those terms, we will explore the concepts derived from scripture by looking at three Christian writers. There are many more who could be cited, but these three stand above the rest. Each one's work builds upon that written before them as evidenced by the citations made by each author.

The works of Clement of Alexandria (Clement), St. Augustine of Hippo (Augustine), and St. Thomas Aquinas (Thomas) are used. Augustine is held in high esteem by both the Catholic and Protestant churches. Luther and Calvin used his works when shaping their theologies, and Clement's writings are evident within Augustine's. Therefore, Clement's and Augustine's views also influenced the Founders through the materials they studied. While Thomas is recognized primarily by the Catholic Church, he often cited Augustine and wrote extensively about law, freedom, personal property, and other matters directly relevant to the topics of this book.

This material is used to develop our second model, one based upon biblical principles.

Questions Posed

Philosophy, whatever the sect, generally attempts to answer some of the same questions. In this book, it is no different. There are some questions whose answers provide direct insight into the minds and beliefs of our Founders. It is those questions we will attempt to ask and answer in each of the next three chapters. The list is likely not complete. In some instances, each writer is silent on a point. We will focus on what each has to say in regards to these questions. As stated earlier, we have made one assumption in this work: There is a creator. It would seem to me that, given our Founder's education and the language within the Declaration, any other thought flies in the face of reason. The existence of a creator being given, the following questions will be explored in the next chapters.

We will open the next chapter with an overview regarding the one and the many. This is the starting point for all discussions about first principles, for it leads to the following questions:

1. Who is the creator?
2. What is his nature?

If there is a creator, there must also be a creation. Not only are there questions about what was created (and how) but also questions about Mankind, and about how we fit into that creation.

1. What did the creator create?
2. Why was Mankind created? Is he different from the rest of creation? If so, how?
3. Does Mankind have a purpose within creation? If so, what is it?
4. What nature did He give Mankind?
5. Did the creator give anything to Mankind? If so, what?
6. Why is there good and evil?

If there is a creator and a creation, then there are also questions about what may go on between them.

1. Can Man know his creator?
2. If so, how can we know Him?
3. Is Man's creator close or distant?

Finally, in conjunction with the last question and the language within the Declaration, there are questions about what, if anything, our Creator expects of us.

1. What are the creator's expectations of Mankind?
    a. What are his laws?
    b. What happens if his expectations and/or laws are violated?
    c. How do we "live rightly?"
    d. What is happiness?
    e. What are truth and faith? How are they related?
    f. Are some virtues more important than others?
        i. If so, which ones?
        ii. Why are they more important?

Summary

Almost all the Declaration's signers received some formal education—a classical education. The goal of classical education was not merely to educate a student, but also to instill morality in him. The purpose of subjects, like history, was to teach how to prevent tyranny by demonstrating models and anti-models of behavior. Our Founders viewed this as necessary in order to build a successful and prosperous society. Successful societies need a solid grounding in both reason and morality—reason alone is insufficient. Our Founders believed in natural law: law based in reason but derived from divine sources and grounded in moral behavior. Finally, the Greek philosophy they studied, which influenced much of their classical educational sources, contained two separate threads of thought: One thread derived from pagan sources and a second derived from the Tanakh and Bible.

Chapter 3

Reason and Faith

Titus Flavius Clement (Clement of Alexandria) lived from approximately 150–220 AD. Within Christianity, only the surviving works of Justin and Irenaeus are older. Clement took a different approach from these earlier writers and was the first to incorporate philosophical thought into his writings. He, like Justin and Irenaeus, wrote at a time when new words were being created in Greek to convey the Christian concepts of faith and truth. While his birthplace is uncertain, he was a pagan philosopher before converting to Christianity. He was a teacher, with his most noted student being Origen.

During Clement's life, Alexandria became the "brain of Christianity." Only Antioch came close to rivaling Alexandria in terms of theological scholarship at this time. Alexandria had been the place where the Tanakh had been translated into Greek, possessed a Jewish community with a long intellectual tradition, and was the site of the renowned ancient library. At this time, North Africa, Rome, and the rest of Western Europe were no more than small outposts of Christian communities.

Christianity was rapidly growing during Clement's life, a time when persecutions also began to occur, but it did not yet have any single, formal, authoritative source. It was encountering new cultures in an ever-widening geographic area. This posed a significant risk to the integrity of its core religious thought, but

> [W]hat is remarkable is the degree of uniformity in fact maintained, despite the new situations, challenges and ideas with which it came to be faced.... Throughout the second

century, local Christian communities were only too likely to be infiltrated by gnostic teachers and ideas, bringing with them a multitude of additional scriptures—further "gospels," and "acts" named after various apostles. What seems striking is the firmness with which they were rejected by the Christian community generally through insistence upon the essential unity of the two covenants and the decisive authority of a limited group of writings known throughout the churches to derive from apostolic times, these centered on the four Gospels and the letters of Paul.[1]

Alexandria was both a source of theological scholarship and heretical gnostic thought. Egyptian gnosticism expressed a mystical dualism and tended to combine paganism with the work of Plato, ignoring the Christian inheritance of the Jewish God and the Tanakh. Some of Clement's writings were specifically aimed at the gnostic teachings of Marcion and Valentinus. Clement developed a concept of the true gnostic based on scripture in his writings to counter the ideas expressed by these other authors. His three surviving works are *Paedagogus* (The Instructor), *Stromateis* (The Miscellanies), and *Protrepticus* (The Exhortation). His works are deliberately unsystematic as he expresses in the following passage:

> Let these notes of ours, as we have often said for the sake of those that consult them carelessly and unskillfully, be of varied character—and as the name itself indicates, patched together—passing constantly from one thing to another, and in the series of discussions hinting at one thing and demonstrating another. "For those who seek for gold," says Heraclitus, "dig much earth and find little gold." But those who are of the truly golden race, in mining for what is allied to them, will find the much in little. For the word will find one to understand it. The Miscellanies of notes contribute, then, to the recollection and expression of truth in the case of him who is able to investigate with reason.[2]

The One and the Many

Clement was responding to Platonic philosophy. There are two concepts that must be understood when discussing Platonic philosophy in this time. The first is philosophical and concerns what is meant by the ambiguous term "the one." The second is divine immanence versus transcendence, which is theological. During Clement's life, these philosophical and theological issues were mixed together. The following is summarized from Chapter 1 of E. F. Osborn's book *The Philosophy of Clement of Alexandria*.[3]

The philosophical concept of the meaning of the one comes from Plato's *Parmenides*. What do we mean when we say a thing "is one?" Is it a simple unity from which nothing can be made from the things that are left, or is it a complex whole of many parts? In the dialogue, a simple unity can only be described in negative terms—in terms of what it is not. The hypothesis for a simple unity is "if the One is to be One, it will neither be a whole nor have parts" (137d).[4] Further properties of a simple unity are the following:

1. It will "have neither a beginning, nor an end nor a middle" (137d).

2. "It is also without shape; for it partakes of neither round nor straight" (137e).

3. It is "not anywhere, if it is neither in itself nor in another" (138a).

4. It is "neither at rest nor in motion" (139b).

5. It "can't be either different from another or the same as itself" (139e).

6. It is "neither like nor unlike another or itself" (140b).

7. It is "neither equal nor unequal to itself or another" (140b).

8. "It has no share of time, nor is it *in* any time" (141d).

9. "Therefore it is not named or spoken of, nor is it the object of opinion or knowledge, nor does anything that is perceive it" (142).

A complex unity, on the other hand, can be described in positive terms—in terms of what it is. The hypothesis for a complex unity is "If One is ... the one that is, must it not itself, since it is one being, be a whole, and the parts of this whole be oneness and being" (142d). A complex unity therefore has both unity and being. An example of a complex unity would be you, the reader. You have many parts, but you are a single human being. Further properties include

1. It is "unlimited in multitude" (144).
2. It is "both one and many, a whole and parts, and limited and unlimited in multitude" (145).
3. It has "a beginning, and end, and a middle" (145 b).
4. "It would partake of some shape ... either straight or round, or some shape mixed from both" (145b).
5. "Insofar as it is a whole, is in another; but insofar as it is all parts, it is in itself" (145e).
6. "Since it is itself always both in itself and in a different thing, must always be both in motion and at rest" (146).
7. It "will be like and unlike the others—insofar as it is different, like, and insofar as it is the same, unlike" (148c).
8. It "both touches and does not touch the others and itself" (149d).
9. It "is both equal to, and greater and less than, itself and the others" (151b).
10. It "will be equal to, and more and fewer than, itself and the others in number" (151e).
11. It has a "past, present, and future ... there would be knowledge and opinion and perception of it" (155d).

These two hypotheses "present us with a pattern of two unities—a unity which is simple, bare, one and nothing but one, and a unity which is infinitely complex, one and many."[5]

The second issue is one of transcendence versus immanence. Is God transcendent, by which is meant remote from the world and beyond the reach of human knowledge? Or is He immanent, present in, and maybe even identical with, the world? In Middle Platonism, to which Clement is responding, the two issues are blended, with simple unity being transcendent and complex unity immanent. However, the blending of these two concepts varied for each philosopher.

Except where noted, the following are excerpts from Clement's writings. As some of the passages are lengthy, some of these quotes appear in italics so that they are easier to follow. This same convention will be used in the following chapters presenting excerpts from Augustine's and Thomas's works.

The Creator's Nature
We will start with the Creator-related questions: Who is He, what is His nature, what did He create, and can we know Him? These are intertwined within Clement's works. The most comprehensive statements Clement makes about the Creator as first principle are contained in *Stromata*, Book V. However, we will start with a reference from Book II where he lays out the problem he faces.

> The professed aim of our philosophy ... leads through Wisdom, ... to the Rule of all, - a Being difficult to grasp and apprehend, ever receding and withdrawing from him who pursues. But He who is far off has ... come very near.... He is in essence remote.... But He is very near in virtue of that power which holds all things in its embrace.... For the power of God is always present, in contact with us, in the exercise of inspection, of beneficence, of instruction.... God is not to be known by human wisdom.... For God is not in darkness or in place, but above both space and time, and qualities of objects.[6]

Clement is laying out his balance between the transcendent and the immanent. The Creator is God. He is transcendent and therefore One, and cannot be known by us through human wisdom. He is outside of time and space, a simple unity. It is God's power which is immanent, and it appears to be a complex unity as there are different positive attributes associated with that power. So what does Clement say about God?

First, that *"God is one."*[7] As the Creator is transcendent, He has been spoken of *"in enigmas, and symbols, and allegories, and metaphors, and such like tropes."*[8] Clement notes, however, that most men think the Creator to be like themselves. They fail to notice that He *"has bestowed on us ten thousand things in which he does not share."*[9] These things include birth, food, growth, long life, and our bodies.

All such references are not literal and should be interpreted symbolically.

But that does not mean that we cannot have some understanding of Him. We know the Creator through a process of confession, contemplation, and analysis that strips away *"not what He is but what He is not."*[10] This stripping away includes all form, motion, position, place, throne, and notions of right hand or left. *"The First Cause is not then in space, but above both space, and time, and name, and conception."*[11]

This process suggests that *"In reasoning, it is possible to divine respecting God,"*[12] by moving within the world of thought. However, reason alone is not enough.

> Should one say that Knowledge is founded on demonstration by a process of reasoning, let him hear that first principles are incapable of demonstration; for they are known neither by art nor sagacity.... Hence ... the first cause of the universe can be apprehended by faith alone.[13]

We come to know our Creator through faith. Knowledge of Him comes not from man, but by His power through the Logos—for *"the grace of knowledge is from Him by the Son."*[14]

Clement finds presenting the absolutely first and oldest principle difficult. The Creator cannot be expressed, as He is not genus, difference, species, an individual, number, event, nor that which is caused by an event.

> No one can rightly express Him wholly. For on account of His greatness he is ranked as the All, and is the Father of the universe. Nor are any parts to be predicated of Him. For the One is indivisible; wherefore also it is infinite, not considered with reference to inscrutability, but with reference to its being without dimensions, and not having a limit. And therefore it is without form and name.[15]

Even though no one can fully or correctly express the Creator, He is not inscrutable.

So why do we use names to describe Him?

We speak not as supplying His name; but for want, we use good names, in order that the mind may have these as points of support, so as not to err in other respects. For each one by itself does not express God; but all together are indicative of the power of the Omnipotent.[16]

The names we do use are good and keep us from going further astray as we are limited in our ability to understand Him, and what we can understand of Him lies within the mind. *"For the God of the universe, who is above all speech, all conception, all thought, can never be committed to writing, being inexpressible even by His own power."*[17]

Moses understood this. That is why he *"set up no image in the temple to be worshipped; showing that God was invisible, and incapable of being circumscribed."*[18] He led the Hebrews to understanding the Creator through the honor of His name alone within the temple. Plato understood this as well. Clement cites the following passages from Plato's *Republic*: *"For it was not from need that God made the world,"*[19] and *"that we ought to make neither temples nor images; for that no work is worthy of the gods."*[20]

> For both it is a difficult task to discover the Father and Maker of this universe; and having found Him, it is impossible to declare Him to all. For this is by no means capable of expression, like the other subjects of instruction," says Plato.[21]

In speaking about the Creator's power, Clement wrote,

> How great is the power of God! His bare volition was the creation of the universe. For God alone made it, because He alone is truly God. By the bare exercise of volition he creates; His mere willing was followed by the springing into being of what He willed.[22]

As the Creator is perfect, "He consequently bestows perfect gifts"[23] and this was fully done for "what He wished came to pass; and there is nothing which God cannot do."[24]

The Creator is described by Clement as a transcendent unity. Per Osborn again, "There are two problems which face an account of God as a transcendent unity. The first is in what way language can be applied to a God who is outside language.... The second problem is how this abstract entity can yet be the first cause, the creator of everything."[25] Clement's response to the first question is unequivocally that language cannot be used to name the Creator. At best, names serve as a crutch for us to use, to keep us from straying further. His answer to the second question is that creation is ex nihilo—an inexplicable mystery. This is the only answer consistent with Clement's arguments.

The Logos

Clement asserts there is a Father and Son (Logos). Both are God, a unity. He also presents two different themes of the Father and Son. One theme is the emphasis on their unity, as in the following passages.

1. "The Son in the Father, and the Father in the Son."[26]

2. "Our Instructor is like His Father God ... the Word who is God, who is in the Father ... and with the form of God is God."[27]

3. "But nothing exists, the cause of whose existence is not supplied by God. Nothing, then, is hated by God, nor yet by the Word. For both are one—that is, God."[28]

4. "And His justice is shown to us by His own Word from there from above, whence the Father was. For before He became Creator He was God."[29]

5. "He Himself being one, the Son of the Father, who is truly one, the beginning and the end of time."[30]

There is only one Creator. Clement draws a contrasting theme indicating distinctions between the Son and Father. Yet even within these distinctions, the Son is still one with the Father—there is still unity. These distinctions include the Son being (1) God's power, (2) God's image, but still one with Him, (3) the creator of all creation, and (4) the key to what we can know about our creator.

1. "God then, being not a subject for demonstration, cannot be the object of science, but the Son is wisdom, and knowledge, and truth, and all else that has affinity thereto. He is also susceptible of demonstration and of description.... And the Son is neither simply one thing as

The Light & the Rod   57

one thing, nor many things as parts, but one thing as all things; whence also He is all things. For He is the circle of all powers rolled and united into one unity."[31]

2. "But the nature of the Son, which is nearest to Him who is alone the Almighty One, is the most perfect, and most holy, and most potent, and most princely and most kingly and most beneficent.... For from His own point of view the Son of God is never displaced; not being divided, not severed, not passing from place to place, being always everywhere, and being contained nowhere, complete mind, the complete paternal light; all eyes, seeing all things, hearing all things, knowing all things, by His power scrutinizing the powers.... He, the paternal Word ... For the Son is the power of God, as being the Father's most ancient Word before the production of all things, and His Wisdom."[32]

3. "He, the Son, is, ... the cause of all good things, being the first efficient cause of motion—a power incapable of being apprehended by sensation.... Being, then the Father's power, He easily prevails in what He wishes, leaving not even the minutest point of His administration unattended to."[33]

4. "And as the Lord is above the whole world, yea, above the world of thought, so the name engraven on the plate has been regarded to signify ... it is the name of God that is expressed; since as the Son sees the goodness of the Father, God the Saviour works, being called the first principle of all things which was imaged forth from the invisible God first, and before the ages, and which fashioned all things which came into being after itself."[34]

5. "And as the unoriginated Being is one, the Omnipotent God; one, too, is the First-begotten, 'by whom all things were made, and without whom not one thing ever was made.'"[35]

6. "'Now the just shall live by faith,' which is according to the covenant and the commandments; since these, which are two in name and time, given in accordance with the

[divine] economy—being in power one—the old and the new, are dispensed through the Son by one God."[36]

7. "For the gates of the Word being intellectual, are opened by the key of faith. No one knows God but the Son ... through whom alone God is beheld."[37]

The Son is immanent as he can be described by us. The Father is transcendent as He is outside of human thought and inexpressible directly.

But how is this possible? Clement says the Father and Son are first principle and creator in different senses of the word, similar to the four causes discussed in Aristotle's *Metaphysics*.[38]

1. "Wherefore the Word is called the Alpha and the Omega, of whom alone the end becomes the beginning, and ends again at the original beginning, without any break....

2. "Now God, who is without beginning, is the perfect beginning of the universe, and the producer of the beginning. As, then He is being, He is the first principle of the department of action, as He is good, of morals; as He is mind, on the other hand, He is the first principle of reasoning and of judgment. Whence also he is Teacher, who is the only son of the Most High Father, the Instructor of men."[39]

3. "The timeless and unoriginated First Principle, and Beginning of existence—the Son— from whom we are to learn the remoter Cause, the Father, of the universe, the most ancient and the most beneficent of all."[40]

God is our creator, the source of all existence, morality, and knowledge. The distinctions Clement lays out are not always consistently maintained. This goes back to his statements about our inability to accurately name or write about Him. These only serve to act as "points of support" because of our limitations.

Clement says very little about the Holy Spirit. What he does say is that (1) the Holy Spirit's power terminates in the Son,[41] (2) the spirit comes to one through faith,[42] (3) wisdom is received through the Holy Spirit after faith,[43] and (4) the soul becomes the Holy Spirit's temple.[44]

In answer to the questions posed earlier about our Creator and creation, Clement says the following:

1. The Creator is One. He is God. Unlimited, all powerful, and through Him all else was created by the mere exercise of His volition. He is the source of all existence.

2. He is the Father, transcendent, a simple unity, and He is the Son who is immanent, a complex unity. They are one unity, yet distinct. The Father is first principle of mind, reason, good, and morals. Through the Son we learn about the Creator. The Son is our instructor, and all powers of the Holy Spirit end in Him.

3. The Son is the Word, the image of the Father. As the Son is immanent, by understanding this image we can have some understanding of the Creator himself.

4. He is not inscrutable. We know the Creator by both reason and faith.

5. He is spoken of in enigmas and allegories. No image of him can be made because He cannot be seen. Names are insufficient to describe Him, but are necessary to keep from straying further in understanding who He is.

Man and Creator

We turn next to questions about Man. What is his nature? Is Man different from the rest of creation? If so, how? Why was Man made? What is Man's purpose? Does God expect anything from us? Does He have any laws? We will first look at Man's nature, then the implications of that nature, and finally at the concept of law governing the relationship between creator and man.

Man's Nature

If God created everything, let's start with asking about creation and man's nature? *"For if the heavenly bodies are not the works of men, they were certainly created for man."*[45] It is not creation itself which is to be worshipped, but its creator. There is separation between creator and creation. While creation was created for Man, it was created for a specific use. *"No one is a stranger to the world by nature, their essence being one, and God one. But the elect man dwells as a sojourner."*[46] We have a common nature but must choose to act as travelers, using what we need while keeping our eyes on an ultimate destination. This life only offers the way toward that ultimate goal.

So why then was creation created for Man? What made Man different from the rest of creation? *"The other works of creation He made by the word of command alone, but man He framed by Himself,"*[47] in His image. We were given life in a very special way, either because this was in itself desirable or because it was desirable on account of something else. The Son is the image of the Father, and in the creation of Man *"there is now a third divine image, made as far as possible like the Second Cause, the Essential Life."*[48] Man is the image of the Son. But this is not meant as a physical resemblance. *"For conformity with the image and likeness is not meant of the body ... but in mind and reason."*[49] This is repeated in another form. *"For the image of God is His Word ... the image of the Word is the true man, the mind which is in man."*[50] Why? Because *"man is made principally for the knowledge of God."*[51] Just as the Son is in the Father, and the Father in the Son; *"God in man, and man in God."*[52]

Man has a special place within creation. Man was created as the image of an image. This image is not physical, but inward, our mind and reason. What are the implications of that nature?

Implications of Man's Nature
Clement notes several: (1) we have a need to know ourselves, (2) we all have an equality of nature, (3) we all have choice, and (4) we all have been given freedom. This of course is not a complete list but are items relevant to the topic at hand. Passages reflecting each of these points follow below.

As to the first point,

> It is then, as appears, the greatest of all lessons to know one's self. For if one knows himself, he will know God; and knowing God, he will be made like God, not by wearing gold or long robes, but by well doing, and by requiring as few things as possible.[53]

We were made to know God, and by knowing Him we fulfill our purpose. This knowing is not evident by how we look, but instead by how we act and live—what we know and do.[54] For *"by thus receiving the Lord's power, the soul studies to be God; regarding nothing bad but ignorance, and action contrary to right reason."*[55]

But knowing someone requires communication and a basis for the relationship. For communication, *"Prayer is, then, to speak more boldly, converse with God."*[56] Through the Son's image we have a basis for a relationship with our Creator. Through prayer we communicate and build a relationship with Him, as it is through our mind by which we have that image. By obtaining knowledge, applying reason, and engaging in prayer, we grow in faith, complete our purpose, and acquire some understanding of our Creator.

On the second point, Clement clearly states all Mankind is equal as God's creation. *"Suffice it for me to say that the Lord of all is God; and I say the Lord of all absolutely, nothing being left by way of exception."*[57] It does not matter whether he is Jew, Gentile, or barbarian.[58] *"For God is not only Lord of the Jews, but of all men."*[59] Neither is there a difference between the sexes, for *"the virtue of man and woman is the same. For if the God of both is one, the master of both is also one."*[60] This does not mean there are not physical differences but that in Man's nature *"there is sameness, as far as respects the soul, she will attain to the same virtue (as man)."*[61]

As for those who would say otherwise, Clement responds,

> For either the Lord does not care for all men; and this is the case either because He is unable (which is not to be thought, for it would be a proof of weakness), or because He is unwilling, which is not the attribute of a good being.... Or He does care for all, which is befitting for Him who has become Lord of all.[62]

In regards to choice, our purpose is to know our Creator, and we have been given mind and reason as our likeness to Him. In discussing faith and free choice, Clement asserts that we are given reason in order to live rationally and rightly, for the Word of the Father is wisdom. How does one live rightly? According to Clement, there are four levels. The first, and lowest, level consists of *"those who manage well the things which occur each day."*[63] The second consists of *"those who behave becomingly and rightly to those who approach them."*[64] The third are *"those who have command of their pleasures."*[65] Finally, the *"fourth—and this is the greatest—those who are not corrupted by prosperity."*[66]

It is only because some choose to dispute and not believe that all *"do not attain to the perfection of the good. For neither is it possible to attain it [faith] without the exercise of free choice."*[67] Not only is the existence of free choice necessary to establish faith, it is also necessary for choosing good. *"For this was the law from the first, that virtue should be the object of voluntary choice."*[68] Further *"the preference and choice for truth is voluntary."*[69] It is voluntary *"since to obey or not is in our own power."*[70] If we do not choose good, *"The Lord clearly shows sins and transgressions to be in our own power."*[71] Truth and obedience are also voluntary.

"'Transgressions catch a man; and in the cords of his own sins each one is bound.' And God is without blame."[72] For *"the individual man is stamped according to the impression produced in the soul by the objects of his choice ... the cause lay in his choosing, and especially in his choosing what was forbidden. God was not the cause."*[73] We alone are responsible for our own choices and those choices leave their imprint on our soul. They are the consequences of the ideas we hold and actions we take. This is free will.

While free will is voluntary, knowledge is required to effectively exercise it. *"Choice and avoidance are exercised according to knowledge; so that it is not pleasure that is the good thing, but knowledge by which we shall choose a pleasure at a certain time, and of a certain kind."*[74] But not all actions are voluntary. Towards involuntary action, Clement states that *"What is involuntary is not a matter for judgment. But this is twofold—what is done in ignorance, and what is done through necessity."*[75] More about involuntary and voluntary actions when discussing good and evil.

Free will is freedom. The ability as individuals to choose our actions without coercion. A gift. Freedom is necessary to fulfill our purpose but requires knowledge for its proper use. We must each use this gift to the best of our ability. In his *Exhortation*, Clement says,

> He (the Creator) offers freedom, you flee into bondage; He bestows salvation, you sink down into destruction; He confers everlasting life, you wait for punishment.[76] Although visited with ignominy and exile, and confiscation, and above

all, death, he [Clement's gnostic] will never be wrenched from his freedom, and signal love to God.[77]

God's freedom endures. It cannot be taken away through any trial, even at the point of death. Further, we have a choice as to whether we accept that freedom or not. It is our choice. We turn next to law.

Law

Law has a defining place within Clement's writings:

> For he who is wise will live concentrating all his energies on knowledge, directing his life by good deeds, despising the opposite, and following the pursuits which contribute to truth. And the law is not what is decided by law (for what is seen is not vision), nor every opinion (not certainly what is evil). But law is the opinion which is good, and what is good is that which is true, and what is true is that which finds "true being" and attains to it.[78]

Further, *"the sense of the law is to be taken in three ways,—either as exhibiting a symbol, or laying down a precept for right conduct, or as uttering a prophecy."*[79] Clement says understanding law is pursuing truth to acquire wisdom. It is a truth that is rooted in "true being," our Creator, which can take several forms.

Regarding Divine Law, Clement says that

> Virtue is a will in conformity to God and Christ in life ... a system of reasonable actions—that is, of those things taught by the Word—an unfailing energy which we have called faith. The system is the commandments of the Lord, which, being divine statutes and spiritual counsels, have been written for ourselves, being adapted for ourselves and our neighbours.[80]

Divine Law comes from our Creator's commands. It has been written specifically for us as a system of negative actions based on reason, with virtue and faith as integral parts.

In regards to natural law he says that

> "Law is monarch of all, both of mortals and immortals," says Pindar. I understand, however, by these works, Him who

enacted law. And I regard, as spoken of the God of all, the following utterance of Hesiod.... "For the Saturnian framed for men this law: Fishes, and beasts, and winged birds may eat Each other, since no rule of right is theirs: But Right (by far the best) to men he gave.

"Whether, then, it be the law which is connate and natural, or that given afterwards, which is meant, it is certainly of God; and both the law of nature and that of instruction are one."[81]

Natural Law also comes from our Creator and is derived from the instructions He has given us. It is based on what is good and right: God's divine law.

The philosophy of law is

divided into four parts—into the historic, and that which is specially called the legislative, which two properly belong to an ethical treatise; and the third, that which relates to sacrifice, which belongs to the physical science; and the fourth, above all, the department of theology.[82]

Clement links law with history, ethics, sacrifice, and theology. The latter we have already defined as involving formal reasoning about our Creator. The next areas discuss good, evil and virtue—morality. These are followed by sections about knowledge, reason, and faith which all support good and virtue, as well as each other.

The relationships between faith, virtue, freedom, love, charity, and God's law are diagrammed below. For the underlying detail see *Collectivism and Charity*[83] and *A Handbook of Natural Rights*.[84]

We have covered much in the way of subject matter and are now at a point where we can summarize the answers posed earlier in this section regarding Man's purpose: what God gave each of us, whether we can have a relationship with Him, and, if we can, what that relationship is like.

1. Creation was made for Man. It is intended to support Man on his journey to his final destination, and we are to exercise good judgment and stewardship while on our journey.

2. Man is made as an image of the Son, but this image is not physical. It is our mind and ability to reason which comprise the image, and that image is reflected in our soul.

3. As we are made in our Creator's image, we can communicate with Him. Our purpose is to know Him, and we have been given reason in order to know Him. We must therefore be able to have a relationship with Him. By knowing the Son, we come to know God.

4. By knowing our self, we come to know Him. We were given reason to acquire knowledge. It is through the inward conversation that is prayer that we have the opportunity to talk with Him. But reason alone is not enough. Faith is required, because a first cause can only be known by faith, and our Creator is the first cause.

5. We are all equal before our Creator. We have free choice, which is necessary to know Him. This free choice is freedom, and it comes solely from our Creator. It cannot be taken from us, but we can each choose not to use it as intended.

6. Divine Law comes from our Creator's commandments and is specifically designed for us, based upon actionable reason, and grounded in faith and virtue. Morality then is also necessary in order to follow Divine Law as it requires virtue.

7. Natural Law is derived from the instructions we have received from our Creator—His Divine Law. They are

not statutes, but are based on the understanding we have from Him of what is good and right.

8. Ethics and theology are components of His Law.

Clement has now answered questions about why creation was made, our purpose, our nature and some of its implications, and what God's laws generally hold for us. As our purpose is to know Him— we will look now as to what that means. He is mind, reason, truth, and good; therefore, we must understand these in relation to Him. His law is grounded in faith and virtue; therefore, we must also understand what these are and if there is any relationship between them. In short, we must understand what it means to "live rightly." We will start by discussing good and evil.

Good and Evil

We saw previously that ethics is connected to law, so a discussion of good and evil is relevant. However, Clement writes that in talking about good and evil, we also need to go back to the questions of "Who is our Creator?" and "What kind of relationship can we have with Him?" We will start by discussing what good is according to Clement, which will lead to discussions about Providence, evil, sin, and sin's consequences.

The Good

In laying out the issue of good Clement discusses what it means to do wrong —the opposite of good.

> To do wrong, then, is not good, for no one does wrong except for some other thing; and nothing that is necessary is voluntary. To do wrong, then is voluntary, so that it is not necessary. But the good differ especially from the bad in inclinations and good desires. For all depravity of soul is accompanied with want of restraint; and he who acts from passion, acts from want of restraint and from depravity.[85]

Doing wrong is voluntary and driven by Man's internal factors.

In discussing good, Clement cites Plato, saying there are two goods:

> Further, Plato the philosopher says that the end is twofold: that which is communicable, and exists first in the ideal forms themselves, which he also calls 'the good'; and that

which partakes of it, and receives its likeness from it, as is the case in the men who appropriate virtue and true philosophy.[86]

The first good is our Creator, as follows:

> For assuredly He does not hate anything, and yet wish that which He hates to exist. Nor does He wish anything not to exist, and yet become the cause of existence to that which he wishes not to exist. Nor does He wish anything not to exist which yet exists. If, then, the Word hates anything, He does not wish it to exist. But nothing exists, that cause of whose existence is not supplied by God. Nothing, then, is hated by God, nor yet by the Word. For both are one—that is, God.... If then He hates none of the things which He has made, it follows that He loves them. Much more than the rest, and with reason, will He love man, the noblest of all objects created by Him, and a God-loving being. Therefore God is loving; consequently the Word is loving.

> But he who loves anything wishes to do it good. And that which does good must be every way better than that which does not good. But nothing is better than the Good. The Good, then, does good. And God is admitted to be good. God therefore does good. And the Good, in virtue of its being good, does nothing else than do good. Consequently God does all good. And He does no good to man without caring for him, and He does not care for him without taking care of him. For that which does good purposely, is better than what does no good purposely. But nothing is better than God. And to do good purposely, is nothing else than to take care of man. God therefore cares for man, and takes care of him.... But the good is not said to be good, on account of its being possessed of virtue ... but on account of its being in itself and by itself good.[87]

For there is one good, the Father.[88]

This has the following implications for His creation:

> God is good on His own account, and just also on ours, and He is just because He is good. And His justice is shown to

> us by His own Word from there from above, when the Father was. For before He became Creator He was God; He was Good.[89]

Even before creation, our Creator was and has always been good. He must also be just because He is good.

It is because our Creator is good that creation was made.

> For God, being good, on account of the principal part of the whole creation, seeing he wishes to save it, was induced to make the rest also; conferring on them at the beginning this first boon, that of existence. For that to be is far better than not to be, will be admitted by every one. Then, according to the capabilities of their nature, each one was and is made, advancing to that which is better.[90]

But our Creator is not only good in and of Himself; his good is active in creation. In Clement's writing, this active good is Providence. This is the second good Plato referenced.

> For God is the cause of all good things; but of some primarily, as of the Old and the New Testament; and of others by consequence, as philosophy. Perchance, too, philosophy was given to the Greeks directly and primarily, till the Lord should call the Greeks.[91]

It is Providence to which we will turn to next.

Providence

Clement says Providence comes from our Creator and is extended to us because of God's love for His creation:

> For the Providence which extends to us from God is not ministerial, as that service which proceeds from inferiors to superiors. But in pity for our weakness, the continual dispensations of Providence work, as the care of shepherds towards the sheep, and of a king towards his subjects.[92]

Providence's existence is self-evident from the works which occur around us and is not subject to question.

> And there are those that deserve punishment, as to ask proofs of the existence of Providence. There being then a

Providence ... the divine Providence being evident from the sight of all its skillful and wise works which, are seen, some of which take place in order, and some appear in order.[93]

As stated earlier, even the activities of those who rebel against the Creator

> are guided by universal Providence to a salutary issue ... It is accordingly the greatest achievement of divine Providence, not to allow the evil, which has sprung from voluntary apostasy, to remain useless, and for no good ... but especially to ensure that what happens through the evils hatched by any, may come to a good and useful issue, and to use to advantage those things which appear to be evils, as also the testimony which accrues from temptation.[94]

The Creator is not only good, but He even turns evil resulting from our voluntary choices into good within His plan. He has given us free will. Being all-knowing and standing outside of time, He has always known what we each will choose. By Providence, He has already taken our choices into consideration within His plan and turns even our choices to do wrong to His good purposes.

Because our Creator is good,

> He is in no respect whatever the cause of evil. For all things are arranged with a view to the salvation of the universe by the Lord of the universe, both generally and particularly.[95] Evil is the opposite of good.[96] Evil has an evil nature, and can never turn out the producer of aught that is good; indicating that philosophy is in a sense a work of Divine Providence.[97]

Our Creator is good, and as good and evil are opposites, He cannot be responsible for evil. Even the theft and falsehoods within Greek philosophy are cited by Clement as works of Providence as it is now being used for good by revealing God's truth.

To summarize, Our Creator is good in two ways. First, He is in and of Himself not only good, but the Good. Second, He is active in His good through Providence, His divine plan which turns even wrong actions into good. As He has also given us free will and law, he does not choose who will receive salvation. We do so through our own choices.

So how is this good reflected in our lives? Clement develops a view of the true gnostic—one who truly has some knowledge and understanding of our Creator—and how this impacts the way one should live. Clement says about the gnostic,

> after that which is reckoned perfection in others, his [the gnostic's] righteousness advances to activity in well-doing. And in whomsoever the increased force of righteousness advances to the doing of good, in his case perfection abides in the fixed habit of well-doing after the likeness of God.[98]
>
> The Gnostic is such, that he is subject only to the affections that exist for the maintenance of the body, such as hunger, thirst, and the like ... who [the Gnostic] is incapable of exercising courage: for neither does he meet what inspires fear, as he regards none of the things that occur in life as to be dreaded; nor can aught dislodge him from this – the love he has towards God.... Nor is he angry; for there is nothing to move him to anger, seeing he ever loves God, and is entirely turned towards Him alone, and therefore hates none of God's creatures.
>
> How, then, has he any more need of fortitude, who is not in the midst of dangers, being not present, but already wholly with the object of love? And what necessity for self-restraint to him who has not need of it? For to have such desires, as require self-restraint in order to their control, is characteristic of one who is not yet pure, but subject to passion. Now, fortitude is assumed by reason of fear and cowardice. For it were no longer seemly that the friend of God ... should fall into pleasures or fears, and be occupied in the repression of the passions. For I venture to assert, that as he is predestinated through what he shall do, and what he shall obtain, so also has he predestinated himself by reason of what he knew and whom he loved.[99]

Our Creator is all-knowing and knew what choices we each would make before the beginning of time, yet he has allowed us the freedom to choose because it is necessary to fulfill His purpose for us. As God allows us to make our own choices, we predestine ourselves through our actions, as we have been given the means to reason and knowledge regarding obedience. This ends the discussion of good and evil. We will next turn to the topics of vice and sin.

Vice and Sin
What is vice? *"To restrain oneself from doing good is the work of vice."*[100] Vice is the voluntary act of choosing *not* to do good.

What is sin? We noted earlier that *"to do wrong, then is voluntary."*[101]

> What is voluntary is either what is by desire, or what is by choice, or what is of intention. Closely allied to each other are these things—sin, mistake, crime.... Sinning arises from being unable to determine what ought to be done, or being unable to do it.... Mistake is a sin contrary to calculation; and voluntary sin is crime; and crime is voluntary wickedness. Sin, then is on my part voluntary.... Mistake is the involuntary action of another towards me, while a crime alone is voluntary, whether my act or another's.[102]

Sin is the voluntary act then of doing what is wrong and has more than one source.

In relation to the gnostic view of law present during Clement's life, he wrote that,

> [T]hose, who denounce fear, assail the law; and if the law, plainly also God, who gave the law. For these three elements are of necessity presented in the subject on hand: the ruler, his administration, and the ruled. If, then, according to hypothesis, they abolish the law; then, by necessary consequence, each one who is led by lust, courting pleasure, must neglect what is right and despise the Deity, and fearlessly indulge in impiety and injustice together, having dashed away from the truth.
>
> Yea, say they, fear is an irrational aberration and perturbation of mind. What sayest thou? And how can this definition be any longer maintained, seeing the commandment is given me by the Word? But the

> commandment forbids, hanging fear over the head of those who have incurred admonition for their discipline.
>
> Fear is not then irrational. It is therefore rational. How could it be otherwise.... But if the law produces fear, the knowledge of the law is the beginning of wisdom; and a man is not wise without law. Therefore those who reject the law are unwise.... Let us see what terrors the law announces. If it is the things which hold an intermediate place between virtue and vice, such as poverty, disease, obscurity, and humble birth, and the like, these things civil laws hold forth, and are praised for so doing.... But the law given to us enjoins us to shun what are in reality bad things—adultery, uncleanness, paederasty, ignorance, wickedness, soul-disease, death ... For these are vices in reality, and the workings that proceed from them are dreadful and terrible.... The law did not cause, but showed sin.[103]

By assailing God's law, we assail our Creator. Fear of our Creator is rational and the beginning of wisdom. Law is designed to save us from real and terrible outcomes.

In regards to sin there are two sources, ignorance and inability. Their correction leads to the same end, a work of Providence.

> Though men's actions are ten thousand in number, the sources of all sin are but two, ignorance and inability. And both depend on ourselves; inasmuch as we will not learn, nor, on the other hand, restrain lust. And of these, the one is that, in consequence of which people do not judge well, and the other that, in consequence of which they cannot comply with right judgment.... Consequently, then there are assigned two kinds of correction applicable to both kinds of sin: for the one, knowledge and clear demonstrations from the testimony of the Scriptures; and for the other, the training according to the Word, which is regulated by the discipline of faith and fear. And both develop into perfect love.[104]

Sin's Consequences
The preceding passage goes on to say, *"But as children are chastised by their teacher, or their father, so are we by Providence. But God does not punish, for punishment is retaliation for evil. He chastises,*

however, for good to those who are chastised, collectively and individually."[105]

So why do we suffer when our Creator is good? Persecution was real in Clement's day. He had two responses to this question. The first is

> It was not that He (our Creator) wished us to be persecuted.... Accordingly, they unwillingly bear testimony to our righteousness, we being unjustly punished for righteousness' sake. But the injustice for the judge does not affect the providence of God. For the judge must be master of his own opinion—not pulled by strings, like inanimate machines, set in motion only by external causes. Accordingly he is judged in respect to his judgment, as we also, in accordance with our choice of things desirable, and our endurance.[106]

This type of punishment results from the voluntary actions of another and is involuntary on the part of the persecuted. Both the persecutor and persecuted are judged accordingly by their Creator. Choice must be present, but all will be turned to His good through Providence.

His second response is that God corrects for three causes.

> First, that he who is corrected may become better than his former self; then that those who are capable of being saved by examples may be driven back, being admonished; and thirdly, that he who is injured may not be readily despised, and be apt to receive injury."[107] As He is good, He is just and "it is not expedient that justice should be neglected on our account. Each one of us, who sins, with his own free-will chooses punishment, and the blame lies with him who chooses. God is without blame.[108]

The ultimate punishment from sin is death. A death by our own choice, as

> Socrates says, "that the law was not made for the sake of the good." ... the commandments by menacing with fear, work love, not hatred. Wherefore the law is productive of the emotion of fear. "So that the law is holy," and in truth "spiritual," according to the apostle. We must, then ... not regard death as evil.... death is the fellowship of the soul in

a state of sin with the body; and life the separation from sin.[109]

Before we proceed to our final topics, let's summarize Clement's thoughts about good and evil. These include the following:

1. There are two types of good, the one and the many. The first is the Good, our Creator—that is, God. The other good relates to Providence which is the good order in which all things are directed to His end. It includes all things within creation as all came from our Creator. Providence exists within the mind of our Creator who has always known the choices we would make from before the beginning of time and turned all actions to His end.

2. As we have free choice, indeed it is required to know Him; it is we who predestine ourselves as we have been given reason and knowledge and were created for the purpose of knowing Him. Our Creator does not choose our outcome; we alone are responsible.

3. Sin is evil and voluntary and occurs from either ignorance or inability. God's law was created to start us on the path to wisdom—knowing our Creator—and to warn us of sin's terrible and final consequences.

4. In response to why people suffer when the Creator is good, Clement had two responses. The first was for those who are innocent: Their suffering is a consequence of the free choice that we have been given. However, both the persecutor and persecuted will be judged by their actions, and even when the innocent suffer, that suffering will be brought to a good end through Providence. The second response concerned correction for those who do wrong by choosing sin. There are three causes for correction: (1) the transgressor might become better, (2) to serve as an example for others, and (3) to prevent injury to the one who has been harmed.

5. Our Creator does not punish from wrath, but from justice. As sin is voluntary, by committing sin we voluntarily choose punishment.

Virtue

Virtue has been mentioned several times. We all have the same virtuous nature. Virtue is voluntary. It is connected to faith, and it is by acquiring virtue that we partake of "the good." From this we can deduce that we have an inclination toward virtue, but it must be acquired, and that through its acquisition we approach "the good." But what is virtue? How do we acquire it? Why do we need it? Is there only one virtue? Clement starts with discussing truth.

"One speaks in one way of the truth, in another way the truth interprets itself. The guessing at truth is one thing, and truth itself is another. Resemblance is one thing, the thing itself is another. And the one results from learning and practice, the other from power and faith."[110] Further, *"The way of truth is therefore one. But into it as into a perennial river, streams flow from all sides."*[111] There is both truth itself and many truths which resemble it. In regards to truth itself, Clement asserts that *"the Word is truth."*[112]

> The instruction which is of God is the right direction of truth to the contemplation of God.... As therefore the general directs the phalanx, consulting the safety of his soldiers, and the pilot steers the vessel, desiring to save the passengers; so also the Instructor [the Word] guides the children to a saving course of conduct.[113]

As to the truths that resemble the truth,

> so while the truth is one, many things contribute to its investigation. But its discovery is by the Son. If then we consider, virtue is, in power one. But it is the case, that when exhibited in some things, it is called prudence, in others temperance, and in others manliness or righteousness. By the same analogy, while truth is one, in geometry there is the truth of geometry; in music, that of music; and in the right philosophy, there will be Hellenic truth.... And each, whether it be virtue or truth, called by the same name, is the cause of its own peculiar effect alone.[114]

Virtue and truth are the same. Again we have the same framework as with our Creator and good. We have another instance of the one and the many. By understanding truth, we understand virtue. Virtue is the means by which we approach God's truth.

> Now, inasmuch as there are four things in which the truth resides—Sensation, Understanding, Knowledge, Opinion,—intellectual apprehension is first in the order of nature; but in our case, and in relation to ourselves, Sensation is first, and of Sensation and Understanding the essence of Knowledge is formed; and evidence is common to Understanding and Sensation. Well Sensation is the ladder to Knowledge; while Faith, advancing over the pathway of the objects of sense, leaves Opinion behind, and speeds to things free of deception, and reposes in the truth.... For knowledge is a state of mind that results from demonstration; but faith is a grace which from what is indemonstrable conducts to what is universal and simple, what is neither with matter, nor matter, nor under matter.[115]

For *"sight, and hearing, and the voice contribute to truth, but it is the mind which is the appropriate faculty for knowing it."*[116] Knowledge comes from reason and demonstration, but faith is not demonstrable. It is the mind which alone can know truth.

The special way in which we have been made allows us to learn virtue. *"Above all, this ought to be known, that by nature we are adapted for virtue; not so as to be possessed of it from our birth, but so as to be adapted for acquiring it."*[117]

In regard to how truth is acquired, *"philosophy, being the search for truth, contributes to the comprehension of truth; not as being the cause of comprehension, but a cause along with other things, and co-operator; perhaps also a joint cause."*[118] Philosophy is one way to discover truths that are demonstrable, God's word is another.

The false should not dissuade us from pursuing the truth.

> On account of the heresies, therefore, the toil of discovery must be undertaken; but we must not at all abandon [the truth]. For, on fruit being set before us, some real and ripe, and some made of wax, as like the real as possible, we are not to abstain from both on account of the resemblance. But by the exercise of the apprehension of contemplation, and by reasoning of the most decisive character, we must distinguish the true from the seeming.

> And as, while there is one royal highway, there are many others, some leading to a precipice, some to a rushing river or to a deep sea, no one will shrink from travelling by reason of the diversity, but will make use of the safe, and royal, and frequented way; so, though some say this, some that, concerning the truth, we must not abandon it; but must seek out the most accurate knowledge respecting it. Since also among garden-grown vegetables weeds also spring up, are the husbandmen, then, to desist from gardening?[119]

Knowing truth is necessary to distinguish the true from the false. Virtue is useful, and it is by our efforts that we acquire them. *"If one loves justice, its toils are its virtues. For temperance and prudence teach justice and fortitude; and [other] than these there is nothing more useful in life to men."*[120]

Summary of Virtue

So virtue and the truth are the same. There are again two truths, the one and the many. We are made in order to acquire virtue, because we are not born with it. We must acquire virtue in order to both know the truth and not to be led astray—to discern good from evil. We should not be deterred by the existence of the false. It is from work in searching for virtue that we acquire it. We obtain some truth from knowledge—that which can be perceived by our senses and understanding. It is one way we can find some understanding of the first cause as the Logos is His image. Truth is also found in faith, which is received by grace. It is simple and direct and also necessary in understanding first cause (God).

Goal of Virtue

As to why we need virtue, *"to the whole human race, then, discipline and virtue are a necessity, if they would pursue after happiness."*[121] *"Now Plato the philosopher, defining the end of happiness, says that it is likeness to God as far as possible."*[122] Virtue is necessary to achieve happiness and the pursuit of happiness ends by becoming as close as possible to the likeness of our Creator. This is our purpose: to become good as our Creator is good.

Virtues Themselves

> Fear [of the Creator], accordingly, leads to repentance and hope. Now hope is the expectation of good things, or an

> expectation sanguine of absent good; and favourable circumstances are assumed in order to good hope, which we have learned leads on to love. Now love turns out to be consent in what pertains to reason, life, and manners, or in brief, fellowship in life.... And akin to love is hospitality.... Philanthropy ... is natural affection, being a loving treatment of men.... As, then, the virtues follow one another, why need I say what has been demonstrated already, that faith hopes through repentance, and fear through faith; and patience and practice in these along with learning terminate in love, which is perfected by knowledge?[123]

Clement writes there are three types of friendship:

> And that of these the first and the best is that which results from virtue, for the love that is founded on reason is firm; that the second and intermediates is by way of recompense, and is social, liberal, and useful for life; for the friendship which is the result of favour is mutual. And the third and last we assert to be that which is founded on intimacy"[124]

The virtues are numerous, and all are connected to one another, but all terminate in love. The virtues are perfected by knowledge, and learning is required to develop them. There are three types of relationships, the best of which is built on virtue.

We have now discussed *the what* about knowing our Creator. We turn next to *the how*. The point has been made several times that both reason and faith are necessary to know Him. It is to those topics we now turn, focusing on how both result in knowledge. As we have just seen, there is also a connection between virtue and faith. What is faith? Why do we need it? What is the connection between virtue and faith? How does it relate to knowledge and the virtues?

Faith

So far we have covered the following concerning faith: Understanding the Creator as first cause can be done by faith alone; free choice is necessary for faith; faith is an integral part of Divine Law; faith brings wisdom through the Holy Spirit; and faith and fear are both used in training those who choose to sin no more. But what is faith? Why do we need it?

As to what faith is,

> For if it [faith] were mere human habit, as the Greeks supposed, it would have been extinguished. But if it grow, and there be no place where it is not; then I affirm, that faith, whether founded in love, or in fear, ... is something divine. For love on account of its friendly alliance with faith, makes men believers; and faith, which is the foundation of love, in its turn introduces the doing of good.[125]

> Our deeds ought to be conformable to reason, and to manifest further that we ought to select and possess what is useful out of all culture. Now the ways of wisdom are various that lead right to the way of truth. Faith is the way.[126]

Faith is divine, the foundation of love, and the way to truth.

As to why faith is needed,

> Without faith it is impossible to please God.... If then it be choice, being desirous of something, the desire is in this instance intellectual. And since choice is the beginning of action, faith is discovered to be the beginning of action.[127] Faith, then, we say, we are to show must not be inert and alone, but accompanied with investigation. For I do not say that we are not to inquire at all.[128]

Faith is the beginning of action and must be accompanied by investigation.

How is faith related to virtue and knowledge? As to virtue,

> And, in truth, faith is discovered, by us, to be the first movement toward salvation; after which fear, and hope, and repentance, advancing in company with temperance and patience, lead us to love and knowledge.... Fear and patience are then helpers of your faith; and our allies are long-suffering and temperance.... so neither can knowledge be attained without faith. It is then the support of truth.[129] Faith is the greatest mother of the virtues.[130]

As to knowledge,

The exercise of faith directly becomes knowledge, reposing on a sure foundation. Knowledge, accordingly, is defined by the sons of the philosophers as a habit, which cannot be overthrown by reason. Is there any other true condition such as this, except piety, of which alone the Word is teacher? I think not.[131] We assert that it is impossible for a man without learning to comprehend the things which are declared in the faith. But to adopt what is well said, and not to adopt the reverse, is caused not simply by faith, but by faith combined with knowledge.[132]

Summary of Faith
Faith then is the way to truth. It is voluntary. It cannot be demonstrated. We've also discussed previously that as first causes cannot be demonstrated, and the Creator is the first cause, the Creator therefore can be apprehended by faith alone. Faith, accompanied by virtue, also leads us to knowledge—but not just faith alone: faith combined with knowledge.

Finally, faith cannot be dissolved by reason:

> For the prophets and disciples of the Spirit know infallibly their mind. For they know it by faith, in a way which others could not easily, as the Spirit has said. But it is not possible for those who have not learned to receive it thus.[133]

Our link with our Creator is our mind and reason, and it is through His image within each of us that He gave us these things also to use in knowing Him. It is once again by knowing Him that we complete our purpose. His law for us is based upon both faith and reason.

We finally move to knowledge and reason.

Knowledge and Reason
As we have already seen, reason is the process by which we obtain knowledge, and it is knowledge of Him we seek. Faith and knowledge, which by reason becomes unshakable, leads to wisdom.

Law is the precept of knowledge. *"The sure seal of knowledge is composed of nature, education, and exercise."*[134] In relation to nature, *"Philosophy is characterized by the investigation into truth and the nature of things."*[135] It is preparatory training:

> The readiness acquired by previous training conduces much to the perception of such things as are requisite; but those things which can be perceived only by mind are the special exercise of the mind. And their nature is triple according as we consider their quantity, their magnitude, and what can be predicated of them.[136]

To the need for learning,

> It is not by nature but by learning, that people become noble and good, as people also become physicians and pilots.... Again, God has created us naturally social and just; whence justice must not be said to take its rise from implantation alone. But the good imparted by creation is to be conceived of as excited by the commandment; the soul being trained to be willing to select what is noblest.[137]

Exercise is needed as

> Use keeps steel brighter, but disuse produces rust in it. For, in a word, exercise produces a healthy condition both in souls and bodies.... For by teaching, one learns more; and in speaking, one is often a hearer along with his audience. For the teacher of him who speaks and of him who hears is one who waters both the mind and the word.[138]

In relation to the Gnostic again, knowledge is predicated on the law. It also consists of understanding the nature of things which alone lie within the province of the mind. Attaining knowledge requires both learning and use of reason.

"We define Wisdom to be certain knowledge, being a sure and irrefragable apprehension of things divine and human, comprehending the present, past, and future.... And it is irrefragable by reason, inasmuch as it has been communicated."[139] Wisdom is sure knowledge that cannot be assaulted or shaken by reason.

"And if, too, the end of the wise man is contemplation ... then, knowledge or wisdom ought to be exercised up to the eternal and unchangeable habit of contemplation."[140] Wisdom is certain knowledge and the end of wisdom is contemplation.

"*Faith is something superior to knowledge, and is its criterion.... Knowledge, accordingly, is characterized by faith; and faith, by a kind of divine mutual reciprocal correspondence, becomes characterized by knowledge.*"[141] Knowledge is also perfected by faith.[142] Unlike faith, "*knowledge is a state of mind that results from demonstration.*"[143] "*Wisdom is intelligence, but all intelligence is not wisdom. And it has been shown, that the knowledge of the first cause of the universe is of faith.*"[144] While faith is the way to knowledge of the first cause, knowledge is perfected by faith and faith becomes knowledge.

> Truth is the knowledge of the true; and the mental habit of truth is the knowledge of the things which are true. Now knowledge is constituted by the reason, and cannot be overthrown by another reason. What we do not, we do not either from not being able or not being willing—or both. Accordingly we don't fly, since we neither can nor wish; we do not swim at present, for example, since we can indeed, but do not choose; and we are not as the Lord, since we wish, but cannot be.[145]

Summary of Knowledge and Reason
The following points can be summarized from Clement on reason and knowledge:

1. Learning is required for a people to become good and noble, and exercising the mind is necessary to keep it sharp.

2. It is by learning that we acquire knowledge, using reason. Knowledge which is planted firmly becomes unshakable. This is the virtue of wisdom, which ends in the contemplation of the truth.

3. Knowledge is characterized by faith, and faith becomes characterized by knowledge.

Connections to Augustine's Writings
Finally, there are several passages within Clement's writing that are developed much further by Augustine in the next chapter. The first idea comes from the following two passages.

> For the Stoics say that heaven is properly a city, but places here on earth are not cities; for they are called so, but are not. For a city is an important thing, and the people a decorous body, and a multitude of men regulated by law as the church by the word—a city on earth impregnable—free from tyranny; a product of the divine will on earth as in heaven.[146]

> But truth is not taught by imitation, but by instruction. For it is not that we may seem good that we believe in Christ ... we are compelled to be Christians in order to be excellent and good. For the kingdom belongs pre-eminently to the violent, who, from investigation, and study, and discipline, reap this fruit, that they become kings.[147]

These passages refer to two kingdoms: one of the Earth built upon violence, the "city of man"; the other which is regulated by the Word, the "city of God."

> The distinction of names and things also in the Scriptures themselves produces great light in men's souls. For it is necessary to understand expressions which signify several things, and several expressions when they signify one thing. The result of which is accurate answering.[148]

This passage refers to Scripture potentially having multiple meanings and the use of multiple words to represent the same thing. Both of these ideas are picked up in the *City of God*, which will be the primary source for the next chapter.

Summary

A few words before we leave this chapter. We have found much in this chapter to lay a foundation for the rest of this book. We will not repeat the same information if it appears in the remaining sources we will be examining. Instead we will focus on what is new, different, or contrary to the content in this chapter. What, exactly, does Clement lay out in his work?

There is one and only one Creator. Clement focuses on the Platonic philosophical concept of the one and the many in his writing. He presents two distinctions as being present within the one unity we call the Creator, and that is the Father and the Son. Consistent with middle platonic thought, the Father is a transcendent and simple unity, while the Son is immanent and complex. However, both distinctions lie within a single unity. He is saying that the Father and Son are first principle and Creator in different senses, similar to the different causes stated by Aristotle, but both are a single unity.

He also presents arguments for considering both good and truth to be instances of the one and the many. In regards to good, the Father is said to be "the Good," a good based "on account of its (the Father's) being in itself and by itself good" and the Creator being the "cause of all good things." There are certainly many types of good which occur in the world: parents caring for their children and parents late in life, friends caring for neighbors, and strangers helping those in need are just a few examples. We have been given free choice by Him and do not always make good choices. However, since our Creator is all-knowing and all-seeing, His mind was able to see all the choices each of us would ever make, even before Creation. He has brought all things to His good end by His plan, which we call Providence. Through Providence even our bad choices are brought to good by God.

As to the case for truth also being an instance of the one and the many, Clement says that "*guessing at truth is one thing, the truth itself is another.*"[149] The "Word is the truth," and the Word is the only way by which the Creator can be known. The Word is His truth, the truth—one truth. He cites many instances of truth from the sciences, the arts, mathematics, etc. Truth resides in four things: sensation, understanding, knowledge, and opinion. Sensation and understanding lead to knowledge, which can be demonstrated, but faith flies over opinion and leads straight to the understanding of what cannot be demonstrated and "conducts to what is universal and simple." Reason is used to acquire knowledge; therefore, both reason and faith are necessary in order to know our Creator.

At first blush, these may not appear to be related, but I do not think that is the case. Clement has provided us with two cases that we can grasp: good and truth. We can realize there is a single underlying good and truth, and at the same time we see that there are many instances of both all around us. He is using our understanding of those things to show how they relate to our Creator, to better understand the distinction between the Father and Son. These distinctions again lie within a single unity similar to Aristotle's notion of different causes: material, efficient, formal, and final.

Clement also said that all creation came about by our Creator. As our Creator is good, creation is also good as evil cannot produce that which is good. Man was created differently from the rest of creation. We were given mind and reason, the image of the Son, who is the image of our Creator. This image is an inward one which is reflected in our soul, and that image is transformed by our choices. Man's purpose is to know his Creator. By His law He gave us free choice, the capacity to make our own unforced choices. This is freedom, and it is necessary in order for us to fulfill our purpose. As such, Man is responsible for his own choices, so our Creator cannot predestine Man in terms of salvation; Man can only predestine himself by his choices and obedience. We are also all created with an equal nature before our Creator. There is no difference between Jew, or Gentile, or pagan, or man, or woman. The same Creator is the God of all.

As our Creator is not only good, but is in fact "the good," He cannot be responsible for evil. For evil is the opposite of good and evil cannot produce good. It is the result of Man's exercising his free choice that evil arises. Man is therefore responsible for evil. Our choices can be voluntary or involuntary. For the involuntary, our Creator will judge both the persecutor and persecuted accordingly. Wrong (disobedient) voluntary choices are sin. Our Creator does not punish but chastises as a parent or teacher. Punishment would be retribution which would be evil. Correction is done out of love for His creation and is done to (1) improve the one making the choice, (2) serve as an example to others, or (3) protect a person from harm. As sin is a voluntary choice, we also choose to be punished when we sin. Therefore, the punishment arising from sin is also our choice, and ours alone. And again, through Providence even evil acts are turned to good within our Creator's plan.

Finally, we found that truth is virtue, the virtues are all related, and all end in love. There is only one true way to truth, what Clement called the royal highway in one of his analogies. Reason and knowledge are needed to acquire virtue by helping to determine the difference between what is true and what is false. It is through the struggle to determine what is true that we build virtue, and we were made in a way to adapt to virtue—but we were not born with it. It is knowledge that has become unshakable through reason that we gain wisdom. Faith is the foundation for all virtues. It is divine, the foundation of love, and the way to the truth. As to why virtue is important, *"discipline and virtue are a necessity, if they would pursue after happiness."*[150] In order to reach happiness, we need the discipline that comes with virtue's development. And the end of happiness is becoming a likeness of our Creator, to the greatest extent that we can.

Chapter 4

The Two Cities

Aurelius Augustinus (St. Augustine of Hippo) is without doubt one of the most influential early theological writer/philosophers of his time. He was born in 354 in what is now Algeria, the son of a pagan father, Patricius, and a Christian mother, Monnica. He was educated in Carthage where he taught until 383 when he went to Rome. He began as a pagan and practiced Manichaeism for a while. He moved to Milan in 384 as a professor of rhetoric. Carthage and Rome were very traditional Roman cities. Milan, however, was under the influence of the Christian scholar Ambrose. While in Milan, Augustine listened to sermons from Ambrose and read Platonist literature and Paul's letters. He was baptized by Ambrose on Easter in 387.

He briefly returned to Rome a second time and began writing against false philosophy and Manichaeism. He returned to Africa in 388 where he founded a monastery. He was ordained Presbyter of Hippo in 389 and became its Bishop in 396, where he stayed until his death in 430. His writings were both significant and influential. He was the greatest intellectual in the west during his life. Like Clement, he also incorporated philosophy into his writing and drew contrasts between his positions and those of Plato and Neo-Platonic philosophers, including Plotinus and his student Porphyry.

But the times had changed. During Clement's life, Rome was at the height of its power and Christianity a new religion which did not yet have a single authoritative source. Since then, the emperor Constantine had converted to Christianity in 313 and made it the Roman Empire's official religion. The empire had split between east and west. Jerome had translated the Hebrew Scriptures into Latin (the Vulgate) in 405. The first two Ecumenical Counsels had occurred at Nicea (325) and Constantinople (381), which denounced Arianism as heresy and adopted and then revised the Nicene Creed. Rome had been sacked by the Goths in 410 and Attila again in 424. By 429, the Vandals had invaded North Africa, and at Augustine's death their fleet lay outside Hippo's harbor. The western Roman Empire was in the final stages of its collapse.

The Two Cities
Many blamed Rome's decline on Christianity's rise as people turned away from the pagan gods they had previously worshipped. Augustine begins the *City of God* by refuting the claims made against Christianity. He reviews Rome's history and all of the calamities occurring while the old gods were worshipped. He uses Varro's writings about the Roman gods to show they were not powerful; it was Man who protected the gods rather than the gods who protected Man. These pagan gods could not grant even the simplest things let alone eternal life. Finally, these gods were, in fact, created by Man as even Varro indicated.

In explaining the Roman Empire's early success, Augustine ties virtue's existence to Providence, showing how that virtue was lost as Rome's success increased, using both Sallust's and Cicero's histories to make his points. Those histories tie success to an increased risk for corruption and a subsequent decline of moral values (a point also made earlier by Clement). Augustine picks up this theme and ties it to the old gods' development as well as the behaviors and worship rituals surrounding them—the state religion society's development discussed in Chapter 1. Augustine argues the Platonic philosopher's natural theology creates inconsistencies when teaching belief in the existence and worship of a single, all-powerful creator god, while at the same time advocating worship of many other smaller gods.

He takes these arguments and uses them to develop the concept of two cities. In his words,

> When, therefore, man lives according to man, not according to God, he is like the devil ... So, then, when a man lives according to truth, he lives not according to himself but

> according to God.... When man lives according to himself, that is to say, according to human ways and not according to God's will, then surely he lives according to falsehood. Man himself, of course, is not a lie, since God who is his Author and Creator could not be the Author and Creator of a lie.... [and] it is a lie not to live as a man was created to live....
>
> For, when we choose to sin, what we want is to get some good or get rid of something bad. The lie is in this, that what is done for our good ends in something bad, or what is done to make things better ends by making them worse. Why this paradox, except that the happiness of man can come not from himself but only from God, and that to live according to oneself is to sin, and to sin is to lose God? When, therefore, we said that two contrary and opposing cities arose because some men live according to the flesh and others live according to the spirit, we could equally well have said that they arose because some live according to man and others according to God.[1]

These two cities are intertwined and have always existed. The first is the "city of man," of which the Roman Empire is an example. The other is the "city of God," which consists of His church's believers. Augustine contrasts them in terms of ideas, knowledge, and actions. It is those contrasts we will examine. We will break them down into the same questions posed before. In addition, at the chapter's end, we will briefly review Neo-Platonic philosophy, particularly that of Plotinus and his student Porphyry. Augustine cited both extensively. We begin covering the questions related to our Creator.

The Creator's Nature
This chapter presents brief sets of passages, noting additions to or differences from Clement's writing. The first focus on our Creator's nature, providence, law, and scripture. A summary outlining the differences is presented at the section's end. In relation to our Creator's nature, the passages below outline Augustine's views.

> There is, accordingly, a good which is alone simple, and therefore alone unchangeable, and this is God. By this Good have all others been created, but not simple, and therefore not unchangeable. "Created," I say—that is, made, not

begotten. For that which is begotten of the simple Good is simple as itself, and the same as itself. These two we call the Father and the Son; and both together with the Holy Spirit are one God.... And He is another than the Father and the Son, for He is neither the Father nor the Son. I say "another," not "another thing," because He is equally with them the simple Good, unchangeable and co-eternal. And this Trinity is one God; and none the less simple ... we say it is simple, because it is what it has, with the exception of the relation of the persons to one another. For, in regard to this relation, it is true that the Father has a Son, and yet is not Himself the Son; and the Son has a Father, and is not Himself the Father.

It is for this reason, then, that the nature of the Trinity is called simple, because it has not anything which it can lose, and because it is not one thing and its contents another.... According to this, then, those things which are essentially and truly divine are called simple, because in them quality and substance are identical, and because they are divine, or wise, or blessed in themselves, and without extraneous supplement. In Holy Scripture, it is true, the Spirit of wisdom is called "manifold" because it contains many things in it; but what it contains it also is, and it being one is all these things. For neither are there many wisdoms, but one, in which are untold and infinite treasures of things intellectual, wherein are all invisible and unchangeable reasons of things visible and changeable which were created by it.[2]

We believe, we maintain, we faithfully preach, that the Father begat the Word, that is, Wisdom, by which all things were made, the only-begotten Son, one as the Father is one, eternal as the Father is eternal, and, equally with the Father, supremely good; and that the Holy Spirit is the Spirit alike of Father and of Son, and is Himself consubstantial and co-eternal with both; and that this whole is a Trinity by reason of the individuality of the persons, and one God by reason of the indivisible divine substance, as also one Almighty by reason of the indivisible omnipotence; yet so that, when we inquire regarding each singly, it is said that each is God and Almighty; and, when we speak of all together, it is said that there are not three Gods, nor three Almighties, but one God Almighty; so great is the indivisible unity of these Three, which requires that it be so stated.³

These descriptions are consistent with Clement's, with the following additions: the Holy Spirit becoming a third distinction with the Father and Son, and the addition of wisdom as an instance of the one and many similar to good and truth.

The Creator is unique and essential for the rest of creation. There is no being contrary to Him.

> For since God is the supreme existence, that is to say, supremely is, and is therefore unchangeable, the things that He made He empowered to be, but not to be supremely like Himself. To some He communicated a more ample, to others a more limited existence, and thus arranged the natures of beings in ranks ... Consequently, to that nature which supremely is, and which created all else that exists, no nature is contrary save that which does not exist. For nonentity is the contrary of that which is. And thus there is no being contrary to God, the Supreme Being, and Author of all beings whatsoever.⁴

Providence

As to providence, philosophers in Augustine's day argued you could only have either foreknowledge or free choice; both could not be present. Augustine uses Cicero's own arguments against him to prove foreknowledge and choice are not mutually exclusive. He first lays out the problem:

> He whose foreknowledge cannot be deceived foreknew that we would choose to do it. This was the fear that made Cicero oppose foreknowledge. It was this fear, too, that led the Stoics to admit that not everything happened of necessity, even though they held that everything happens by fate.⁵

He draws their argument's implications and refutes them in the following passage:

> Thus, his (Cicero's) motives for rejecting foreknowledge of the future was to avoid unworthy, absurd and dangerous

implications for human society. He narrows down the choices of a devout mind to one or other of these alternatives: either the power of choice or foreknowledge. It seemed to him impossible that both could exist. If one stands, the other falls. If we choose foreknowledge, we lose free choice; if we choose free choice, we must lose knowledge of the future.... Cicero made his choice. He chose free choice. To make certain, he denied foreknowledge. Thus to make men free, he made them give up God.

A man of faith wants both. He professes both and with a devout faith he holds both firmly. But how, one asks? ... [We] say that God knows all things before they happen; yet, we act by choice in all those things where we feel and know that we cannot act otherwise than willingly. And yet, so far from saying that everything happens by fate—for the simple reason that the word fate means nothing.... God spoke once and for all because He knows unalterably all that is to be, all that He is to do. In this way, we might use the word 'fate' to mean what God has 'spoken' (fatum), except that the meaning of the word has already taken a direction in which we do not want men's minds to move.

However, our main point is that, from the fact that to God the order of all causes is certain, there is no logical deduction that there is no power in the choice of our will. The fact is that our choices fall within the order of the causes, which is known for certain to God and is contained in His foreknowledge—for, human choices are the causes of human acts. It follows that He who foreknew the causes of all things could not be unaware that our choices were among those causes which were foreknown as the causes of our acts.

In this matter it is easy enough to refute Cicero by his own admission, namely that nothing happens without a preceding efficient cause. It does not help him to admit that nothing happens without a cause and then to argue that not every cause is fated, since some causes are either fortuitous or natural or voluntary. He admits that nothing happens without a preceding cause; that is enough to refute him.[6]

Implications

The existence of both free will and foreknowledge has implications for our choices and actions:

> As He is the Creator of all natures, so is He the giver of all powers—though He is not the maker of all choices. Evil choices are not from Him, for they are contrary to the nature which is from Him. Thus, bodies are subject to wills. Some bodies are subject to our wills – to the wills of all mortal animals, but especially those of men rather than of beasts ... And absolutely all bodies are subject to the will of God; as indeed, are all wills, too, since they have no power save what He gave them.
>
> Thus, God is the Cause of all things—a cause that makes but is not made. Other causes make, but they are themselves made ... Material causes which are rather passive than active are not to be included among efficient causes.... It does not follow, therefore, that the order of causes, known for certain though it is in the foreknowing mind of God, brings it about that there is no power in our will, since our choices themselves have an important place in the order of causes.
>
> And so, let Cicero argue with those who hold that this order of causes is fixed by fate, or, rather, is the reality they call fate.... Cicero must either deny that God exists ... or else, if he admits God's existence while denying His foreknowledge what he says amounts to nothing more than what "The fool hath said in his heart: There is no God." The fact is that one who does not foreknow the whole of the future is most certainly not God.[7]

Consistent with Clement's writing, our Creator has foreknowledge, *and* we each have free choice as to the decisions that we make. To think otherwise is inconsistent and stands against the very nature God must have to be God.

The Law

> The law is indeed good, because it is prohibition of sin, and death is evil because it is the wages of sin; but as wicked men make an evil use not only of evil, but also of good things, so the righteous make a good use not only of good, but also of

evil things. Whence it comes to pass that the wicked make an ill use of the law, though the law is good, and that the good die well, though death is an evil.[8]

The (Divine) law is good, and the righteous use it for good and also make good use of the evil Man chooses that is contrary to it.

Scripture

>Accordingly, though the obscurity of the divine word has certainly this advantage, that it causes many opinions about the truth to be started and discussed, each reader seeing some fresh meaning in it, yet, whatever is said to be meant by an obscure passage should be either confirmed by the testimony of obvious facts, or should be asserted in other and less ambiguous texts. This obscurity is beneficial, whether the sense of the author is at last reached after the discussion of many other interpretations, or whether, though that sense remain concealed, other truths are brought out by the discussion of the obscurity.[9]

>All of us who read strive to trace out and understand what he whom we read actually meant, and since we believe him to speak the truth, we dare not assert that he spoke anything we know or think to be false. Therefore, while every man tries to understand in Holy Scripture what the author understood therein, what wrong is there if anyone understand what you, O light of all truthful minds, reveal to him as true, even if the author he reads did not understand this, since he also understood a truth, though not this truth?[10]

Multiple truths can be contained within the same scripture. These truths can exist both across individuals at a point in time or at different points in time. Man's capacity limits his ability to understand scripture's truth. To expand his ability, Man must work at acquiring virtue, leading to wisdom.

The above passages about our Creator's nature can be summarized as follows:

>1. Our Creator is One, but the Holy Spirit is added as another distinction.

2. Wisdom is added as another instance of the one and the many.

3. There is no being contrary to our Creator. He is unique and essential to all creation.

4. Our Creator has absolute foreknowledge of the choices we will make, and we have the power of the free choice of our will. Both are true and consistent with our Creator's nature and necessary to our purpose.

5. Only good comes from our Creator. Evil is the result of Man's choices when he turns away from his Creator to his own desires.

6. Good makes use of both good and evil through providence.

7. Multiple truths can be derived from the same passage of scripture as the source of all scripture is our Creator.

Man's Nature
The relevant passages related to Man lie in the areas of Man's nature, free will, freedom, and rights. A summary outlining the differences will again be provided at the section's end. We open the discussion of Man's nature with Augustine's comments on God's image Man received from his Creator:

> We ourselves can recognize in ourselves an image of God ... of course, it is merely an image and, in fact, a very remote one. There is no question of identity nor of co-eternity nor, in one word, of consubstantiality with Him. Nevertheless, it is an image which by nature is nearer to God than anything else in all creation, and one that by transforming grace can be perfected into a still closer resemblance.

> For, we are, and we know that we are, and we love to be and to know that we are. And in this trinity of being, knowledge, and love there is not a shadow of illusion to disturb us. For, we do not reach these inner realities with our bodily senses as we do external objects ... But, without any illusion of image, fancy, or phantasm, I am certain that I am, that I know that I am, and that I love to be and to know.[11]

> For He speaks to that part of man which is better than all else that is in him, and than which God Himself alone is better. For since man is most properly understood (or, if that cannot be, then, at least, believed) to be made in God's image, no doubt it is that part of him by which he rises above those lower parts he has in common with the beasts, which brings him nearer to the Supreme.[12]

It is through that which is unique to Man, his mind and reason, that our Creator speaks to us. Even though the image we have is remote, it is still closer to our Creator than anything else within all creation. Augustine then proceeds to that nature's inherent equality.

> We have already stated in the preceding books that God, desiring not only that the human race might be able by their similarity of nature to associate with one another, but also that they might be bound together in harmony and peace by the ties of relationship, was pleased to derive all men from one individual, and created man with such a nature that the members of the race should not have died, had not the two first (of whom the one was created out of nothing, and the other out of him) merited this by their disobedience; for by them so great a sin was committed, that by it the human nature was altered for the worse, and was transmitted also to their posterity, liable to sin and subject to death.[13]

Man was created with free choice, and Adam's choice brought Man death. All Man was derived from one person so we would know we share the same nature, both toward our Creator and each other. Further, this nature comes from our Creator alone.

> Now, if we were the cause of our own nature, then, indeed, we would be the fathers of our own wisdom and would not need to get an education from our teachers. And if we were the source and the only object of our love, we would be self-sufficient and would need enjoyment of no other good to make us happy. But, in fact, God is the Author of the existence of our nature and, therefore, He must be our Teacher if we are ever to be wise, and He must be the Source of our inmost consolation if we are ever to be happy.[14]

By our very nature we are not self-sufficient. We require education in order to gain wisdom, and the Word is our teacher. This goes back again to Clement's arguments for reason, faith, knowledge, virtue, and wisdom. This counters the argument of Man and Man alone, that there is either no Creator or He is not involved in Man's affairs.

Augustine goes on to say,

> It is He, then, who has given to the human soul a mind, in which reason and understanding lie as it were asleep during infancy, and as if they were not, destined, however, to be awakened and exercised as years increase, so as to become capable of knowledge and of receiving instruction, fit to understand what is true and to love what is good. It is by this capacity the soul drinks in wisdom, and becomes endowed with those virtues by which, in prudence, fortitude, temperance, and righteousness, it makes war upon error and the other inborn vices, and conquers them.... For over and above those arts which are called virtues, and which teach us how we may spend our life well, and attain to endless happiness ... has not the genius of man invented and applied countless astonishing arts, partly the result of necessity, partly the result of exuberant invention ... What wonderful—one might say stupefying—advances has human industry made in the arts of weaving and building, of agriculture and navigation! With what endless variety are designs in pottery, painting, and sculpture produced, and with what skill executed! What wonderful spectacles are exhibited in the theatres, which those who have not seen them cannot credit! How skillful the contrivances for catching, killing, or taming wild beasts! ... Who could tell the thought that has been spent upon nature, even though, despairing of recounting it in detail, he endeavored only to give a general view of it? In fine, even the defence of errors and misapprehensions, which has illustrated the genius of heretics and philosophers, cannot be sufficiently declared. For at present it is the nature of the human mind which adorns this mortal life which we are extolling, and not the faith and the way of truth which lead to immortality.[15]

By our Creator, we are adapted in such a way as to use our mind and reason to learn and acquire knowledge. Our free choice allows us to overcome and conquer vices and increase our virtue. There is no end to what virtue can accomplish. Augustine lists examples of many innovations which have occurred in the arts and sciences, and that even the genius of the heretics proclaim the existence and use of those gifts—even if they do not profess what Augustine considers truth. We'll next consider Augustine's views of the human will and how that will is changed—for good or for evil.

Free Will

Augustine begins his free will discussion with the notion that Man initially possessed a good will, but it changes with his consent through the choices we each make.

> Accordingly God, as it is written, made man upright, and consequently with a good will. For if he had not had a good will, he could not have been upright. The good will, then, is the work of God; for God created him with it. But the first evil will, which preceded all man's evil acts, was rather a kind of falling away from the work of God to its own works than any positive work. And therefore the acts resulting were evil, not having God, but the will itself for their end; so that the will or the man himself, so far as his will is bad, was as it were the evil tree bringing forth evil fruit. Moreover, the bad will, though it be not in harmony with, but opposed to nature, inasmuch as it is a vice or blemish, yet it is true of it as of all vice, that it cannot exist except in a nature, and only in a nature created out of nothing, and not in that which the Creator has begotten of Himself, as He begot the Word, by whom all things were made.[16]

> But the character of the human will is of moment; because, if it is wrong, these motions of the soul will be wrong, but if it is right, they will be not merely blameless, but even praiseworthy. For the will is in them all; yea, none of them is anything else than will.[17]

Further regarding the will and consent,

> But when consent takes the form of seeking to possess the things we wish, this is called desire; and when consent takes

> the form of enjoying the things we wish, this is called joy. In like manner, when we turn with aversion from that which we do not wish to happen, this volition is termed fear; and when we turn away from that which has happened against our will, this act of will is called sorrow. And generally in respect of all that we seek or shun, as a man's will is attracted or repelled, so it is changed and turned into these different affections. Wherefore the man who lives according to God, and not according to man, ought to be a lover of good, and therefore a hater of evil.[18]

> If the further question be asked, What was the efficient cause of their evil will? There is none. For what is it which makes the will bad, when it is the will itself, which makes the action bad? And consequently the bad will is the cause of the bad action, but nothing is the efficient cause of the bad will. For if anything is the cause, this thing either has or has not a will. If it has, the will is either good or bad. If good, who is so left to himself as to say that a good will makes a will bad? For in this case a good will would be the cause of sin; a most absurd supposition ... How, then, can a good thing be the efficient cause of an evil will? How, I say, can good be the cause of evil? For when the will abandons what is above itself, and turns to what is lower, it becomes evil—not because that is evil to which it turns, but because the turning itself is wicked. Therefore it is not an inferior thing which has made the will evil, but it is itself which has become so by wickedly and inordinately desiring an inferior thing.[19]

Man's character is the result of his will—what he chooses. It can become good or evil. When Man's desires turn him away from his Creator, Man's will becomes evil. There is no efficient cause for such a will.

In fact, an evil will is one that is deficient:

> Let no one, therefore, look for an efficient cause of the evil will; for it is not efficient, but deficient, as the will itself is not an effecting of something, but a defect. For defection from that which supremely is, to that which has less of being,—this is to begin to have an evil will. Now, to seek to

> discover the causes of these defections,—causes, as I have said, not efficient, but deficient,—is as if some one sought to see darkness, or hear silence.[20]

The cause of an evil will is therefore a defect in Man's character. The source for this is not visible and can only be found within Man himself. Actions stemming from the ideas and desires Man chooses for himself.

"For if man despise the will of God, he can only destroy himself; and so he learns the difference between consecrating himself to the common good and reveling in his own. For he who loves himself is abandoned to himself."[21] A man who loves himself turns to himself, and in the end will have nothing but himself. Such a man separates himself from his Creator and leads himself to his own destruction. Augustine's views on free will bear themselves out in his discussions on Man's freedom to act, outlined next.

Freedom
Again, many philosophers of Augustine's day expressed the view that one could only have either the freedom to act or be subject to the Creator's prescience. He refutes their arguments and asserts in the following passages that both must be present to both know and do well, fulfilling our purpose.

> Among those things which they (Stoics) wished not to be subject to necessity they placed our wills, knowing that they would not be free if subjected to necessity ... But if we define necessity to be that according to which we say that it is necessary that anything be of such or such a nature, or be done in such and such a manner, I know not why we should have any dread of that necessity taking away the freedom of our will.... So also, when we say that it is necessary that, when we will, we will by free choice, in so saying we both affirm what is true beyond doubt, and do not still subject our wills thereby to a necessity which destroys liberty. Our wills, therefore, exist as wills, and do themselves whatever we do by willing, and which would not be done if we were unwilling. But when any one suffers anything, being unwilling by the will of another, even in that case will retains

> its essential validity ... for we resolve it into the power of God....
>
> Therefore we are by no means compelled, either, retaining the prescience of God, to take away the freedom of the will, or, retaining the freedom of the will, to deny that He is prescient of future things, which is impious. But we embrace both. We faithfully and sincerely confess both. The former, that we may believe well; the latter, that we may live well. For he lives ill who does not believe well concerning God. Wherefore, be it far from us, in order to maintain our freedom, to deny the prescience of Him by whose help we are or shall be free. Consequently, it is not in vain that laws are enacted, and that reproaches, exhortations, praises, and vituperations are had recourse to; for these also He foreknew, and they are of great avail, even as great as He foreknew that they would be.... For a man does not therefore sin because God foreknew that he would sin. Nay, it cannot be doubted but that it is the man himself who sins when he does sin, because He, whose foreknowledge is infallible, foreknew not that fate, or fortune, or something else would sin, but that the man himself would sin, who, if he wills not, sins not. But if he shall not will to sin, even this did God foreknow."[22]

Both freedom and God's providence are needed to believe and live well, to have faith leading to good actions, to know and do well.

He goes on to state that this presence of good within society is more profitable than evil:

> In this world, therefore, the dominion of good men is profitable, not so much for themselves as for human affairs. But the dominion of bad men is hurtful chiefly to themselves who rule, for they destroy their own souls by greater license in wickedness; while those who are put under them in service are not hurt except by their own iniquity. For to the just all the evils imposed on them by unjust rulers are not the punishment of crime, but the test of virtue. Therefore the good man, although he is a slave, is free; but the bad man, even if he reigns, is a slave, and that not of one man, but,

> what is far more grievous, of as many masters as he has vices.[23]

God gave Man the freedom to use his will in making his choices. This freedom is unconditional, as our wills come from our Creator. As all men are descended from the first man, we share the same nature. This freedom is shared equally by all regardless of race, gender, station in life, or any other distinction. Freedom is not based upon our physical appearance or what we have, but by the Creator's image we each possess: our minds and reason. But our ability to effectively use this gift is influenced by our ability to master reason and not be drawn by want or passion. *"Thus, a person who evaluates according to reason has far more freedom of choice than one who is driven by want or drawn by passion."*[24]

So far we've seen that our freedom is a gift from our Creator; we are to use reason in its proper exercise; we have a special nature and equality in that nature; and we are subject to God's laws. The source of all of this is our Creator. All of this comes to us from Him. Does this mean that we can do whatever we want or are there limits to our behavior if we are fulfilling our purpose? This leads to Augustine's discussions on rights and governance, which are next. We begin with defining a "people."

Rights

> Scipio defines the people as "a multitude bound together by a mutual recognition of rights and a mutual co-operation for the common good." As the discussion progresses, he explains what he means by "mutual recognition of rights," going on to show that a republic cannot be managed without justice, for, where there is not true justice there is no recognition of rights.

> For what is rightly done is justly done; what is done unjustly cannot be done by right. We are not to reckon as right such human laws as are iniquitous, since even unjust lawgivers themselves call a right (ius) only what derives from the fountainhead of justice (iustitia), and brand as false the wrong-headed opinion of those who keep saying that a right (ius) is whatever is advantageous (utile) to the one in power.

> It follows then that, wherever true justice is lacking, there cannot be a multitude of men bound together by a mutual recognition of rights; consequently, neither can there be a "people" in the sense of Scipio's definition. Further, if there is no "people," there is no will of the "people," or commonwealth, but only the weal of a nondescript mob undeserving of the designation "the people."
>
> Let us see. Justice is the virtue which accords to each and every man what is his due. What, then, shall we say of a man's "justice" when he takes himself away from the true God?[25]

All rights are founded on moral grounds—what is just. Justice is a virtue, one concerned with receiving our due. We already have seen that all virtues must be acquired; are a means of partaking of the good, another name for truth; end in love; and are necessary if one is to pursue happiness—the fulfillment of our purpose. That purpose is knowing and becoming like our Creator, to the extent we are able. Further, those rights must be held in common if there is to be a people. This follows from the previous discussion that we all share the same nature and freedom, both of which also come from our Creator. Finally, without justice there can be no commonweal. As justice is a virtue, it can only exist when Man is turned toward his Creator, the source of all morality, and attempts to fulfill his purpose. The implications of turning away from God in relation to rights, justice, virtue, and freedom are discussed in Chapter 6.

We can summarize the above passages on Man's nature as follows:

1. It is through reason and our mind that Man is unique and our Creator speaks to us.

2. All Man is derived from one man, Adam, so we might understand we all share the same nature and a common kinship. That nature comes from our Creator.

3. Man is not self-sufficient by nature. We must look to our Creator for wisdom if we are to be truly happy.

4. A man who follows his Creator should be a lover of good and therefore a hater of evil.

5. Man's evil acts are the result of his will and therefore exist only in a nature created out of nothing by Man himself. This is the result of Man abandoning what is above him and turning to what is lower. This choosing to turn away from good is itself evil.

6. Both our Creator's foreknowledge and our freedom are necessary for our Creator to be who He is and for us to be who we are, the former that we may believe well, the latter that we may live well. The claim that these are mutually exclusive is false.

7. Rule by good men is profitable for human affairs as the virtue of justice exists. Justice is necessary for a multitude of men to be a people. Without justice there can be no mutual recognition of the rights our Creator endowed us with or a mutual cooperation for the common good, because without virtue they will not exist.

We are now ready for the topic of human governance and the "city of man."

Human Governance

Augustine states, using the words of Sallust and Cicero, that Rome was never a republic in accordance with Scipio's definition mentioned above:

> But if our adversaries ... pooh-pooh the testimony of Sallust to its "utterly wicked and profligate" condition, what will they make of Cicero's statement, that even in his time it [the republic] had become entirely extinct, and that there remained extant no Roman republic at all? He introduces Scipio (the Scipio who had destroyed Carthage) discussing the republic ... [Scipio] gave it as his opinion that ... no progress could be made in discussing the republic unless it was established ... that [not only the maxim] "the republic cannot be governed without injustice," was false, but also that the truth is, that it cannot be governed without the most absolute justice.
>
> Scipio ... repeats with commendation his own brief definition of a republic, that it is the weal of the people. "The

> people" he defines as being not every assemblage or mob, but an assemblage associated by a common acknowledgment of law, and by a community of interests. Then he shows the ... "weal of the people," then exists only when it is well and justly governed, whether by a monarch, or an aristocracy, or by the whole people. But when the monarch is unjust, or ... a tyrant; or the aristocrats are unjust, and form a faction; or the people themselves are unjust, and become ... themselves the tyrant, then the republic is not only blemished, but by legitimate deduction from those definitions, it altogether ceases to be. For it could not be the people's weal when a tyrant factiously lorded it over the state; neither would the people be any longer a people if it were unjust, since it would no longer answer the definition of a people—"an assemblage associated by a common acknowledgment of law, and by a community of interests."[26]
>
> According to the definitions in which Cicero himself, using Scipio as his mouthpiece, briefly propounded what a republic is, and what a people is ... Rome never was a republic, because true justice had never a place in it. But accepting the more feasible definitions of a republic, I grant there was a republic of a certain kind, and certainly much better administered by the more ancient Romans than by their modern representatives. But the fact is, true justice has no existence save in that republic whose founder and ruler is Christ, if at least any choose to call this a republic; and indeed we cannot deny that it is the people's weal.[27]

Justice only exists when a people is turned toward God. Justice does not exist when Man turns to himself.

> Justice being taken away, then, what are kingdoms but great robberies? For what are robberies themselves, but little kingdoms? The band itself is made up of men; it is ruled by the authority of a prince, it is knit together by the pact of the confederacy; the booty is divided by the law agreed on. If, by the admittance of abandoned men, this evil increases to such a degree that it holds places, fixes abodes, takes possession of cities, and subdues peoples, it assumes more plainly the name of a kingdom, because the reality is now

> manifestly conferred on it, not by the removal of covetousness, but by the addition of impunity.[28]

The form of government in such a case doesn't matter, "For, as far as this life of mortals is concerned, which is spent and ended in a few days, what does it matter under whose government a dying man lives, if they who govern do not force him to impiety and iniquity?"[29]

A republic can only exist where the people's weal is present. For a people to exist, the following characteristics must be present: a multitude must possess a common acknowledgement of law, there must be a community of interests, and justice must be present in order for there to be a mutual recognition of rights and shared commitment for the common good. Governing can be done by a single individual, group, or everyone, but regardless of the number of people in power, the rule must be virtuous and just. If lacking, there will be no weal and no people, and the governing body will be no more than a pack of robbers and thieves, regardless of what they call themselves. Any government forcing its people to turn from their Creator is itself evil as it becomes the cause of turning others toward evil. When placed within a position where he must choose, Man is to obey his Creator rather than Man. Consider some of the issues dividing America today: abortion, gender confusion, redefining marriage, etc. When we lose our way, we lose our purpose.

Regarding the presence of virtue, Augustine goes on to state that,

> Where there is not this righteousness whereby the one supreme God rules the obedient city according to His grace, so that it sacrifices to none but Him, and whereby, in all the citizens of this obedient city, the soul consequently rules the body and reason the vices in the rightful order, so that, as the individual just man, so also the community and people of the just, live by faith, which works by love, that love whereby man loves God as He ought to be loved, and his neighbor as himself,—there, I say, there is not an assemblage associated by a common acknowledgment of right, and by a community of interests. But if there is not this, there is not a people, if

our definition be true, and therefore there is no republic; for where there is no people there can be no republic.[30]

Unless faith and virtue are present within a society, there can be no people and no republic as defined, for there will be no basis for a community of interests to exist. This includes the republic known as America.

Therefore, if the people wish to be governed by a republic, they must possess virtue, and virtue will only be found if that people are turned toward their Creator. It is therefore imperative that no constraints be placed on the people's ability to fulfill their purpose—knowing their Creator—for in this way virtue develops and wisdom is obtained. Fulfilling one's purpose requires negative rights and freedom, which are only present when Man is turned toward his Creator.[31] It also requires a true education as we are not born with this knowledge; it must be learned, as Clement demonstrated.

Man does wrong when turned to himself:

> For it is the wrongdoing of the opposing party which compels the wise man to wage just wars; and this wrongdoing, even though it gave rise to no war, would still be a matter of grief to man because it is man's wrong-doing. Let every one, then, who thinks with pain on all these great evils, so horrible, so ruthless, acknowledge that this is misery. And if any one either endures or thinks of them without mental pain, this is a more miserable plight still, for he thinks himself happy because he has lost human feeling.[32]

Wars are contrary to a virtuous man's nature, but are just when compelled by the wrongdoing of other men, who, by waging war, show they lack virtue. Even if war does not result, such wrongdoing would inflict anguish on the virtuous—it would be morally wrong.

We can summarize these passages on human governance and a republic's requirements as follows:

1. A republic only exists in the presence of true justice, for there must be a people for there to be a republic, regardless of the governance form.

2. A republic can only exist where virtue is present. *Justice is a virtue.* As virtue takes us towards our Creator, a republic can only exist where a people are turned toward their Creator. Therefore, the common acknowledgement of law will at a minimum be His law and the community of interests achieved by fulfillment of His law: to know Him, to love Him, and to love our fellow man.
3. War is justified only against those who do wrong against the Creator or their fellow man, for this violates His law.

The topics of good and evil are next, followed by more on why virtue and truth matter. Summaries are provided at the end of each section.

Good and Evil

As to good's nature,

> Accordingly we say that there is no unchangeable good but the one, true, blessed God; that the things which He made are indeed good because from Him, yet mutable because made not out of Him, but out of nothing.... And since this is so, then in this nature which has been created so excellent, that though it be mutable itself, it can yet secure its blessedness by adhering to the immutable good ... in this nature, I say, not to adhere to God, is manifestly a fault. Now every fault injures the nature, and is consequently contrary to the nature. The creature, therefore, which cleaves to God, differs from those who do not, not by nature, but by fault; and yet by this very fault the nature itself is proved to be very noble and admirable. For that nature is certainly praised, the fault of which is justly blamed. For we justly blame the fault because it mars the praiseworthy nature.[33]

In talking about the things of the earth (creation) Augustine says,

> These things, then, are good things, and without doubt the gifts of God. But if they neglect the better things of the heavenly city ... and so inordinately covet these present good things that they believe them to be the only desirable things, or love them better than those things which are believed to be better,—if this be so, then it is necessary that misery follow and ever increase.[34]

> Thus, all those who are called unclean spirits are no longer light in the Lord but darkness in themselves, being deprived of a participation in His eternal light. For, evil has no positive nature; what we call evil is merely the lack of something that is good.[35]

While evil is a lack of good, both good and evil have ultimate ends, which Augustine discusses in the following passage.

> Philosophers have expressed a great variety of diverse opinions regarding the ends of goods and of evils, and this question they have eagerly canvassed, that they might, if possible, discover what makes a man happy. For the end of our good is that for the sake of which other things are to be desired, while it is to be desired for its own sake; and the end of evil is that on account of which other things are to be shunned, while it is avoided on its own account. Thus, by the end of good, we at present mean, not that by which good is destroyed, so that it no longer exists, but that by which it is finished, so that it becomes complete; and by the end of evil we mean, not that which abolishes it, but that which completes its development. These two ends, therefore, are the supreme good and the supreme evil.[36]

Good is both of the body and spirit, and must be grounded in virtue.

> Man is neither the body alone, nor the soul alone, but both together. And therefore the highest good, in which lies the happiness of man, is composed of goods of both kinds, both bodily and spiritual. And consequently he thinks that the primary objects of nature are to be sought for their own sake, and that virtue ... is the most excellent of spiritual goods ... Now, of all goods, spiritual or bodily, there is none at all to compare with virtue. For virtue makes a good use both of itself and of all other goods in which lies man's happiness; and where it is absent, no matter how many good things a man has, they are not for his good, and consequently should not be called good things while they belong to one who makes them useless by using them badly. The life of man, then, is called happy when it enjoys virtue and these other spiritual and bodily good things without which virtue is

> impossible. It is called happier if it enjoys some or many other good things which are not essential to virtue; and happiest of all, if it lacks not one of the good things which pertain to the body and the soul. For life is not the same thing as virtue, since not every life, but a wisely regulated life, is virtue; and yet, while there can be life of some kind without virtue, there cannot be virtue without life. This I might apply to memory and reason, and such mental faculties; for these exist prior to instruction, and without them there cannot be any instruction, and consequently no virtue, since virtue is learned.[37]

Living rightly requires bodily and spiritual goods. Virtue is the ultimate spiritual good we are to seek. This living rightly can be achieved in several ways:

> As to these three modes of life, the contemplative, the active, and the composite, although, so long as a man's faith is preserved, he may choose any of them without detriment to his eternal interests, yet he must never overlook the claims of truth and duty. No man has a right to lead such a life of contemplation as to forget in his own ease the service due to his neighbor; nor has any man a right to be so immersed in active life as to neglect the contemplation of God.... And, in active life, it is not the honors or power of this life we should covet, since all things under the sun are vanity, but we should aim at using our position and influence, if these have been honorably attained, for the welfare of those who are under us.[38]

Man must live by recognizing both truth and duties—that is, rights and responsibilities, regardless of the mode of life he elects to live.

Man becomes corrupted when he fails to recognize both truth and duties. This corruption begins when one's will turns away from its Creator and toward Man himself.

> But if any one says that the flesh is the cause of all vices and ill conduct, inasmuch as the soul lives wickedly only because it is moved by the flesh, it is certain he has not carefully considered the whole nature of man. For "the corruptible body, indeed, weigheth down the soul." ... We are then

> burdened with this corruptible body; but knowing that the cause of this burdensomeness is not the nature and substance of the body, but its corruption ... they are in error who suppose that all the evils of the soul proceed from the body.... For the corruption of the body, which weighs down the soul, is not the cause but the punishment of the first sin; and it was not the corruptible flesh that made the soul sinful, but the sinful soul that made the flesh corruptible. And though from this corruption of the flesh there arise certain incitements to vice, and indeed vicious desires, yet we must not attribute to the flesh all the vices of a wicked life ... For it is not by having flesh ... but by living according to himself,—that is, according to man,—that man became like the devil.[39]

This corruption has its roots in pride.

> Our first parents fell into open disobedience because already they were secretly corrupted; for the evil act had never been done had not an evil will preceded it. And what is the origin of our evil will but pride? And what is pride but the craving for undue exaltation? ... But man did not so fall away as to become absolutely nothing; but being turned towards himself, his being became more contracted than it was when he clave to Him who supremely is. Accordingly, to exist in himself, that is, to be his own satisfaction after abandoning God, is not quite to become a nonentity, but to approximate to that.... For it is good to have the heart lifted up, yet not to one's self, for this is proud, but to the Lord, for this is obedient, and can be the act only of the humble.... therefore it is that humility is specially recommended to the city of God as it sojourns in this world ... while the contrary vice of pride ... specially rules his adversary the devil. And certainly this is the great difference, which distinguishes the two cities of which we speak.[40]

As Adam's corruption affected Man's nature, it has been passed on to all men:

> For God, the author of natures, not of vices, created man upright; but man, being of his own will corrupted, and justly condemned, begot corrupted and condemned children. For

we all were in that one man, since we all were that one man, who fell into sin by the woman who was made from him before the sin.... And thus, from the bad use of free will, there originated the whole train of evil.[41]

We can summarize this section as follows:

1. Our nature comes from our Creator, so it is good. It is our turning away from Him that creates evil, and this Augustine calls a defect. This is consistent with Clement's view that evil is an absence of good, and that absence is caused by Man's free choice.

2. There is a supreme good and supreme evil at the ends of both good and evil. Neither the supreme good nor the supreme evil are found in this life, and the philosophers erred in thinking both could be so.

3. The supreme good provides us with true happiness, and is acquired by pursuing both virtue and the objects of our nature for their own sakes.

4. However, there are goods and evils in this life that lead us to one or the other of the supreme good or evil. Concerning good in this life, nothing compares to the spiritual good called virtue, because it makes use of both itself and all other goods in which our happiness lies. However, goods in the absence of virtue do not provide happiness. Virtue contributes to the quality of life, and so also do memory and reason.

5. Evil does not come from the flesh. It is the soul that makes the flesh corruptible when Man lives according to himself. This is the root of what has been termed "Original Sin," Man turning from his Creator and toward himself. This brought not only physical death, but the potential for spiritual death.

6. Man's duty is not only to himself but to his neighbor and those under him should he rule.

Virtue and Truth

Just as with good, virtue, turned inward toward Man himself also leads to corruption.

> Philosophers,—who place the end of human good in virtue itself, in order to put to shame certain other philosophers, who indeed approve of the virtues, but measure them all with reference to the end of bodily pleasure, and think that this pleasure is to be sought for its own sake, but the virtues on account of pleasure,—are wont to paint a kind of word picture, in which Pleasure sits like a luxurious queen on a royal seat, and all the virtues are subjected to her as slaves.
>
> There is nothing, say our philosophers, more disgraceful and monstrous than this picture, and which the eyes of good men can less endure. And they say the truth. But I do not think that the picture would be sufficiently becoming, even if it were made so that the virtues should be represented as the slaves of human glory ... [It] is unworthy of the solidity and firmness of the virtues to represent them as serving this glory.... For their virtue,—if, indeed, it is virtue at all,—is only in another way subjected to human praise; for he who seeks to please himself seeks still to please man.[42]

Man must voluntarily choose to submit himself to his Creator, using His image of reason to build virtue.

> In this, then, consists the righteousness of a man, that he submit himself to God, his body to his soul, and his vices, even when they rebel, to his reason, which either defeats or at least resists them; and also that he beg from God grace to do his duty, and the pardon of his sins, and that he render to God thanks for all the blessings he receives.[43]

The proof of what he says lies in the dissension between philosophers versus the prophet's consistency.

> But let us ... return to the philosophers from whom we digressed to these things. They seem to have labored in their studies for no other end than to find out how to live in a way proper for laying hold of blessedness. Why, then, have the disciples dissented from their masters, and the fellow-disciples from one another.... Now, although there might be among them a desire of glory ... yet I may grant that there were some ... whose love of truth severed them from their teachers or fellow-disciples, that they might strive for what

> they thought was the truth, whether it was so or not. But what can human misery do, or how or where can it reach forth, so as to attain blessedness, if divine authority does not lead it? Finally, let our authors, among whom the canon of the sacred books is fixed and bounded, be far from disagreeing in any respect.[44]

As stated before, virtue makes use of both good and evil.

> Here, indeed, we are said to be blessed when we have such peace as can be enjoyed in a good life; but such blessedness is mere misery compared to that final felicity. When we mortals possess such peace as this mortal life can afford, virtue, if we are living rightly, makes a right use of the advantages of this peaceful condition; and when we have it not, virtue makes a good use even of the evils a man suffers. But this is true virtue, when it refers all the advantages it makes a good use of, and all that it does in making good use of good and evil things, and itself also, to that end in which we shall enjoy the best and greatest peace possible.[45]

Following good leads to peace. True peace. Eternal peace.

> The peace of the body then consists in the duly proportioned arrangement of its parts. The peace of the irrational soul is the harmonious repose of the appetites, and that of the rational soul the harmony of knowledge and action. The peace of body and soul is the well-ordered and harmonious life and health of the living creature. Peace between man and God is the well-ordered obedience of faith to eternal law. Peace between man and man is well-ordered concord. Domestic peace is the well-ordered concord between those of the family who rule and those who obey. Civil peace is a similar concord among the citizens.... The peace of all things is the tranquillity of order. Order is the distribution which allots things equal and unequal, each to its own place. And hence, though the miserable ... do certainly not enjoy peace ... they are by their very misery connected with order. They are not, indeed, conjoined with the blessed, but they are disjoined from them by the law of order. And though they are disquieted, their circumstances are notwithstanding

adjusted to them, and consequently they have some tranquillity of order, and therefore some peace. But they are wretched because, although not wholly miserable, they are not in that place where any mixture of misery is impossible. They would, however, be more wretched if they had not that peace which arises from being in harmony with the natural order of things. When they suffer, their peace is in so far disturbed; but their peace continues in so far as they do not suffer, and in so far as their nature continues to exist. As, then, there may be life without pain, while there cannot be pain without some kind of life, so there may be peace without war, but there cannot be war without some kind of peace, because war supposes the existence of some natures to wage it, and these natures cannot exist without peace of one kind or other.[46]

We can summarize Augustine's relevant thoughts about virtue and truth as follows:

1. Virtues are not to be sought for pleasure in and of themselves. This leads to Man turning inward toward himself. Instead, righteousness is realized by turning toward our Creator and submitting. It is by turning to Him that virtue leads to happiness.

2. The proof is in the dissension and dissonance among the philosophers stacked up against the consistency of the prophets. Philosophy comes from Man; scripture comes from our Creator.

3. We can have peace in this life, and virtue takes advantage of, and makes good use of, peace. It even makes good use of the evils that are suffered. This is an aspect of providence.

4. Peace is a well-ordered and harmonious existence for Man. What is true of peace for an individual applies to families, communities, and kingdoms.

5. Order is the distribution of things to their rightful place, for both the equal and unequal. Order provides some peace to those in misery, though it is less than those

who've been blessed. Peace can exist without war, but war cannot exist without peace.

6. Righteous peace is gained inwardly through the mind, knowledge, and actions. Peace of the body through being consumed with things. This latter peace is not righteous.

The City of Man

The differences discussed so far distinguish the citizens of the "city of God" from those of the "city of man." In describing the "city of man" itself, Augustine said,

> And this is the characteristic of the earthly city, that it worships God or gods who may aid it in reigning victoriously and peacefully on earth not through love of doing good, but through lust of rule. The good use the world that they may enjoy God: the wicked, on the contrary, that they may enjoy the world would fain use God,—those of them, at least, who have attained to the belief that He is and takes an interest in human affairs.[47]

The city of man will not last because it seeks human good and earthly peace. Both are perishable:

> But the earthly city, which shall not be everlasting ... has its good in this world, and rejoices in it with such joy as such things can afford. But as this is not a good which can discharge its devotees of all distresses, this city is often divided against itself by litigations, wars, quarrels, and such victories as are either life-destroying or short-lived. For each part of it that arms against another part of it seeks to triumph over the nations through itself in bondage to vice. But the things which this city desires cannot justly be said to be evil, for it is itself, in its own kind, better than all other human good. For it desires earthly peace for the sake of enjoying earthly goods, and it makes war in order to attain to this peace; since, if it has conquered, and there remains no one to resist it, it enjoys a peace which it had not while there were opposing parties who contested for the enjoyment of those things which were too small to satisfy both. This peace is purchased by toilsome wars.... But if they neglect the better things of the heavenly city, which are secured by eternal

victory and peace never-ending, and so inordinately covet these present good things that they believe them to be the only desirable things, or love them better than those things which are believed to be better,—if this be so, then it is necessary that misery follow and ever increase.[48]

Take a good long look around. Isn't this the path we've placed ourselves on today? Man sets this course for himself by abandoning morality—and its source: God.

> When, therefore, the Roman republic was such as Sallust described it, it was not "utterly wicked and profligate," as he says, but had altogether ceased to exist, if we are to admit the reasoning of that debate maintained on the subject of the republic by its best representatives. Tully himself, too, speaking not in the person of Scipio or any one else, but uttering his own sentiments, uses the following language in the beginning of the fifth book, after quoting a line from the poet Ennius, in which he said, "Rome's severe morality and her citizens are her safeguard." "This verse," says Cicero, "seems to me to have all the sententious truthfulness of an oracle. For neither would the citizens have availed without the morality of the community, nor would the morality of the commons without outstanding men have availed either to establish or so long to maintain in vigor so grand a republic with so wide and just an empire. Accordingly, before our day, the hereditary usages formed our foremost men, and they on their part retained the usages and institutions of their fathers. But our age, receiving the republic as a chef-d'oeuvre of another age which has already begun to grow old, has not merely neglected to restore the colors of the original, but has not even been at the pains to preserve so much as the general outline and most outstanding features. For what survives of that primitive morality which the poet called Rome's safeguard? It is so obsolete and forgotten, that, far from practising it, one does not even know it. And of the citizens what shall I say? Morality has perished through poverty of great men; a poverty for which we must not only assign a reason, but for the guilt of which we must answer as criminals charged with a capital crime. For it is

> through our vices, and not by any mishap, that we retain only the name of a republic, and have long since lost the reality." This is the confession of Cicero, long indeed after the death of Africanus.[49]

Abandoning virtue, the greatest spiritual good, leads to division and corruption. much as we see today because we no longer teach the things truly enabling us to succeed.

> But if we discard this definition of a people, and, assuming another, say that a people is an assemblage of reasonable beings bound together by a common agreement as to the objects of their love, then, in order to discover the character of any people, we have only to observe what they love. Yet whatever it loves, if only it is an assemblage of reasonable beings and not of beasts, and is bound together by an agreement as to the objects of love, it is reasonably called a people; and it will be a superior people in proportion as it is bound together by higher interests, inferior in proportion as it is bound together by lower. According to this definition of ours, the Roman people is a people, and its weal is without doubt a commonwealth or republic. But what its tastes were in its early and subsequent days, and how it declined into sanguinary seditions and then to social and civil wars, and so burst asunder or rotted off the bond of concord in which the health of a people consists, history shows, and in the preceding books I have related at large. And yet I would not on this account say either that it was not a people, or that its administration was not a republic, so long as there remains an assemblage of reasonable beings bound together by a common agreement as to the objects of love. But what I say of this people and of this republic I must be understood to think and say of the Athenians or any Greek state, of the Egyptians, of the early Assyrian Babylon, and of every other nation, great or small, which had a public government. For, in general, the city of the ungodly, which did not obey the command of God that it should offer no sacrifice save to Him alone, and which, therefore, could not give to the soul its proper command over the body, nor to the reason its just authority over the vices, is void of true justice.[50]

When Man turns toward himself in virtue, he experiences some success, as evidenced by Rome's early days. However, this state doesn't last as it is not grounded in the ultimate good, but rather Man's changeable will.

> If He had also withheld from them the terrestrial glory of that most excellent empire, a reward would not have been rendered to their good arts ... So also these despised their own private affairs for the sake of the republic, and for its treasury resisted avarice, consulted for the good of their country with a spirit of freedom, addicted neither to what their laws pronounced to be crime nor to lust. By all these acts, as by the true way, they pressed forward to honors, power, and glory; they were honored among almost all nations; they imposed the laws of their empire upon many nations; and at this day, both in literature and history, they are glorious among almost all nations. There is no reason why they should complain against the justice of the supreme and true God,—"they have received their reward."[51]

These differences within the "city of man" play themselves out in a number of ways.

The City of Man's Fruits

The "city of man" seeks the material rather than the spiritual. This produces division, deception, a thirst for power, and war—its ideas provide an environment for vices to develop.

> Our City is as different from theirs as heaven from earth, as everlasting life from passing pleasure, as solid glory from empty praise, as the company of angels from the companionship of mortals, as the Light of Him who made the sun and moon is brighter than the light of sun and moon.[52]

Desiring Earthly Things

> But since those Romans were in an earthly city, and had before them, as the end of all the offices undertaken in its behalf, its safety, and a kingdom, not in heaven, but in earth,—not in the sphere of eternal life, but in the sphere of demise and succession, where the dead are succeeded by the dying,—what else but glory should they love, by which they

wished even after death to live in the mouths of their admirers?[53]

Division

Now what people, senate, power, or public dignity of the impious city has ever taken care to judge between all these and other well-nigh innumerable dissensions of the philosophers, approving and accepting some, and disapproving and rejecting others? Has it not held in its bosom at random, without any judgment, and confusedly, so many controversies of men at variance, not about fields, houses, or anything of a pecuniary nature, but about those things which make life either miserable or happy? Even if some true things were said in it, yet falsehoods were uttered with the same licence; so that such a city has not amiss received the title of the mystic Babylon. For Babylon means confusion, as we remember we have already explained.[54]

Oppression

The society of mortals spread abroad through the earth everywhere, and in the most diverse places, although bound together by a certain fellowship of our common nature, is yet for the most part divided against itself, and the strongest oppress the others, because all follow after their own interests and lusts, while what is longed for either suffices for none, or not for all, because it is not the very thing. For the vanquished succumb to the victorious, preferring any sort of peace and safety to freedom itself; so that they who chose to die rather than be slaves have been greatly wondered at. For in almost all nations the very voice of nature somehow proclaims, that those who happen to be conquered should choose rather to be subject to their conquerors than to be killed by all kinds of warlike destruction. This does not take place without the providence of God.[55]

Man Serving Himself

Within the "city of man," Man's interests are drawn toward things which prevent him fulfilling his purpose.

This is our concern, that every man be able to increase his wealth so as to supply his daily prodigalities, and so that the powerful may subject the weak for their own purposes. Let the poor court the rich for a living, and that under their protection they may enjoy a sluggish tranquillity; and let the rich abuse the poor as their dependants, to minister to their pride. Let the people applaud not those who protect their interests, but those who provide them with pleasure. Let no severe duty be commanded, no impurity forbidden. Let kings estimate their prosperity, not by their righteousness, but by the servility of their subjects. Let the provinces stand loyal to the kings, not as moral guides, but as lords of their possessions and purveyors of their pleasures; not with a hearty reverence, but a crooked and servile fear. Let the laws take cognizance rather of the injury done to another man's property, than of that done to one's own person.[56]

Domination

There is assuredly a difference between the desire of human glory and the desire of domination; for, though he who has an overweening delight in human glory will be also very prone to aspire earnestly after domination, nevertheless they who desire the true glory even of human praise strive not to displease those who judge well of them.[57]

Man Becomes Creator

Even the gods of the "city of man" were created by him to serve his purposes.

The generations of the gods ... certainly seems to have been done for no other cause except that it was the business of such men as were prudent and wise to deceive the people in matters of religion, and in that very thing not only to worship, but also to imitate the demons, whose greatest lust is to deceive.[58]

Deception

It is recorded that the very learned pontiff Scævola had distinguished about three kinds of gods—one introduced by the poets, another by the philosophers, another by the statesmen. The first kind he declares to be trifling, because many unworthy things have been invented by the poets concerning the gods; the second does not suit states, because it contains some things that are superfluous, and some, too, which it would be prejudicial for the people to know. It is no great matter about the superfluous things ... But what are those things which do harm when brought before the multitude? "These," he says, "that Hercules, Æsculapius, Castor and Pollux, are not gods; for it is declared by learned men that these were but men, and yielded to the common lot of mortals." What else? "That states have not the true images of the gods; because the true God has neither sex, nor age, nor definite corporeal members." The pontiff is not willing that the people should know these things; for he does not think they are false. He thinks it expedient, therefore, that states should be deceived in matters of religion; which Varro himself does not even hesitate to say in his books about things divine. Excellent religion! to which the weak, who requires to be delivered, may flee for succor; and when he seeks for the truth by which he may be delivered, it is believed to be expedient for him that he be deceived.[59]

Separation

While the "city of man" too has several different levels, its ends are all the same.

> After the state or city comes the world, the third circle of human society,—the first being the house, and the second the city. And the world, as it is larger, so it is fuller of dangers, as the greater sea is the more dangerous. And here, in the first place, man is separated from man by the difference of languages. For if two men, each ignorant of the other's language, meet, and are not compelled to pass, but, on the contrary, to remain in company, dumb animals, though of different species, would more easily hold intercourse than they, human beings though they be. For their common nature is no help to friendliness when they are prevented by diversity of language from conveying their sentiments to one another; so that a man would more readily hold intercourse with his dog than with a foreigner. But the imperial city has endeavored to impose on subject nations

not only her yoke, but her language, as a bond of peace, so that interpreters, far from being scarce, are numberless. This is true; but how many great wars, how much slaughter and bloodshed, have provided this unity! And though these are past, the end of these miseries has not yet come. For though there have never been wanting, nor are yet wanting, hostile nations beyond the empire, against whom wars have been and are waged, yet, supposing there were no such nations, the very extent of the empire itself has produced wars of a more obnoxious description—social and civil wars—and with these the whole race has been agitated, either by the actual conflict or the fear of a renewed outbreak. If I attempted to give an adequate description of these manifold disasters, these stern and lasting necessities, though I am quite unequal to the task, what limit could I set? But, say they, the wise man will wage just wars. As if he would not all the rather lament the necessity of just wars, if he remembers that he is a man; for if they were not just he would not wage them, and would therefore be delivered from all wars.[60]

War

Whoever gives even moderate attention to human affairs and to our common nature, will recognize that if there is no man who does not wish to be joyful, neither is there any one who does not wish to have peace. For even they who make war desire nothing but victory,—desire, that is to say, to attain to peace with glory. For what else is victory than the conquest of those who resist us? And when this is done there is peace. It is therefore with the desire for peace that wars are waged, even by those who take pleasure in exercising their warlike nature in command and battle. And hence it is obvious that peace is the end sought for by war. For every man seeks peace by waging war, but no man seeks war by making peace. For even they who intentionally interrupt the peace in which they are living have no hatred of peace, but only wish it changed into a peace that suits them better. They do not, therefore, wish to have no peace, but only one more to their mind. And in the case of sedition, when men have separated themselves from the community, they yet do not effect what

> they wish, unless they maintain some kind of peace with their fellow-conspirators. And therefore even robbers take care to maintain peace with their comrades, that they may with greater effect and greater safety invade the peace of other men. And if an individual happens to be of such unrivalled strength, and to be so jealous of partnership, that he trusts himself with no comrades, but makes his own plots, and commits depredations and murders on his own account, yet he maintains some shadow of peace with such persons as he is unable to kill, and from whom he wishes to conceal his deeds. In his own home, too, he makes it his aim to be at peace with his wife and children, and any other members of his household; for unquestionably their prompt obedience to his every look is a source of pleasure to him. And if this be not rendered, he is angry, he chides and punishes; and even by this storm he secures the calm peace of his own home, as occasion demands. For he sees that peace cannot be maintained unless all the members of the same domestic circle be subject to one head, such as he himself is in his own house. And therefore if a city or nation offered to submit itself to him, to serve him in the same style as he had made his household serve him, he would no longer lurk in a brigand's hiding-places, but lift his head in open day as a king, though the same covetousness and wickedness should remain in him. And thus all men desire to have peace with their own circle whom they wish to govern as suits themselves. For even those whom they make war against they wish to make their own, and impose on them the laws of their own peace.[61]

The preceding are powerful and truthful words. While we could examine each passage by itself, the message is much clearer when presented as a whole. The "city of man" is focused on material things. This outward focus leads to divisions through vice. War becomes a means to obtain a kind of peace a particular man finds attractive to himself. The cost of this peace is endless war, based upon covetousness. Rome was a "city of man," one which fell further after its successes. Virtue was lost as Man turned toward his own self-interest. This same sequence of events happened to the Greeks, Egyptians, Assyrians, and others. So why did the "city of man" which was Rome succeed? Because of the virtue initially present in its people, even if they were not turned toward their Creator. Because they were focused only on Man, they drifted and became lost. They entered Babylon (confusion).

The strongest oppress the weak for their own pleasure, even though we share a common nature: equality. The "city of man" attempts to destroy and distort our nature, and therefore ignores that equality. Its men love their own glory and seek to dominate others. All this occurs within Providence, though, and even this evil is brought to good. *In the "city of man," the truth about our Creator is actually known by the wise, but it must be suppressed as it is dangerous to those in power, for they do not rule justly.* Instead, they establish false gods for the people to worship. The suppression of religion seeks to deprive those who need it most—the poor and the weak—from receiving hope. We will see more about this in developing the final two models in the next volume.

The cost of the "city of man" is high and becomes greater the more powerful and expansive this city becomes. The miseries persist long after war has ended. But these wars don't normally end. Once external wars cease, internal wars manifest themselves as factions strive for more of what they desire. But all men desire peace. Those of the "city of man," however, desire "their" peace, one based on their own outward desires, and ultimately this peace is never achieved.

Summary
Summarizing the differences between these two cities, Augustine states,

> Two cities have been formed by two loves: the earthly by the love of self, even to the contempt of God; the heavenly by the love of God, even to the contempt of self. The former, in a word, glories in itself, the latter in the Lord. For the one seeks glory from men; but the greatest glory of the other is God, the witness of conscience.... In the one, the princes and the nations it subdues are ruled by the love of ruling; in the other, the princes and the subjects serve one another in love, the latter obeying, while the former take thought for all.[62]

The table below summarizes the differences between the two cities discussed in this chapter.

	City of God	City of Man
Creator's Nature	• Was, Is, and Always Will Be. • Existed before creation.	• Gods are Man's creation.
Creation	• All created by Creator.	• Has always existed. • Goes through endless cycles of death and rebirth.
Law	• Creator's laws are supreme. • Man's laws lie below.	• Man's laws supreme.
Scripture	• Creator's Word.	• N/A
Good	• The Good and many goods.	• Many goods.
Truth	• The Truth and many truths.	• Many truths.
Free Will/Freedom	• Creator gave Man the freedom to make his own choices, which was necessary for him to fulfill His purpose.	• Freedom is only for specific groups of individuals and is oriented toward fulfilling the state's goals.

	City of God	City of Man
Man's Nature	<ul><li>Image of our Creator.</li><li>Image is mind and reason.</li><li>Purpose is to know Creator.</li><li>Man has equal nature.</li></ul>	<ul><li>Man is self-sufficient.</li><li>Strong oppress the weak.</li><li>Man's pursuit of his glory and self-interest.</li></ul>
Rights	<ul><li>Divine rights come from our Creator and can only be changed by our Creator.</li><li>Other rights can come from the people, but must be aligned with divine rights.</li><li>Rights can only exist when true justice is present.</li></ul>	<ul><li>Rights come from the state and can be changed at any time by the state based upon its goals and needs.</li><li>The virtue of justice cannot exist when Man has turned away from his Creator.</li></ul>
Virtue	<ul><li>Obedience to Creator's will.</li><li>Man created to adapt to virtue.</li><li>Ultimate end of virtue is love.</li></ul>	<ul><li>Man's obedience to Man.</li><li>Man's will to dominate.</li><li>Knowledge of Creator repressed.</li><li>False gods used to deceive.</li></ul>

	City of God	City of Man
Rule	• Weal of the People. • Just governance. • Existence of mutual rights. • Just wars waged when compelled.	• Divided people. • Rule by domination. • Elite determines rights. • Unity from bloodshed and war.

Neo-Platonism

Augustine opposed the ideas expressed by Neo-Platonic thought. Two of its most influential philosophers were Plotinus and Porphyry, and Augustine mentions both extensively within the *City of God*. While Augustine thought the Platonic philosophers were in error, they were the ones who had come closest to the truth within philosophy. We will look briefly at both Plotinus and Porphyry as we will come back to their ideas several times before we are finished.

Plotinus and Porphyry

Plotinus was born about 205 AD in what is now the Nile delta region of Egypt. He studied in Alexandria under the teacher Ammonius from about 232 to 244, only a few years after the death of Clement. Little is known about what Ammonius taught, but interestingly Clement's student Origen is also said to have attended some of Ammonius's lectures while in Alexandria. After his studies, Plotinus left Alexandria and joined an army going into Persia to learn more about Chaldean and Indian philosophy. The Roman army was defeated, and with difficulty Plotinus made his way back into Roman territory, and from there eventually went to Rome itself.

Plotinus taught philosophy in Rome for about 26 years before his death in 270. He is primarily known for his development of three principles: the One, the Intellect (Mind), and the Soul. These principles are Plotinus's view of the one and the many. In general, his writings have a flair for the mystical.

Plotinus found gnostic teachings to be

> untraditional, irrational, and immoral. They despise and revile the ancient Platonic teaching and claim to have a new and superior wisdom of their own: but in fact anything that is true in their teaching comes from Plato, and all they have done themselves is to add senseless complications and pervert the true traditional doctrine.... They claim to be a privileged cast of beings, in whom alone God is interested, and who are saved not by their own efforts but by some dramatic and arbitrary divine proceeding; and this ... leads to immorality. Worst of all, they despise and hate the material universe and deny its goodness and the goodness of its maker.[63]

Plotinus taught not only against the gnostics, but also opposed Christianity. He

> maintained not only the goodness of the material universe but also its eternity and its divinity. The idea that the universe could have a beginning and end is inseparably connected in his mind with the idea that the divine action in making it is arbitrary and irrational. And to deny the divinity ... of the World-Soul, and of those noblest of embodied living beings the heavenly bodies, seems to him both blasphemous and unreasonable.[64]

Plotinus was a pagan and polytheist. He believed that creation was eternal, without a beginning or end. In his view of the one and the many, he also looked at the Intellect and Soul as separate gods.

Porphyry was born in Tyre in 234 AD. He was a student of Plotinus in Rome for about six years from 263 to 269. Toward the end of his life, he assembled his master's treatises into the *Enneads*. He died in about 301. He was a staunch Neo-Platonist, defender of paganism, and opponent of Christianity. His work *Introduction to Categories* was used as a standard textbook during the Middle Ages and was translated into Arabic where it became an introductory textbook in logic for the study of philosophy and theology. Let us take a look at Plotinus's idea of the one and the many.

Plotinus's Three Hypostases
Plotinus believed in the following three primary *hypostases*:

> Whenever we say "the One" and whenever we say "the Good," we must think that the nature we are speaking of is the same nature, and call it "one" ... we call it First in the sense that it is simplest, and Self-Sufficient, because it is not composed of a number of parts ... If then, it is not from something else or in something else or any kind of compound, it is necessary that there should be nothing above it. So, we must not go after other first principles but put this first, and then after it Intellect, that which primally thinks; and then Soul after Intellect (for this is the order which corresponds to the nature of things).[65]

A few key passages for each *hypostasis* are provided. Then each is discussed along with their relationship to the others.

About the One he writes,

> Well then, as for the one, if it is the absolutely One to which nothing else is added, not soul, not intellect, not anything at all, this could not be predicated of anything, so that it is not a genus.... if it is undifferentiated in itself how could it make specific forms? ... For how could there be divisions? For in dividing you will make many ... for there could be no differentiation in the one.[66]

> That which is altogether simple and self-sufficient needs nothing.[67]

> The Intelligible (the One) remains by itself and is not deficient, like that which sees and thinks ... the Principle abides "in its own proper way of life" ... for that Principle is "beyond being."[68]

> The Good is without activity ... for it has nothing to think: it is itself the first.... But what is "beyond being" must be beyond thinking; it is not then absurd if he does not know

himself; for he has nothing in himself which he can learn about, since he is one.[69]

Then it has no perception of itself and is not even conscious of itself, and does not even know itself.[70]

[The One] has no shape, not even intelligible shape. For since the nature of the One is generative of all things it is not any one of them ... it is not at movement or rest, not in place, not in time, but "itself by itself of single form," or rather formless, being before all form.[71]

For that One is not absent from any, and absent from all, so that in its presence it is not present except to those who are able and prepared to receive it.[72]

"But one should not enquire whence it comes, for there is no "whence"; for it does not really come or go anywhere, but appears or does not appear."[73]

But how did he give what he does not have? ... Now what comes from him could not be the same as himself. If then it is not the same, it cannot of course be better.... It must then be worse.... It has been said elsewhere that there must be something after the first, and in a general way that it is power, and overwhelming power.[74]

Therefore, Plato says, "it cannot be spoken or written." But we speak and write impelling towards it and wakening from reasonings to the vision of it.[75]

The One is simple and the principle of all things.... [T]his marvel of the One, which is not existent, so that "one" may not here also have to be predicated of something else, which in truth has no fitting name, but if we give it a name, "one" would be an appropriate ordinary way of speaking of it.[76]

This is what one must do if one is going to philosophise about the One.... one must become Intellect and entrust one's soul to and set it firmly under Intellect, that it may be awake to receive what that sees, and may by this Intellect behold the One.[77]

The One is simple and transcendent. It is found through the Intellect and Soul. This one is the source of all else. It gives what it does not have by its power.

As for Intellect,

> Intellect exists in the realm of thought as a universal whole, which we call the intelligible universe, and since there also exist the intellectual powers contained in this and the individual intellects – for Intellect is not only one, but one and many.[78]

> Intellect is as it is, always the same, resting in a static activity. Movement towards it and around it is already the work of Soul, and a rational principle proceeding from Intellect to Soul and making Soul intellectual, not making another nature between Intellect and Soul.[79]

> If someone admires this perceptible universe ... let him ascend to its archetypal and truer reality and there see them all intelligible and eternal in it, in its own understanding of life; and let him see pure Intellect presiding over them, and immense wisdom, and the true life of Kronos ... For he encompasses in himself all things immortal, every intellect, every god, every soul, all for ever unmoving.[80]

> Intellect is all things. It has therefore everything at rest in the same place, and it only is, and its "is" is for ever, and there is no place for the future for then too it is—or for the past—for nothing there has passed away—but all things remain stationary for ever, since they are the same.... But each of them is Intellect and Being, and the whole is universal Intellect and Being, Intellect making Being exist in thinking of it, and Being giving Intellect thinking and existence by being thought ... they both therefore have a cause other than themselves. For they are simultaneous and exist together and one does not abandon the other, but this one is two things, Intellect and Being and thinking and thought, Intellect as thinking and Being as thought.[81]

> This, we may say, is the first act of generation: the One ... overflows as it were, and its superabundance makes

> something other than itself. This, when it has come into being, turns back upon the One and is filled, and becomes Intellect by looking towards it. Its halt and turning towards the One constitutes being, its gaze upon the One, Intellect.[82]

> He [the One] will be above Intellect itself which contemplates him. For Intellect will be standing first to its contemplation, looking to nothing but the Beautiful, all turning and giving itself up to him, and motionless, and filled somehow with strength, it sees first of all itself become more beautiful, all glittering, because he is near.[83]

> Intellect, the cause of knowledge, has become present in the soul.[84]

Intellect is immanent. It lies in the realm of thought and is described in terms of what it is rather than what it is not. Intellect brings Being into existence, but its source is the One.

Finally, as to the Soul,

> There had to be many souls and one soul, and the many different souls springing from the one, like the species of one genus, some better and others worse, some more intelligent, and some whose intelligence is less actualized.[85]

> For as there are two reasons why the soul's fellowship with the body is displeasing, that body becomes a hindrance to thought and that it fills the soul with pleasures, desires, and griefs, neither of these things could happen to a soul which has not sunk into the interior of its body, and is not anyone's property, and does not belong to the body, but the body belongs to it.[86]

> Now these must come to an understanding of the soul, in other ways and especially that it derives from Intellect.[87]

The Soul is an instance of the one and many, and its understanding is derived from Intellect.

Plotinus's view of the One, the Intellect, and the Soul influenced his thoughts on free will and freedom. He asserts finding the One and Intellect are negations. In his view, free will and freedom are not positive gifts from a creator, but rather the absence of a negative. He lays out his case in the following passages.

In relation to free will, we must first determine "whether anything does happen to be in our power."[88]

> "Being in their power" is to be applied to other gods and to the first beings.... I myself think that, when we are pushed around among opposing changes and compulsions and strong assaults of passions possessing our soul, we acknowledge all these things as our masters and are enslaved to them ... and so are in doubt whether we are not nothing and nothing is in our power.[89]

If we wish something and "nothing opposes our wishes, this would be in our power. But if this is so, our idea of what is in our power would be something enslaved to our will and would come to pass (or not) to the extent we wished it."[90] He begins with the notion that free choice involves the imposition of something that is within one's own power onto something else.

He next asks,

> How in general can we have the mastery where we are led? ... For sense-perception does not give mastery of the work since it only sees. But if by knowledge, if it is by knowledge of what is being done, here too it only knows, but something else leads to action.... And if reason itself makes another desire, we must understand how; but if it puts a stop to the desire and stands still and this is where what is in our power is, this will not be in action, but will stand still in Intellect; since everything in the sphere of action, even if reason is dominant, is mixed and cannot have being in our power in a pure state.[91]

Things are in our power—we have mastery of them—when they are within the realm of our reason. Our power over all action is mixed. This is connected to Intellect and inaction.

As to the source of our power,

> we traced back what is in our power to will ... but perhaps we ought to add to "correct" [discourse] that it belongs to

rational knowledge; for if someone had a right opinion and acted on it he would not indisputably have the power of self-determination if he acted, without knowing why his opinion was right, but led to his duty by chance or some imagination.[92]

However,

> we shall grant voluntary action to one whose doings depend on the activities of Intellect and who is free from bodily affections. We trace back what is in our power to the noblest principle, the activity of Intellect, and shall grant that the premises of action derived from this are truly free, and that the desires roused by thinking are not involuntary, and we shall say that the gods who live in this way have self-determination.[93]

Our power comes from our will, grounded in rational knowledge. To Plotinus, true freedom is found within the Intellect and not in our actions.

However,

> a difficulty must be raised about Intellect itself, whether, when its activity is what it is by nature and as it is by nature, it could be said to have freedom and anything in its power, when it does not have it in its power not to act.... But then how is there freedom when even these higher beings are slaves to their own nature? ... For the involuntary is a leading away from the good and towards the compulsory ... and that is enslaved which is not master of its going to the Good, but since something stronger than it stands over it, it is enslaved to that and led away from its own goods. For it is this reason that slavery is ill spoken of, not where one has no power to go to the bad, but where one has no power to go to one's own good but is led away to the good of another.[94]

Intellect's to act, nature is to act, even if it is a slave to its own nature. Slavery is defined as the leading away from one's own good to that of another. In this respect Intellect could be considered as being enslaved by the One, as the One is the source of Intellect: "Intellect, is not of alien form; it is not chance, but each and every part of it is rational principle and cause, but that One is cause of the cause."[95]

Yet again,

> even if Intellect does have another principle, it is not outside it, but it is in the Good [the One]. And if it is active according to the Good, it is much more in its own power and free; since one seeks freedom and being in one's own power for the sake of the Good. If then it is active according to the Good, it would be still more in its own power; for it has already what goes from itself to it, and in itself what would be better for it, being in it, if it is directed towards it.[96]

As Intellect is active according to the Good (the One), it is free since it is active for the sake of the Good. Free will and freedom is therefore to be found in Intellect through reason. Is it found elsewhere? Plotinus turns next to a discussion of the soul and virtue.

> Is self-determination and being in one's own power, then, only in Intellect when it thinks, that is, pure intellect, or is it also in soul when it is active according to intellect and engaged in practical action according to virtue? ... Since virtue is always being compelled to do this or that to cope with what turns up. For certainly if someone gave virtue itself the choice ... it would choose to rest from its practical activities because nothing needed its curative action.... In what way then are we saying that being good is in our power and "virtue has no master"? Yes, it is if we wish and choose it; or because when virtue comes to be in us it constructs freedom and being in our own power and does not allow us to be any more slaves of what we were enslaved to before. If then virtue is a kind of other intellect, a state which in a way intellectualizes the soul, again, being in our power does not belong to the realm of action but in intellect at rest from actions.[97]

Even virtue leads us back to Intellect through reason, contemplation, and inaction.

> Further, we shall assert that virtue and intellect have the mastery and that we should refer being in our own power and

> freedom to them; and since these have no master, intellect is independent and virtue wishes to be independent by supervising the soul to make it good, and up to this point is free itself and makes the soul free ... being in our own power is not referred to practice and outward activity but to the inner activity of virtue itself, that is, its thought and contemplation. But one must say that this virtue is a kind of intellect and not count in with it the passions which are enslaved and limited by the reason ... It is still clearer that the immaterial is free, and it is to this that being in our power is to be referred and the will which has the mastery and is independent, even if something directs it by necessity to what is outside. All therefore that comes from this will and is done according to it is in our power, when it is acting externally and when it is by itself ... Intellect is what is in its own power in this way, that its work in no way depends on another, but it is all turned to itself and its work is itself and it rests in the Good.... For will wants the Good; but thinking is truly in the Good.... If then we allot being in our power to willing the Good, surely that which is already firmly settled in what its will wants must possess it. Or else it must be assumed to be something greater.[98]

Therefore,

> the soul, then becomes free when it presses on without hindrance to the Good by means of Intellect, and what it does through his [Intellect] is in its power; but Intellect is free through itself; but the nature of the Good is the very goal of the striving and that through which the others have what is in their power.[99]

It is through Intellect that the soul and virtue find freedom. However, it is through striving for the Good that the Intellect, soul, and virtue attain it. For the One is the source of all; the Good is reached by one's removing attributes.

"But we see self-determination not as that Good's incidental attribute but itself by itself, by taking away the opposing factors from the self-determinations in other things."[100] It is again by the process of removal through contemplation and reason that we find our own power for self-determination, and our freedom. For

> good ... having its transcendence of Intellect not as something brought in from outside; surely, when we ascend to this and become this alone and let the rest go, what can we say of it except that we are more than free and more than independent?[101]

It is only when we let go of all to reach the One that we find freedom, because all things are slaves to the One.

> But he [the One], since he has the highest place, or rather does not have it, but is himself the highest, has all things as slaves; he does not happen to them, but they to him, or rather they happen around him; he does not look to them, but they to him; but he is, if we may say so, borne to his own interior, as it were well pleased with himself, the "pure radiance."[102]

> And further ... we affirm that each and every thing in the all, and this All here itself, is as it would have been if the free choice of its maker had willed it, and its state is as if this maker proceeding regularly in his calculations with foresight had made it according to his providence.... [S]o their rational principles also always rest among the things which exist all together, standing still in a better order; so that the things there transcend providence and transcend free choice.... That Intellect is there standing still before this All, and this All here is from and according to Intellect.[103]

This is not the free choice, the freedom of the will described by Clement and Augustine, but is instead the freedom achieved through contemplation and reason—as a slave of the One acting in accordance to the Good. To Plotinus, freedom is the imposition of one's will over something else. As the One is the source of all, everything is dependent on it. When we strive to reach the Good, we become aligned to it and we become free. In this sense, freedom does not reside within us, but only through submission to the One. In this sense, freedom is the absence of coercion through submission. All are slaves to the One. We will see these same thoughts again when developing the final model based on Islam's principles in the next volume.

To summarize, the One is a simple transcendent unity. Intellect and Soul are both complex unities. In comparing Clement and the Christian writer Philo with Plotinus, E. F. Osborn writes:

> Despite the clarity and penetration of Plotinus's account, there appear to be certain inconsistencies. Perception, life, and consciousness are attributed to the One. It is the power of all things and identical with the Good. These are an indication of a readiness to talk about the One which is not consistent with its ineffability.... The inevitable result is that his successors postulate some still more mysterious principle behind the Monad.
>
> When we turn to Plotinus's account of the One as first cause and producer of all things, we find again an acute awareness of the problems involved. The One is above speech, thought, and sensation, yet it gives these things to us. How can the one give them to us if it does not have them? How can it have them and yet be simple? ... Plotinus then gives us an explanation in terms of power. The One is an infinitely great power. It must have produced everything because nothing else has the power to do this and because what produces must be simpler than the thing it produces. Plotinus is not as satisfied with this explanation when he has finished as he was when he began.... To say that the One is a great power, is the Good, or is an overflowing perfection, to place a One-many as a second first principle, does not explain the puzzle.... It is disappointing that despite a clear statement of the problem Plotinus really does imagine that he shows how the many proceed from the One.
>
> From this comparison of Clement, Philo, and Plotinus it would appear that in Clement's treatment of the problems arising from the ineffability and creative activity of the One the most consistent account given. Clement is more ready to accept the consequences of the ineffability of the one and the inexplicability of the method of creation. It is possible that Clement was less inclined to put forward bad solutions of philosophical problems because the existence of the problem was less painful to him than it was to Philo and Plotinus.[104]

Maybe because Clement found his solution in the need for both faith and reason, instead of reason alone.

Chapter 5

The Scholastic Master

You may wonder why the material presented so far was selected. I've already mentioned that the authors were considered to be the best minds of their respective times. However, another relationship exists between the texts covered and corresponds with Christianity's development. Clement's writings are the most basic and discuss our Creator and the individual. He includes discussions about who they are, the relationship between them, Man's purpose, and how Man fulfills his purpose. Augustine's writing expands this material to include communities of individuals, specifically two communities: one focused on the Creator as our end and a second focused on Man as his own end, using Rome as an example of the latter city. The two cities are intertwined in this world. He wrote about the differences between these two communities, which included thoughts about freedoms, rights, and what it means to have a republic.

This chapter focuses on St. Thomas Aquinas (Thomas) *Summa Contra Gentiles* and *Summa Theologicae*. Thomas was a master of scholasticism, the basis for the classical education our Founders received. This education attempted to reconcile faith with reason, and scripture with Aristotle (not Plato or the Neo-Platonists as in the earlier chapters), but Thomas did not consider himself to be a philosopher. While he is recognized primarily by the Catholic Church, as already noted there was little difference between the classical education programs, purposes, materials, and emphases between Catholic and Protestant institutions.

Both *Summas* were Thomas's effort to create a compilation of theological thought. As such, these works generally collected existing information, whereas Clement's and Augustine's works were more developmental in nature. Thomas poses, rebuts, and answers various questions within both works. He started work on the sixty volume *Summa Theologicae* in about 1265 and left it, unfinished, a year before his death in 1273.

The two *Summas* share similar structures but have different purposes. The *Summa Contra Gentiles* was intended for understanding and defending one's faith. Written for missionaries entering Moorish (Islamic) Spain. The *Summa Theologicae* was a more comprehensive work aimed at teaching students theology. While both works are wide-ranging, we will concentrate on a narrower set of topics. As mentioned above, Chapter 3 covered the individual and Chapter 4 two communities and their differences. This chapter focuses on topics related to freedom and how individual's in the "city of God" are meant to live and govern themselves. We will therefore look at subjects such as law, governance, justice, rights, and virtue. We will also cite Thomas's thoughts on material covered earlier where they add to, or differ from, the other authors.

Thomas was born in 1225 AD in southern Italy to noble parents. Against their wishes, he entered the Dominican order at the age of nineteen. He started his studies in Paris and later completed them in Cologne. He returned to Paris as a teacher in 1252 for a time. He later went to Italy where he spent about ten years teaching before returning to Paris a final time in 1268 to combat the rise of Averroism that was taking place in the Paris universities. He left that post in 1272 and died in 1274.

It should be noted that Thomas was born ten years after the signing of the *Magna Charta* in England, indicating that freedom was already afoot in Europe. More will be presented on Averroism and freedom's development in Europe in the second volume.

We begin this chapter with material related to providence and grace, which Thomas relates to free choice. We'll proceed next to a brief section on Man's nature, focused on the difference between a likeness and an image, before entering the main topics of law and governance. Afterward, we will return to the topic of virtue before closing with some implications for Man's behavior.

Providence

Thomas makes a distinction between the Creator's plan and how it is executed. His view of providence at one level is similar to both Clement's and Augustine's, but from this distinction he develops concepts for both divine and human governance and law presented in this chapter:

> There are two sides to providence, namely the idea or planned purpose for things provided, and its execution, which is called government. As for the first, God provides for all things immediately and directly, His mind holds the reason for each of them, even the very least.... Consequently, the whole of their design down to every detail is anticipated in His mind.
>
> As for the second, divine Providence works through intermediaries. For God governs the lower through the higher, not from an impotence on His part, but from the abundance of his goodness imparting to creatures also the dignity of causing.[1]

Our Creator's providence consists of His plan, as discussed by both Clement and Augustine, and its execution through His divine governance.

Other properties of divine providence include

1. "Since God is the cause of all existing things, giving being to all, the order of His providence must embrace all things."

2. He "intends some of His effects to be established by way of necessity, and others contingently."

3. "If God foresees that this event will be, it will happen ... but it will occur in the way that God foresaw that it would be."

4. "It does not follow that, if everything be done by divine providence, nothing is within our power. For the effects are foreseen by God, as they are freely produced by us."

5. "For God Himself operates in all things, and in accord with the decision of His will.... Hence, it is appropriate

to His providence sometimes to permit defectible causes to fail, and at other times to preserve them from failure."[2]

On to grace before we discuss free choice.

Grace

Thomas uses an example of the king's grace: gifts given out of love evoking a corresponding love. It's all about love. We have a moral duty, responsibility, to show love for love given. We have the free will to choose otherwise, but such a choice is morally wrong—it is unrighteous. This concept relates to the natural rights we've received from God. They too are His gifts to us. When accepting those gifts, we also incur a moral obligation. Refusing those gifts leaves Man to his own devices.[3]

> In common usage, "grace" is usually taken in three senses. Firstly, it stands for the love of someone, as we might say that this soldier has the king's grace and favour.... Secondly, it is used to refer to a gift given gratis ... Thirdly, it is used to refer to the display of gratitude for benefits given gratis.... The second of these three senses depends on the first; for out of the love with which someone regards another favourable, it comes about that he bestows something on him gratis. The third sense rises from the second, since expression of gratitude arises in response to benefits bestowed gratis.
>
> As to the two latter senses it is clear that grace sets up something in the one who receives the grace: firstly, the gift itself given gratis; secondly, the gratitude for this gift. But as to the first sense, we must note a difference between God's grace and man's. For since the goodness of the creature issues from the divine will, it is out of God's love by which he wills good for the creature that any goodness arises in the creature. Man's will, on the other hand, is moved by goodness already existing in things; and so it is that man's love does not wholly cause the thing's goodness, but presupposes it either in whole or in part.[4]

This grace can come only from our Creator as

> No being can act beyond the limits of its specific nature, since the cause must always be of a higher potency than its

effect. Now the gift of grace surpasses every capacity of created nature, since it is nothing other than a certain participation in the divine nature, which surpasses every other nature. And so it is impossible that a creature should cause grace.[5]

Again, grace is a gift which comes only from our Creator and is not given based on our merits, but His love alone. There is separation between Creator and creation.

Free Choice

Man's nature requires God's grace as Man is not inherently good. Only God is inherently good, so His nature makes His principles superior to Man's. As grace is love freely given, Man must be willing to voluntarily accept it. What our Creator offers is good because God is good.

Thomas relates free choice to grace by stating,

> Man is the master of his acts, including those of willing and of not willing, because of the deliberative activity of his reason, which can be turned to one side or the other. But that he should deliberate or not deliberate, supposing that we were master of this too, would have to come about by a preceding deliberation. And since this may not proceed to infinity, one would finally have to reach the point at which man's free decision is moved by some external principle superior to the human mind, namely by God.... Thus the mind even of a healthy man is not so much the master of its acts as not to need to be moved by God. Much more the free decision of a man become weak after sin.[6]

Also,

> Grace is spoken of in two ways, sometimes as God's gift in the form of a habit, sometimes as the assistance of God moving the soul towards the good. In the first sense, some preparation for grace is demanded in advance.... But if we speak of grace in the sense of the assistance of God moving man towards the good, no preparation as it were anticipating the divine assistance is required on man's part.... In this sense, that good movement of free choice itself, by which a

> man prepares to receive the gift of grace, is the action of a free choice moved by God.... The principal agent is God moving the free choice; and in this sense it is said that *man's will is prepared by God*, and *man's steps are directed by the Lord*.[7]

While Man is master of his own actions and will, he has a need to be moved by His Creator. Grace is this movement within Man by our Creator. It creates a moral obligation, but Man has the free choice to choose otherwise.

> The preparation for grace in man is from God as mover, and from free choice as moved. Therefore preparation may be considered in two ways. Firstly, as arising from free choice; and in this sense it can lay no necessary claim to obtain grace, since the gift of grace surpasses any preparation of human virtue. In a second sense preparation may be considered as arising from God as mover. And then it does lay a necessary claim to what is ordained by God, not coercively but infallibly; for God's intention cannot fail. So Augustine too says that *whoever is liberated by the acts of God's mercy is liberated with the utmost certainty*. Thus if it is by intention of God as mover that the man whose heart he moves should obtain grace, the man obtains it infallibly.[8]

This movement is always present, not coercive, and infallible. God's word always returns to Him fulfilled because of His foreknowledge and providence. Grace does not override our free choice, nor are we deserving of it. It is freely given to those He foreknew would turn toward Him in fulfillment of our purpose—for this leads to true happiness. To summarize, our Creator's predestination is his foreknowledge of our choices—choices we freely make of our own will. In this sense there is no fate, only the responsibility that comes with making our own choices.

Thomas uses the term "elect" in relating choice to reason, will, and decisions:

> The term "election" implies a quality of intellect and a quality of will; Aristotle refers to it being both understanding as desirous and desire as understanding. Now whenever two elements combine to compose a unity, one of them is like a

> form or shaping principle with respect to the other.... It is clear that reason comes before will and directs its activity, in that the will tends towards its object in the setting of reason, which presents to it the object of desire. Accordingly then, that will-act which turns towards an object proposed to it as being good, that is, as being reasonably subordinate to the end, is "materially" one of will, but "formally" one of reason. To appetite belongs the texture of the act, to knowledge its shape. In this sense choice is substantially an act of will, not of reason.... The conclusion of a practical syllogism is the work of reason; it is the decision, called the sentence or judgment, from which choice follows. Accordingly it is related to choice as a consequence.[9]

Choice is primarily an act of will which reason directs. A decision is a consequence of choice.

Since

> We have noted that choice follows the decision or verdict which, as it were, is a conclusion to a practical syllogism. It is this which offers the object of choice. Now in matters of practice then end stands like a principle, not a conclusion, as Aristotle observes. Therefore an end is not, as such, a matter of choice.
>
> However, in matters of practice, why should not the principle of one scientific argument in turn also be the conclusion of another? – though of course the first indemonstrable principles of thought cannot themselves be arrived at like the conclusions of scientific demonstration.... Happiness is the ultimate end of all the virtues, and their proper ends are subordinate to that, which is why they fall into our field of choice.... There is but one last end. There can be choice with respect to other ends which confront us inasmuch as they are ordained to a further end.[10]

Our choices for virtue lead toward the fulfillment of our purpose, the attainment of happiness—our final end. All other ends have a further end. As noted by Augustine, there is a final end for both good and evil.

> Our choice always concerns our own actions. Now whatever we do is possible for us. We must needs conclude that choice falls only on the possible.[11] Man does not choose of necessity. This is because a possible-not-to-be is not a bound-to-be. Why it is possible for a man to choose or not to choose may be gathered from a double ability. First, to be able to will or not and to act or not; second, to will and act thus or thus.... choice is of the means, not the end, it is about particular goods, not the perfect good, which is happiness. On these grounds we say that choice is free, not necessary.[12]

Choices are limited to what is possible and are made freely. Choices matter because they are the means used to attain an end.

Finally, from a common sense perspective Thomas states, "Man is free to make decisions. Otherwise counsels, precepts, prohibitions, rewards and punishments would all be pointless."[13]

Man's Nature

As to Man's nature, Thomas draws a distinction between likeness and image:

> Augustine says, *Wherever you have an image you have a likeness, but wherever you find likeness you do not necessarily find image.* This shows that the idea of image involves likeness, and that "image" adds something to "likeness" ... But man is both said to be "the image," because of his likeness to the original, and "after the image" because the likeness is imperfect.[14]

He concludes that the Creator's image in Man is contained within three separate stages as follows:

> But things are likened to God, first and most generally in so far as they are; secondly in so far as they are alive; thirdly and lastly in so far as they have discernment and intelligence. It is these latter, as Augustine says, which are *so close in likeness to God that there is nothing closer in all creation.* Thus it is clear that only intelligent creatures are properly speaking after God's image.[15]

Reason was given to Man alone and it is in this intelligence and ability to discern that Man has a likeness to his Creator.

We are to use this image to discern good from evil (we'll come back to in discussing virtue and vice). God is love, and grace about love. Man is most aligned with this image when loving God, himself, and his fellow man, an alignment Man must himself choose.

> Since man is said to be after God's image in virtue of his intelligent nature, it follows that he is most completely after God's image in that point in which such a nature can most completely imitate God. Now it does this in so far as it imitates God's understanding and loving of *himself*.
>
> Thus God's image can be considered in man at three stages: the first stage is man's natural aptitude for understanding and loving God, an aptitude which consists in the very nature of the mind, which is common to all man. The next stage is where a man is actually or dispositively knowing and loving God, but still imperfectly; and here we have the image by conformity of grace. The third stage is where a man is actually knowing and loving God perfectly.... The first stage of image then is found in all men, the second only in the just, and the third only in the blessed.... God's image is found equally in both man and woman as regards that point in which the idea of "image" is principally realized, namely an intelligent nature.... But as regards a second point, God's image is found in man in a way in which it is not found in woman; for man is the beginning and end of woman, just as God is the beginning and end of all creation.[16]

Thomas's first point on equality is consistent with both Clement and Augustine, but his second point is not. It appears this last point is not supported. Based upon Thomas's own logic, one can also assert that woman is the beginning and end of man, as man is born of woman—with the exception of Adam. What would be correct to state is that in Adam is the beginning of all man and woman as Adam's creation was unique, and Eve's creation was done in a way to show kinship with all man. This has already been discussed by Clement and Augustine.

Law

Thomas outlines several categories of law and how they are related to each other. These include eternal, divine, natural, and human law.

Law is meant to direct people. It is developed using reason supporting the common good by the authority(s) charged with caring for the community. Law and rights are not the same. Law is about rights; rights are the things themselves. All rights have either a divine or human source.[17]

He first defines the role of law as follows:

> Law is laid on subjects to serve as a rule and measure. This means that it has to be brought to bear on them. Hence to have binding force ... it has to be applied to the people it is meant to direct. This application comes about ... by the fact of promulgation. Hence this is required for a measure to possess the force of law.

> To sum up ... the following definition can be gathered. Law is nought else than an ordinance of reason for the common good made by the authority who has care of the community and promulgated. Hence, natural law is promulgated by God's so instilling it into men's minds that they can know it because of what they really are. Those who are not present when a law is promulgated are obliged to its observance in that ... the law is or can be brought to their attention by others. Promulgation in the present stretches into the future through being perpetuated in a written code.[18]

He mentions natural law coming from our Creator. So what is encompassed within each type of law? Who creates each type? Is there a relationship between them? What does Thomas mean by the common good? Creating law is discussed in the governance section. The types of law, their sources, and how they relate to each other are laid out first.

Eternal Law
Eternal law is the ultimate source of all law.

> Law is nothing but a dictate of practical reason issued by a sovereign who governs a complete community. Granted that the world is ruled by divine Providence ... it is evident that the whole community of the universe is governed by God's mind. Therefore the ruling idea of things which exists in God as the effective sovereign of them all has the nature of law.

> Then since God's mind does not conceive in time, but has an eternal concept ... it follows that this law should be called eternal.
>
> Hence, while not as yet existing in themselves things nevertheless exist in God in so far as they are foreseen and preordained by him.... Thus the eternal concept of divine law bears the character of a law that is eternal as being God's ordination for the governance of things he foreknows.
>
> Promulgation is made by words spoken or written down; in both ways an Eternal Law is proclaimed by God's utterance, since the Divine Word and the Book of Life are eternal.[19]
>
> Since the Eternal Law is the governing idea in the sovereign of the universe, from that all the governing ideas in lower rulers derive. Such are all laws apart from the Eternal Law. Consequently all laws in so far as they share in right reason to that extent derive from the Eternal Law.[20] All law proceeds from the reason and will of the lawgiver; divine and natural law from the intelligent will of God, human law from the will of man regulated by reason.[21]

Our Creator is the source of all law. His law is both supreme and eternal. Divine and natural law are also derived from the Creator's will. Human law is derived solely from Man, and therefore lies below both divine and natural law. In addition, human law is to be determined by use of reason, which in turn is rightly oriented toward our Creator. This means justice and virtue are aligned with our Creator's expressed law, leads to happiness, and should be the end of human law.

Divine Law

Divine law is needed to guide human conduct, because our nature is not inherently good, so human law alone is insufficient. Divine law orders Man to God and directs Man's behavior with his fellow man, thereby supporting justice and our purpose.

In regards to Man's need for divine law, Thomas states,

> The guidance of human conduct required a divine law besides natural law and human law. And for four reasons. First, because law directs men to the actions matching what

> they are made for. Were they destined only to an end not beyond their natural abilities they would need no directive of reason over and above natural law and human law built on it.... Second, because of the untrustworthiness of human judgment ... different people come to differing decisions about human conduct, with the result that diverse and conflicting laws are passed.... Third, men can make laws on matters on which they are competent to judge. They cannot pronounce on inward motions which are hidden, but only on outward and observable behavior. Nevertheless full virtue means that a man is right in both. Since human law is not enough, the complement of divine law is needed.... Fourth, Augustine remarks that human law cannot forbid or punish all wrongdoing, for were it to try to do away with all evils it would also take away much that was good.... Hence, the need of a divine law which misses nothing and leaves no evil unforbidden or unpunished.[22]

We are destined for an end greater than we can achieve on our own. That end was discussed previously. Divine law is needed to help direct us as our nature and human law are insufficient. The final point touches on an implication of positive and negative rights, taken up in the next chapter.

Divine law comes from our Creator and serves two purposes. First, "It is evident that every lawmaker intends to direct men by means of laws toward his own end, principally.... But the end which God intends is God Himself. Therefore, the divine law principally looks to the ordering of man toward God."[23] And, "since man is best able to cling to God through love, it must be that the intention of divine law is primarily ordered to an act of love."[24] The intent of this first purpose is to instill love towards our Creator.

Second,

> The next point after this is that divine law intends the love of neighbor. For there should be a union in affection among those for whom there is one common end. Now, men share in common the one ultimate end which is happiness, to which they are divinely ordered. So, men should be united with each other by mutual love.[25]

Therefore, the ordering of divine law is two-fold: first, ordering Man toward his Creator, and second, ordering Mankind toward one another for the common good.

As to the ordering of Man to each other, Thomas says,

> Now, an ordered concord is preserved among men when each man is given his due, for this is justice.... Therefore, by divine law precepts had to be given, so that each man would give his neighbor his due and would abstain from doing injuries to him. Moreover, among men a person is most in debt to his parents ... each man must render what he owes, both to his parents and to other persons.... Next to be put down are the precepts commanding abstinence from causing various sorts of harm to one's neighbor.[26] Man must be so ordered by divine law that his lower powers may be subject to reason, and his body to his soul, and so that external things may subserve the needs of man. Besides, any law which is rightly established promotes virtue. Now, virtue consists in this: that both the inner feelings and the use of corporeal things be regulated by reason. So, this is something provided for by divine law.[27]

Man is ordered to repay his debts and do no harm to others. Right law promotes virtue, including justice, and creates alignment between Man's inner feelings and his right use of those things he's been given dominion over.

> Now, that he [man] may observe this kind of justice which is prescribed by divine law man is impelled in two ways: in one, from within; in the other way, from without. From within, of course, man is voluntary in regard to observing what divine law prescribes. In fact, this is accomplished by man's love of God and his neighbor.... But since some people are not disposed internally ... they must be forced from without to fulfill the justice of the law. Of course, since this is done only from fear of punishment, they do not fulfill the law in freedom, but in servility.[28]

Obedience to divine law has both internal and external aspects. Laws are created for the sake of those who do not choose to obey.

For those who are internally motivated to fulfill the law,

> The first, then, "are a law unto themselves," for they have charity which impels them in place of law, and makes them act with liberality. So, it was not necessary to promulgate an external law for their sake, but for the sake of those who are not inclined to themselves toward the good.[29]

As for what determines whether Man is oriented toward his Creator, there are three things: "First is his faithful subjection to him ... second is for Man to show him respect ... and the third, to give him service."[30]

Divine Law consists of the Old Law and the New Law. The Old Law includes the Ten Commandments cited within the Old Testament. The New Law consolidates the Old Law into the two commandments within the Gospels:

> The New Law does not differ from the Old Law, because both have the same end, which is that men should be subject to God; now there is only one God.[31] The Old Law, which was given to the imperfect, i.e. those who have not yet obtained spiritual grace, was called *the law of fear*, inasmuch as it induced men to observe its precepts by the threat of various penalties.... And so the New Law, consisting primarily in spiritual grace itself implanted to men's hearts, is called *the law of love*; and it is said to contain spiritual and eternal promises, which are the objects of virtue, especially charity. And so men are drawn to them intrinsically, not as to what is external to them but as to what is their very own. This too is why the Old Law is said to restrain *the hand, not the mind*, since someone who abstains from sin through fear of penalty does not, simply speaking, withhold his consent to sin, as does someone who abstains from sin for love of justice. And for this reason the New Law, which is the law of love, is said to *restrain the mind*.[32]

Finally, in regards to the New Law,

> And so each individual is free as regards works of this kind to decide what it is best for him to do or avoid doing; and each man in authority is free to make arrangements for his

> subjects in such matters as to what they should do or avoid doing. And so even in this respect the law of the Gospel is called the *law of freedom*; for the Old Law prescribed many things and left human freedom only a few things to decide.[33]

Another implication of positive and negative rights is discussed in the next chapter.

> The New Law, then, is called the law of freedom in two senses. Firstly, because it does not constrain us to do or to avoid anything apart from what itself is necessary or contrary to salvation, falling under the precept or the prohibition of the law. Secondly, because even such precepts or prohibitions it makes us fulfill freely, inasmuch as we fulfill them by an inner stirring of grace.[34]

Both Clement and Augustine noted that free choice is necessary for Man. Thomas goes further in that free choice is a part of divine law. While those choices are foreknown by our Creator, they are ours to make without coercion. As such, our choices merely fulfill His foreknowledge. This is truly freedom, and it comes from our Creator as part of His divine law.

Natural Law
Natural law (1) is derived from Eternal Law, (2) like divine law comes from divine will and cannot be changed by Man, (3) requires divine or human law to be applied, and (4) relates to moral precepts—that is, virtue.

> Since all things are regulated and measured by eternal Law ... it is evident that all somehow share in it, in that their tendencies to their own proper acts and ends are from its impression. Among them intelligent creatures are ranked under divine Providence.... Thus they join in and make their own the Eternal Reason through which they have their natural aptitudes for their due activity and purpose. Now this sharing in the Eternal Law by intelligent creatures is what we call "natural law."[35]

> Divine and natural law proceed from the divine will ... and hence cannot be altered by custom proceeding from the will of man; change can come only by divine authority.

> Accordingly no custom can acquire the force of law against divine or natural law.[36] It is the function of divine law to regulate relationships between men, and the relationship of men to God. Now, as a matter of general principle both of these relationships are subject to the dictates of natural law, to which the moral precepts relate. But both of them require to be applied to the concrete by a further law, either divine or human.[37]

> These precepts are called *moral*, since human morals are derived from reason. Other precepts there are which do not bind from the dictate of reason ... their binding force arises from some enactment, divine or human.[38] Both the moral and the judicial precepts have the function of directing human life. It is for this reason that both of them are included under a single head.... Judgment imports the carrying out of what is just.... Hence the judicial precepts have something in common with the moral ones to the extent that they have their source in reason.[39]

Moral precepts have their basis in reason and have justice as an end. Therefore, morals relate also to virtue, and virtue relates to natural law as follows:

> There are two ways to referring to acts about virtue, the first, in so far as they are virtuous, the other in so far as they are acts of a certain specific kind. If we are speaking of them as virtuous, then all of them are matters for natural law.... But if we are speaking of them as acts of specific virtues in themselves ... then not all of them are of natural law. For many of them are not immediately prompted by nature, but have to be investigated and reasoned out before they are held to be helpful to the good life.[40]

> The objects to which men have a natural tendency are the concern of natural law.[41] And so this is the first command of law, "that good is to be sought and done, evil to be avoided"; all other commands of natural law are based on this. Accordingly, then, natural-law commands extend to all doing or avoiding of things recognized by the practical reason of itself as being human goods.

> Now since being good has the meaning of being an end, while being an evil has the contrary meaning, it follows that reason of its nature apprehends the things towards which man has a natural tendency as good objectives.... The order in which commands of the law of nature are ranged corresponds to that of our natural tendencies. Here there are three stages. There is in man, first, a tendency towards the good of the nature he has in common with all substances.... Natural law here plays a corresponding part, and is engaged at this stage to maintain and defend the elementary requirements of human life.
>
> Secondly, there is in man a bent towards things which accord with his nature considered more specifically, that is in terms of what he has in common with other animals. Thirdly, there is in man an appetite for the good of his nature as rational, and this is proper to him, for instance, that he should know truths about God and about living in society."[42]
>
> To sum up: as for its common principles, here natural law is the same for all in requiring a right attitude towards it as well as recognition. As for particular specific points ... here also natural law is the same for most people in their feeling for and awareness of what is right. Nevertheless in fewer cases either the desire or the information may be wanting. The desire to do right may be blocked by particular factors ... and the knowledge also of what is right may be distorted by passion or bad custom or even by racial proclivity.[43]

Natural rights encompass both the laws of nature and nature's God. The first relates to creation, much of which Man shares with it. The second is unique to Man because of Man's reason and God's revelations to him. Man can choose to make additions, but rarely, if ever, should there be deletions, as Man's will lies below God's.

> You speak of something being according to natural right in two ways. The first is because nature is set that way; thus the command that no harm should be done to another. The second is because nature does not bid the contrary; thus we might say that it is of natural law for man to be naked, for nature does not give him clothes; these he has to make by

art. In this way common ownership and universal liberty are said to be of natural law, because private property and slavery exist by human contrivance for the convenience of social life, and not by natural law. This does not change the law of nature except by addition.[44]

A change can be understood to mean either addition or subtraction. As for the first, there is nothing against natural law being changed, for many things over and above natural law have been added, by divine law as well as by human laws, which are beneficial to social life.

As for change by subtraction ... here there is room for a distinction. The first principles of natural law are altogether unalterable. But its secondary precepts ... though not unalterable in the majority of cases where they are right as they stand, can nevertheless be changed on some particular and rare occasions ... because of some special cause preventing their unqualified observance.[45]

Natural law cannot be cancelled in the human heart, nevertheless it can be missing from a particular course of action, when the reason is stopped from applying the general principle there, because of lust or some other passion.... As for its other and secondary precepts, natural law can be effaced either by wrong persuasions—thus also errors occur in theoretical matters concerning demonstrable conclusions—or by perverse customs and corrupt habits.... Sin cancels natural law on some specific point, not as in general principles, unless perhaps with regard to secondary principles.... Though grace is more powerful than nature, nevertheless nature is more essential to man, and therefore more permanent.[46]

Consistent with virtue, natural law is intended to promote good and avoid evil. It is, except in rare circumstances, the same for everyone, as it has its basis in divine will. It is possible for divine and human law to add to natural law, but very rare for something to be taken away from it—and then only involving its secondary precepts. Its primary precepts are manifold and lie in the single root of providing good.

Human Law
Human law is to be consistent with the divine will through divine and natural law, and supports the common good. Unjust laws are contrary to God's rights. In these cases, Man is to obey God. Positive law is a part of human law. Human laws are also subject to change as they have their basis in Man's nature, but they should be sanctioned by the people. Finally, human law is to be applied equally to all.

> The purpose of human law is to be useful to men ... namely that it is consistent with religion as corresponding with divine law, that it agrees with good discipline as corresponding to natural law, and that it furthers our welfare as corresponding to human usefulness.[47]

A second

> purpose of human law is to bring people to virtue, not suddenly but step by step. Therefore it does not all at once burden the crowd of imperfect men with the responsibilities assumed by men of the highest character.[48] One may speak of an act of virtue in two senses. First, to refer to the deed of virtue, thus, for instance, the fair dealing in which justice is engaged ... this is what the law prescribes for those acts of virtue it deals with. Secondly, to refer to its being done in the virtuous style of a good man; as such it always springs from virtue, and does not fall under the precept of the law, but is the end to which the lawgiver intends the law to lead.[49]

This is consistent with virtue and natural law discussed earlier.

> First of all, to depend on natural law is of the essence of human law.... on this head positive law and justice is divided into the *jus gentium* and civil law.... Those precepts belong to the *jus gentium* which are drawn like conclusions from the premises of natural law, such as those requiring justice in buying and selling and so forth, without which men cannot live sociably together; this last is a condition of natural law, since ... man is by nature a sociable animal. Constructions, however, put upon natural law are proper to civil law, and here each political community decides for itself what is fitting.

> Secondly, it is of the essence of human law to be ordered to the benefit of the commonwealth.... Thirdly, it is of the essence of law to be instituted by the governor of the political community ... namely that *which men of birth together with the common people have sanctioned.* Fourthly, it is of the essence of law to be the directive of human acts.[50]

Human law is to be in accord with divine and natural law; it is intended to create virtue within the society and be instituted based on agreement between the ruler and the people. Human laws can be just or unjust:

> Human laws are either just or unjust. If they are just, they have binding force in the court of conscience from the Eternal Law from which they derive.... Now laws are said to be just on three counts; from their end, when they are ordered to the common good, from their authority, when what is enacted does not exceed the lawgiver's power, and from their form, when for the good of the whole they place burdens in equitable proportion on subjects.[51]

> Laws are unjust in two ways, as being against what is fair in human terms and against God's rights. They are contrary to human good on the three counts made above; from their end ... from their author ... and from their form.... These are outrages rather than laws.[52] Laws can be unjust because they are contrary to God's rights; such are the laws of tyrants which promote idolatry or whatsoever is against divine law. To observe them is in no wise permissible ... *We must obey God rather than men.*[53]

Unlike divine and natural law, which are just as they come from the divine will, human law can either be just or unjust. If a human law conflicts with higher law then the human law should not be observed.

> Law of its nature has the double role of being a guide for human acts and of possessing the power of constraint. Hence a man can be subject to a law on these two counts, first, of being guided by a ruling principle, and second, of being constrained by an enforcing principle.

> In the first manner all who are subject to a governing authority are subject to the law it makes. There can be two reasons why a person is not subject, first because he owes no allegiance ... and second, because he comes under a higher law.... In the second manner a person is said to be subject to law as being constrained by an enforcing principle. Thus virtuous and upright men are not bound by law, but only wicked men. What is constrained and forced is contrary to one's own will.[54]

> Reflect on this, however, that commands can be traced to natural law in two ways; one, drawn deductively like conclusions from premises; two, grounded on it like constructional implementations of general directives.... Both processes are at work in human positive law. Commands, however, that issue according to the first have part of their force from natural law, and not only from the fact of their enactment. Whereas commands that issue according to the second have their force only by human law.[55]

Commands, in some circumstances, can have the force of human law. However, like human law, they must be consistent with divine and natural law for them to have the authority of law.

> Law is laid down for a great number of people, of which the majority have no high standard of morality. Therefore it does not forbid all the vices, from which upright men can keep away, but only those grave ones which the average man can avoid, and chiefly those which do harm to others and have to be stopped if human society is to be maintained, such as murder, theft, and so forth.[56]

> Yet of his own will a sovereign is subject to the directive power of the law, according to the Decretals, *Whoever establishes a law for another, the very same he should practice himself.* And a wise authority says, *Be open yourself to the law you produce.* Our Lord reproaches those who do not practice what they preach.... Before God's judgment, then, the sovereign is not exempt from the law's directive power, and he ought to fulfill the law, freely not forcedly. Yet he is above the law in that he can change it if expedient,

and grant dispensations from it adapted to place and season.⁵⁷

Human law is not comprehensive, and even the lawmaker should follow whatever law he produces.

Changes may be required in human law as

> 1. "[T]hose who first attempted to draw up useful regulations for the human community were of themselves unable to take everything into consideration."⁵⁸
> 2. "Law may be justly altered because of changed conditions of life, which make for differences in what is beneficial."⁵⁹
> 3. "Human reason, however, is imperfect and mutable, so as well, therefore, is the law it makes."⁶⁰
> 4. "A measure should be as permanent as possible. Yet in a world of change there can be nothing that is altogether and immutably stable. Consequently human law cannot be entirely unalterable."⁶¹

Human law is rightly altered so far as this will provide for the common benefit. Now a change in the law, looked at merely as a change, inflicts a kind of loss on the common well-being ... when law is altered the restraining power of law is weakened in so far as custom is done away with. Hence a human law should never be altered, unless the gain to the common well-being on one head makes up for what has been lost on another.⁶²

Exemptions can be granted to human law, but these need to be for the common good:

> Now it happens at times that some precept that is for people's benefit in most cases is not helpful for this particular person or in this particular case, either because it stops something better from happening or because it brings in some evil.... To leave the decision to anybody's discretion would be dangerous, except perhaps where there is an evident emergency.... Therefore he whose office it is to rule

the people has the power to grant dispensations from the human laws that rest on his authority.... If, however, he grants permission without these reasonable grounds and of his own pleasure, then he will not dispense faithfully and he will be unwise; untrustworthy if his intention is not the common good, foolish if he disregards the reason for dispensation. Hence:

1. When a person is dispensed from observing the usual law this is not done to the prejudice of the common good, but with the intention of advancing it.
2. There is not respect for persons if unequal people are not equally treated. When a person's condition is such as to deserve special treatment, there is no unfair favouritism if special regard is shown him.
3. In so far as natural law contains common precepts which never fail it does not allow of dispensation.... Each man comes under the divine law as a private person comes under the public law of which he is a subject. Correspondingly, as dispensation from human public law cannot be granted except from him from whom law has its authority, so from the precepts of divine law, which come from God, no one can grant a dispensation except God or a man entrusted with his particular commission in the matter.[63]

Governance

Just as he did with law, Thomas makes a distinction between divine and human governance. Divine governance is supreme, and it is human governance's purpose to secure the common good by instilling virtue in its citizens, which it is to do through enacting human law. This body of law is to reflect Man's natural rights.

We'll look at some general statements about governance, then divine and human governance, before closing with virtue and societal implications.

> For we observe among beings of nature that what is best comes to pass either always or most of the time. This would not be the case were not there some providence guiding such beings to an end, the good. Such guidance is what

> government means.... Now the highest perfection of any being consists in the attaining of its end. Hence it is appropriate to God's goodness that, as he has brought things into being, he also guides them towards their end. This is what governing them means.[64]

And for our Creator, that end is the good, and it encompasses providence. God governs creation toward His end.

> We gain a good in many ways. One is by its becoming a quality inhering in us.... A second is by the good's being something produced by us.... A third way is by the good's being held or owned by us.[65] The Law excluded no race from the worship of God and from whatever conduced to the salvation of the soul.[66]

We all have the opportunity to know our Creator by fulfilling our purpose of becoming good.

"Note this difference, however, that what creatures receive from God constitutes their natures; what a man imposes artificially on the beings of nature is a coercion."[67] What comes from our Creator is the very nature of who we are; what comes from human governance at best provides only guidance as it builds atop our Creator's foundation. Human governance is normally a coercion through law. So what is provided by divine and human government?

Divine Government

Creation is under one ruler, its Creator, and His governance directs Man toward Himself as both individuals and one single community. This direction is accomplished through Man choosing to develop virtue, using his reason acting in obedience toward fulfilling his purpose.

In answering whether the world has one ruler, Thomas says,

> The only answer is that the world is under the one ruler. The reason: because the purpose of the world's being governed is the good by essence, i.e. the optimum the governing of the world must be the best possible. Now the best form of government is government by one. The proof is this: to govern means nothing else but to guide those governed towards an end, i.e. towards some good. Unity, however, is

> an essential characteristic of goodness.... And we perceive that any reality as far as possible resists being divided and that its dissolution results from some defect in it. The conclusion is that unity or peace is the aim intended by the ruler of any group.... It stands to reason, then, that the government of the universe, the most perfect instance of government, is by the one ruler.[68]

> There are, then, three ways of regarding the effect of God's governing action. One is from the standpoint of its end.... Secondly, the effect of governance can be viewed in terms of the influences whereby creatures are being guided towards a likeness to God ... first, to the degree that the creature is good it imitates God ... secondly, to the degree that one creature brings about good in another it imitates God.... Thirdly, the effects of God's rule can be viewed, in detail; from this aspect they are beyond reckoning.[69]

This is one place natural rights and law enter the picture. These rights are almost exclusively negative, and their influence is voluntary—that is, subject to Man's choices. More about this at the end of Chapter 6.

> The way God is the governor of things matches the way he is their cause.... God is not simply a particular cause with respect to one class of things, but the universal cause of all being. Therefore even as nothing can exist that is not created by God, so also nothing can exist that is not ruled by him.... Inane, therefore, was the opinion of those maintaining that either the corruptible things of earth or singulars or even the affairs of men are not ruled by God.[70]

> But the community for which the divine law is given is that of men in relation to God, whether in the present or the future life. The divine law, therefore, lays down precepts about all matters which affect man's right disposition for communication with God. Now man is joined to God by his reason or mind, in which the image of God is present; and therefore the divine law lays down commands about whatever disposes human reason aright. This comes about through acts of all the virtues; for the intellectual virtues

> rightly dispose the acts of reason in themselves and the moral virtues dispose them aright in regard to the inward passions and outward actions."[71]

> Precepts of human law direct man in regard to the human community, so those of the divine law direct him in regard to a kind of community or commonwealth of men under God. Now for the proper conduct of any community there are two requirements: the first is that each member should behave rightly towards its head; the second, that he should behave rightly to the rest of his fellows and partners in the community. Consequently, the divine law ought, in the first place, to contain precepts regulating man's relations to God; and, in the second place, others regulating his relations to the other members, his neighbours all living under God.[72]

Our Creator governs all creation to His end, happiness, which is achieved by becoming virtuous and beginning to imitate Him as far as our nature allows. To reach that end requires the right use of reason as it is through our mind and reason that we have His image. It is the purpose of divine government to govern a people's relationship with their Creator and through that relationship the relationships he has with his fellow men. So how should human government fit in?

Human Government
Human governance's chief purpose is planning for the community's common good, and it is the entire community's business.

> The chief and main concern of law properly so called is the plan for the common good. The planning is the business of the whole people or of their vicegerent. Therefore to make law is the office of the entire people or of the public personage who has care of them.[73]

> Now human law is ordained for one kind of community, divine law for another. Human law is ordained for the civil community, which involves relationships of men to one another; and men are ordered to one another by outward acts, whereby they communicate with each other. It is this kind of communication that comes under justice, whose essential function is to direct the human community. Consequently,

the precepts of human law are concerned only with acts of justice; and if they prescribe the acts of other virtues, that is, only in so far as they take on the character of justice.[74]

Human government is intended to assist divine government through law regulating men's relationships to one another and toward the common good. As such it and its laws are subordinate to divine government and its law. Its chief precept is the virtue of justice, although it can and should reflect other virtues in relation to justice.

The type of human governance can vary, but the best is a mixture as outlined in the following:

> Law can be divided according to the type of the regime. One is kingship or royalty ... another is aristocracy, or the rule of the best ... another is oligarchy, where a few rich or powerful men are in control ... another is popular rule, called democracy, and from this comes decrees of the commonality. Another regime is tyranny, which is so thoroughly corrupt that it affords no law. There is another type of regime blended of the others, and this is the best, and provides law as Isidore understood it, namely that *which men of birth together with the common people have sanctioned.*[75]

> There are two things to be observed concerning the right ordering of rulers in a state or people. One is that all should have some share in government; this makes for peace among the people, and commends itself to all.... The other regards the kind of government, or how the rulers are instituted. There are various kinds of regimen ... but the principal ones are monarchy, in which one man rules as specially qualified, and aristocracy, that is the rule of the best.... Hence the best system in any state or kingdom is one in which one man, as specially qualified, rules over all, and under him are others governing as having special endowments, yet all have a share inasmuch as those are elected from all, and also are elected by all. This is the best form of constitution, a mixture of monarchy, in that one man is at the head, or aristocracy, in that many rule as specially qualified, and democracy, in that the rulers can be chosen from the people and by them. This was the form established by divine law.[76]

What Thomas described as the best type of human government is what America's Founders created. We have a blended government made up of an executive with some powers of a monarch and a legislative body with special endowments of power to counter the executive power. This legislative body was intended to be the rule of the best, with the states selecting the members of the Senate and the people the members of the House. All members of the government are to be drawn from the people and be freely elected by the people. The compact between the people and the human government was documented within the social contracts called America's Declaration of Independence and its Constitution, both of which are covered in the second volume.

In more general terms about human government, Thomas states,

> A human group with its own customs can be in one of two conditions, self-governing or not. If it is a free country, where people are able to make their own laws, their common consensus about a particular observance, expressed in custom, is more important than the authority of the ruler, who has the power of making law only in so far as he represents the people; a whole people can make law, not a single individual. If, however, people are not free to make their own laws, or to put aside a law laid down for them by superior authority, then all the same a prevailing custom among them obtains the force of law when it is allowed by those whose office it is to make laws for them; by this very fact authority seems to approve what has been brought in by custom.[77]

In a free society, the rule-making capability of the human government derives from the customs the people themselves develop. In other words, people's individual decision-making orders society rather than human government's law. Even in a society which is not free, those customs should have the power of law when they are allowed by the human government, so long as those customs do not violate divine laws.

> As Augustine says, quoting Cicero, *a nation is a body of persons joined together in acceptance of a law for the good of all*. Thus it is of the essence of a nation that the mutual

The Light & the Rod

> relations of its members be governed by just laws. Now such relations are of two kinds: those set up by the authority of the rulers, and those established by the will of private persons. Since whatever is subject to an individual's power can be used as he wills, and the individual is subject to the ruler, it follows that by the latter's authority judgment must be exercised between man and man, and punishment inflicted on evildoers. On the other hand, the private individual has power over the things he possesses, and therefore he can deal with them as he will, buying, selling, giving, and so forth.
>
> Now the Law was perfectly adequate in regard to both kinds of relations. It established judges.... It also prescribed justice in administering the Law.... Moreover, it removed an occasion of unjust judgment by forbidding judges to accept gifts. It prescribed the number of witnesses, two or three, and definite penalties for various crimes.[78]

A separate branch of human government is advocated for the judicial. Its power should be separated from law-making. Specific judicial precepts are outlined below. It is intended that law-making provide for general cases and judicially apply to specific instances where injustice occurs. These precepts can change if the people or their human government changes. More on this in the next chapter.

> In any people we find four different types of order. There is the order of rulers to their subjects, of the subjects to one another, of the citizens to foreigners, and the order within the household, that of father to son, wife to husband, and master to servant. According to these four orders the judicial precepts of the Old Law may be distinguished. Some are about the institutions of the rulers and their duties, and about the respect to be shown them.... There are also some regarding the relations of citizens to one another, such as about buying and selling, judgments and penalties; this is the second part of the judicial precepts. Further, there are some regarding foreigners, such as about wars against enemies, and the reception of travellers and strangers; this is the third part of the judicial precepts. Finally, there are precepts

regarding domestic life, such as those about servants, wives and children; this is the fourth part of the judicial precepts.[79]

> The judicial precepts ordained by men bind for ever, so long as the regimen remains the same; but should the State or the agent pass over to a different one, then the laws have to be changed. The same laws are not appropriate in a democracy, where the power is in the hands of the people, and in an oligarchy, when it is in those of the rich.... Consequently, once the state of that people had changed, the judicial precepts had also to change.[80]

As to a preference for law over judges,

> Aristotle says, *it is better that all issues be regulated by law than to be left to the decision of judges*. Three reasons may be given. First, because it is easier to find the few wise men who suffice to frame rightful laws than the many required to judge aright about every single case. Secondly, because framing the laws allows for a long time during which to ponder over what they should enforce. . . . Thirdly, because lawgivers judge on the general lie of the land and with an eye to the future.[81]

Finally, in regards to a people's ruler, whether he be divine or human, Thomas states,

> Now there are three things man owes to the head of the community: fidelity, reverence, and service.... As to his neighbours, man has obligations to some in particular and also to the generality. In particular, as regards those to whom he is indebted.... To all men in general he is obliged to refrain from doing harm, whether by deed, word, or thought.[82]

> But the rulers, as we have said, were taken from the people in general, and so had their own property on which they could live. Another, the principal, reason was that the Lord forbade even the king to have extensive wealth or indulge in pomp and splendor, both because otherwise he could hardly avoid pride and tyrannical conduct, and also because, if the rulers were not very wealthy, and their office involved much

hard work and anxiety, it would not be much sought after by ordinary people; thus one cause of sedition was removed.[83]

Those participating in human government are there in order to guide the people in virtue and should reflect virtue themselves. They are to come from the people—and be selected by the people—in order to serve the people. They thereby also serve God. Therefore, they should live from their own means and not off the people so they do not become corrupted.

The Final End: Happiness

We've mentioned several times that the final end is good—by which we obtain happiness. But what is happiness and where is it found? According to Thomas, happiness is not found in wealth,[84] honors,[85] fame or glory,[86] power,[87] bodily good,[88] pleasure,[89] the good of the soul,[90] or any created good.[91] Happiness then,

> is to be found, not in any creature, but in God alone.[92] Happiness means gaining the Perfect Good.... That man has the capacity appears from the fact that his mind can apprehend good which is universal and unrestricted and his will can desire it. Therefore he is open to receive it.[93]

As to this life,

> The partial happiness we can hold in this life a man can secure for himself ... Now all knowing according to a manner of created thing falls short of seeing what God really is, for the divine infinitely surpasses every created nature. Consequently neither man nor any creature can attain final happiness through their natural resources.[94] For he [man] has been endowed with freewill, so that he can be turned to God who can make him happy ... "what we can do through our friends can, in a sense, be done through ourselves."[95]

Virtue

Virtue is the path. Thomas classified virtues into the theological, intellectual, and moral. He names three theological virtues. Relevant moral virtues include justice, obedience, and truth. These stand above the other moral virtues within his writing. We'll conclude this chapter with some implications for how Man should live with virtue in accord with divine requirements and Man's nature. But first we'll look at a couple of passages about virtue and sin (vice).

> Virtue and sin do not arise from the same source. Sin springs from the desire for transient goods; and consequently the desire for that good which helps towards the attainment of all other temporal goods is called the root of all sin. Virtue, conversely, derives from the desire for the changeless good; thus charity, the love of God, is described ... as the root of all virtue.[96]

As to the source of sin, "Because the nature of moral evil begins in turning away from God, pride is called sin's 'beginning.'"[97]

As for virtue,

> Aristotle teaches that the requirements of a virtuous act are that it is done, first, knowingly, second, from choice and for a fitting end, and third, unwaveringly. The first is included in the second.... Hence the definition starts with the *will* in order to show that the act ... has to be voluntary, and qualifies this as *lasting and constant* in order to indicate the firmness of the act.[98]

As sin and virtue are contrary, each virtue has a corresponding sin, and "an inclination towards one of two contraries necessarily diminishes any inclination towards the other. Since sin is the contrary of virtue, that good of nature which is the inclination to virtue is lessened by the fact of a person's sinning."[99] Virtue is the desire for the changeless good (God), whereas sin is a desire for transient (material) goods. Each virtue has a corresponding vice (sin). We can only choose one or the other. They are mutually exclusive choices.

The distinction between the theological, intellectual, and moral virtues is the difference in their objects. The theological virtues have God as their object; all others have Man as their object. Intellectual virtues relate to Man's use of reason, and the moral virtues to Man's controlling his desires.

"Now the object of the theological virtues is God Himself, Who is the last end of all, as surpassing the knowledge of our reason. On the other hand, the object of the intellectual and moral virtues is something comprehensible to human reason."[100] The intellectual virtues are

> the habits of the speculative intellect [and] do not perfect the appetitive part, nor affect it in any way, but only the intellective part; they may indeed be called virtues in so far as they confer aptness for a good work, viz. the consideration of truth.[101]

Between intellectual and moral virtues,

> Reason is the first principle of all human acts.... Accordingly for a man to do a good deed, it is requisite not only that his reason be well disposed by means of a habit of intellectual virtue; but also that his appetite be well disposed by means of a habit of moral virtue. And so moral differs from intellectual virtue, even as the appetite differs from the reason. Hence just as the appetite is the principle of human acts, in so far as it partakes of reason, so are moral habits to be considered virtues in so far as they are in conformity with reason.[102]

The intellectual virtues include wisdom, prudence, science, and understanding, which have been covered to some extent previously. We will look briefly at the theological virtues of faith, hope and charity,[103] and the moral virtues of justice, obedience, and truth. These all impact our relationships with each other as they impact the relationship we have with our Creator. The moral virtues place constraints on our behavior toward each other. We will then conclude this chapter with some implications for moral behavior derived from law, governance, and virtue.

Theological Virtues

The theological virtues all orient us toward the Creator. Faith is the beginning for hope and charity, and all other virtues. Faith looks to the past as well as the future, and can have good or evil as its objects—although the faith that believes them is not evil, but good.[104] Hope looks only to the future and has good as its object. Charity can also be translated as *love*. All virtues end in acts of charity performed out of love, both for our Creator and fellow man. This is agape.

As to faith,

> There are two requisites for faith. The one is the proposal of what is to be believed.... The second requisite is assent to what is proposed. As to the first, God is necessarily the cause of faith. The reason: the things of faith surpass man's understanding and so become part of his knowledge only because God reveals them.... As to the assent of the matters of faith, we can look to two types of cause. One is a cause that persuades from without, e.g. a miracle witnessed.... Another kind of cause must therefore be present, an inner cause, one that influences a person inwardly to assent to the things of faith.[105]

> It is clear that in the case of man the term virtue means a resource making a human act to be good. Any habit, then, that is in every case the source of a good human act can be called a virtue in man. Formed faith is such a habit.[106]

Further, "Of its nature faith is first among all the virtues. The reason: Because, as shown, in all matters of action the end has primacy, the theological virtues, having the final end as object, are necessarily prior to other virtues."[107]

In regards to hope, Thomas states,

> Hope's object is a good that lies in the future and that is difficult but possible to attain.... When it is a case, then, of hoping for something as possible to us precisely through God's help, such hope, by reason of its very reliance upon God, reaches God himself. Evidently, then it is a virtue.[108]

Hope is a theological virtue in that its end is our Creator himself. Hope looks only to good and the future.

And finally, in regards to charity,

> Now always a being through itself is fuller than a being through another. But faith and hope attain to God according as from him comes knowledge of truth or possession of good, but charity attains God himself so as to rest in him without looking for any gain. This is why charity is higher than faith and hope, and consequently than all the virtues. By

a like argument prudence, which appertains to the reason itself, is better than the other moral virtues.[109]

In regards to charity and faith, he further states, "This good, the end of faith's act, is the divine good, the proper object of charity. This is why charity is called the form of faith, namely because the act of faith is completed and shaped by charity."[110] Also, "Faith belongs to the cognitive power, whose act is of such a kind that the things known are in the knower. Charity, on the contrary, has its seat in the affective power, which reaches out to the things themselves as they exist in reality."[111] Thomas appears to be making a distinction between faith and charity, whereby they are each ranked first as one relates to intellect (knowing) and the other to the completion of a voluntary external act (doing), performed out of love for another.

Justice

Justice is different from the other moral virtues. It governs Man's dealings with others. Justice is also a natural right.[112] Justice is essential for trust to exist, and therefore for society to exist. Justice is also dependent on the judge and the decisions they make.

As for the moral virtue of justice,

> The proper characteristic of justice, as compared with the other moral virtues, is to govern a man in his dealings towards others. It implies a certain balance of equality.... Equality is relative to another. The other moral values, however, compose a man for activities which befit him considered in himself. So then that which is correct in their working and which is the proper object of their bent is not thought of save in relation to the doer. Whereas with justice, in addition to this, that which is correct is constituted by a relation to another ... as with the payment of a fair wage for a service rendered.[113] A man is called just because he safeguards right.[114]

Justice can be defined as "the habit whereby a person with a lasting and constant will renders to each his due."[115] Justice is the greatest of the moral virtues as it properly relates to that which is correct between more than one individual. Thomas asserts that other moral virtues pertain only to activities which befit a Man himself.

> Well then, since we are called just in that we do something rightly ... it must needs be that justice is seated in some power of that sort. That power is twofold, namely of will, which is in the reason, and of feeling, which follows sense perception, and is divided into the emotive of desire and that of tackling the difficult.... The act of rendering each his due cannot spring from the emotional appetite, because sense perception does not go so far as to look into the relationship of one thing to another; this is proper to reason. Therefore justice cannot be seated in the desirous or the spirited emotional powers, but only in the will.[116]

As for its objective,

> for justice especially, in comparison with other virtues, an impersonal objective is fixed. We call it *the just thing*, and this indeed is a right. Clearly, then, right is the objective of justice.[117] The right and just is a work that is commensurate with another person according to some sort of fairness. This can be measured in two ways. One, from the very nature of the case ... this is called natural right. The other, the commensurate to the other is settled by agreement or mutual consent.... And this may come about in two ways. First, by private engagement ... and second, by public agreement, as when the whole civil community or State fixes what is adequate and commensurate or when this is so ordained by the sovereign authority who has charge over and personifies the people: this is called positive right.[118]

Right is the object of justice and its basis is God's natural rights and positive (human) rights, the latter determined by agreement between parties.

> Hence, that which is natural to a thing with an immutable nature is necessarily constant always and everywhere. Man's nature, however, is variable. And so that which is natural to him can fail to meet the situation sometimes.[119] By mutual agreement the human will can establish that which is just in matters which of themselves do not conflict with natural justice. It is here that positive right has its place.... However if anything conflict with natural right, human will cannot

> make it just.[120] That which is divinely promulgated is termed divine right. Partly it is of matters that belong to natural right, though their justice is hidden from men and not recognized, and partly of matters that are made just by divine institution.[121]

Man's nature is variable. Again, we have an ordering of the divine, through natural law, over the human law where these two conflict due to our variable nature.

Thomas cites the following as an example:

> We have said that natural right or the naturally just is that which of itself is adequate to and commensurate with another. There are two ways of arriving at this. First, by looking at it purely and simply in itself.... Second, by looking at the natural matching of one with another, not absolutely or in the abstract, but as involving a consequence. Take the ownership of property; considered in itself there is no reason why this field should belong to this man rather than to that man, but when you take into account its being put under cultivation and farmed without strife, then as Aristotle makes clear, it tallies with being owned by this not that individual.[122]

Natural rights are derived based on looking at the things themselves and at the consequences derived from them, specifically whether good is attained or not.

There is a relationship between justice and charity: "For as charity may be called a general virtue because it sets the activities of all the virtues towards the divine good, so it is with legal or general justice which sets them towards the common good."[123] Charity and justice both order Man to good, the first the divine good and the second the common good.

While justice is the first of the moral virtues, it covers only Man's external actions.

> All whatsoever that can be ruled aright by reason are matters for moral virtue, which is defined by right reason.... All the same it is through external actions and things, through which men mutually communicate, that the order of one to another

is observed, whereas in a man's interior feelings you take note of his uprightness within himself. Since it is directed to others, justice consequently is not about the whole field of moral virtue, but only about external deeds and things.[124]

Finally, the decision rendered by justice is judgment.

> The word judgment which in its original usage meant the right determination of what is just, has been stretched to cover the right determination on any matter whether theoretical or practical. Yet there are always two requirements. One is the power or ability of producing a judgment: as to this, judgment is an act of reason.... The other relates to the disposition of the one who judges, on this depends his aptness to judge aright.[125]

Judgment is a consequence of justice and dependent on both the power and ability to make a decision and the judge himself.

Obedience

God gave Man the freedom to make his own choices, but he has an obligation to obey his superiors, another instance of a moral duty extending from grace. Our actions are to be oriented toward good, and God is the ultimate good. Human goods Man can give up in pursuing God's good are his possessions, his body, and—most importantly—his will.

As to why obedience is necessary,

> God left man in the hand of his own counsel, not in the sense that he could do whatever he pleases, but that he approach every act, not under the stricture of a natural necessity, in the way non-rational creatures do, but out of free choice issuing from his own counsel. Just as he should undertake everything else from this personal decision, so should he face obeying superiors.[126]

As we have seen, acts are the carrying out by will of the choices we make. But those choices, and therefore the corresponding acts, are to be oriented towards good.

There are two ways whereby something can be viewed as an act of good will: first of all, looking to the deed itself ... secondly, looking to the person acting.... Now the main reason why any deed is virtuous, honourable and meritorious is that it issues from the will. For this reason, even though to obey is an obligatory act, this still does not diminish its merit if the person obeying does so willingly.[127]

Obedience ranks highly within the moral values as follows:

> The classes of human goods a person can forgo in his quest for God are three. The least important is that good in external possessions; next is that of physical well-being; above all others is that of endowments of soul. Among such endowments, the will, in one sense, holds first place.... In these terms, the virtue of obedience is more praiseworthy than other moral virtues, seeing that by obedience a person gives up his own will for God's sake and by other moral virtues something less.[128]

This ranking is consistent with Plato's assertions noted in Chapter 3. For

> just as God is the primary mover over all beings that are subject to the forces of nature, so he is over all wills. This parallel, therefore, is established: as all the elements in nature are by the exigencies of nature subject to God moving, so all wills are bound under the demands of moral rightness to obey God ruling.[129]

While obedience is generally ranked highly among the moral virtues, it is obedience to God which ranks highest.

But there are instances where obedience should not be observed:

> There are two ways in which it can happen that some sub-rational being is not moved by its mover. The first is interference coming from the stronger power of another moving force.... The second comes from a lack of complete subjection in a recipient to its moving force....

> Carrying over the parallel: there are two ways it can happen that a subordinate is not bound to obey a superior in everything. The first is because of the precept of a higher superior.... The second way is for a command to be given in

> a matter where no subjection to the superior exists. Seneca's remark is to the point, *He is mistaken who supposes that slavery takes in the whole person. It touches not the better part; the body may be subject and consigned to an owner, but thoughts are free.* The force of this is that we are not bound to obey man but God alone in matters which concern the inner life of the will.
>
> Those matters in which one man is bound to obey another are outward actions involving the body. Even so, he is not bound to obey humans but God alone in regard to what belongs to the very nature of physical life, since in these matters all men are equal.[130]

Again, we are bound first to our Creator on internal matters and again to Him on external matters based on the equality of our nature. Obedience to Man must be consistent with obedience to our Creator.

Thomas emphasizes this point again in that

> Man is subject to God utterly and in all matters, internal and external; thus he is bound to a universal obedience. In contrast, subjects are not under their superiors in all regards, but only within fixed limits; here superiors are mediators between God and the subject. In other respects subjects are under the authority of God directly, who manifests his will through law, natural and positive.[131]

Governance stands between Creator and Man, but its scope is limited. It is to serve the people and thereby serve Him by fairly and impartially supporting the common good.

Truth
The virtue of truth concerns speaking it. This virtue is related to justice as human justice cannot exist without it, because human justice rests on what Man can judge: our external acts alone. Only God and divine justice sees the heart also.

> "Truth" can have two meanings. In the first it is the quality by which a thing is said to be "true," and it is not a virtue but the objective or the end for virtue.... In its second sense "truth" can be taken as that by which a person speaks the truth; it is the reason for his being called "truthful." So

understood, truth or truthfulness has to be a virtue, for to speak the truth is a morally good act and that which makes its possessor and his actions good is a virtue.[132]

Truth relates to justice as

> any virtue is allied to justice as a subordinate to its principal, when it coincides in part with justice, but in part falls short of the full meaning. The virtue of truth has two points in common with justice. The first is that justice has reference to another person, and what we have determined the act of truth to be, namely a communication, has reference to someone else.... The second is that justice establishes a certain objective quality. So does truth, making as it does signs match facts.[133]

Insofar as

> truth in justice, this can have two meanings. The first is that justice itself is a certain rightness measured by conformity to divine law. In this regard truth in justice is different from truth in life: truth in life means that someone keeps his own life upright; truth in justice, that someone keeps the requirements of law in the judgments he passes on others....
>
> In a second sense truth in justice can be taken to indicate that out of respect for justice someone makes known the truth, expressing it or bearing true testimony in a legal case. This kind of truth is one special act of justice and does not have direct bearing upon the truth now being discussed.[134]

Truth is a moral virtue required for law to be effective as justice involves at least two parties and therefore requires communication in addition to adhering to divine law's requirements.

Moral Implications

Man's Dominion

Man's dominion concerns his use and management of what God has blessed him with. This dominion is natural to Man because of reason, God's image given to Man. God's providence orders all things to His good end. This includes the recognition of private property as each person takes greater care for what they are responsible and is more organized when each has their own responsibility. These lead to greater peace and contentment with our work: securing the common good.

> We can consider external things in two ways. Looked at first of all from the point of view of their nature, this is not subject to man's power, but only to God's sovereign power. Alternatively, they can be looked at from the point of view of their use and management, and in this regard man has a natural dominion over external things, for he has a mind and a will with which to turn them to his own account. They seem to be made for him in so far as imperfect things are for the sake of the more perfect, as we have already observed. And this is the reason Aristotle uses to prove that the possession of external things is natural to man. Further, this dominion over the rest of creation, which is natural to man as a creature possessed of the reason in which his imagehood of God consists, is manifested in the very creation of man.[135]

> God has pre-eminent dominion over all things, and in his providence he ordered certain things for men's material support. This is why it is natural for man to have dominion over things in the sense of having the power to use them.[136]

> Man has a twofold competence in relation to material things. The first is the title to care for and distribute the earth's resources. Understood in this way, it is not merely legitimate for a man to possess things as his own, it is even necessary for human life, and this for three reasons. First, because each person takes more trouble to care for something that is his sole responsibility than what is held in common or by many—for in such a case each individual shirks the work and leaves the responsibility to somebody else, which is what happens when too many officials are involved. Second, because human affairs are more efficiently organized if each person has his own responsibility to discharge; there would be chaos if everybody cared for everything. Third, because men live together in greater peace where everyone is content with his task. We do, in fact, notice that quarrels often break out amongst men who hold things in common without distinction.

> Man's other competence is to use and manage the world's resources. Now in regard to this, no man is entitled to manage things merely for himself, he must do so in the interest of all, so that he is ready to share them with others in case of necessity.[137]
>
> Hence, [the] community of goods is said to be part of the natural law not because it requires everything to be held in common and nothing to be appropriated to individual possession, but because the distribution of property is a matter not for natural law but, rather, human agreement, which is what positive law is about.... The individual holding of possessions is not, therefore, contrary to the natural law; it is what rational beings conclude as an addition to the natural law.[138]

Man has been given dominion over creation in order to care for it and thereby provide the means for his own existence. Each man has a responsibility both for himself and others. Individual ownership is a means for fulfilling that responsibility, and is subject to human agreement in compliance with both divine and natural law. This responsibility exists not only for our current time, but across time—a form of charity toward the future.

The Distribution of Goods

Distribution of goods is the responsibility of the one who has dominion (stewardship). This is a form of justice. Justice requires that we, as individuals, fairly distribute from our own abundance the goods we produce for the benefit of others. This cannot be accomplished by the state. As a form of charity, it can only be realized through individuals. Virtue is required to enable people to execute this obligation effectively.

> The act of distributing common goods is the office of him who is their guardian. Nevertheless distributive justice is also in subjects in that they are content with the fair sharing out. Yet note that distributive justice may be from the common goods of the family, not the State, and this dispensing can be done by the authority of a private person.[139]

The dictates of human law cannot derogate from natural or divine law. The natural order established by God in his providence is, however, such that lower things are meant to enable man to supply his needs. A man's needs must therefore still be met out of the world's goods even though a certain division and apportionment of them is determined by law. And this is why according to natural law goods that are held in superabundance by some people should be used for the maintenance of the poor.... At the same time those who suffer want are so numerous and they cannot all be supplied out of one stock, and this is why it is left to each individual to decide how to manage his property in such a way as to supply the wants of the suffering.[140]

Use of Force

Further, sovereigns are entrusted with public authority so that they might be guardians of justice. They may, therefore, use violence and coercion only to the extent that the principles of justice permit, whether by way of fighting enemies or of punishing malefactors. Anything taken away by this sort of violence, therefore, does not fall within the definition of robbery, since it is not contrary to justice. On the other hand, those who exercise the public authority entrusted to them by using violence to take away others property in a manner that is contrary to justice do wrong and commit robbery, and they are bound to make restitution.[141]

Those with public authority are bound by the same justice as individuals, except when dispensation has been given for fighting enemies and those who disobey the law. However, human law is to be consistent with divine and natural law.

Market Price

Exchange of goods should be based on a fair price to both parties. That fair price should represent a just or market price between buyer and seller and can include the loss of value associated with not having an item.

As to the exchange of goods between parties,

It is otherwise in exchanges between persons. There something is rendered to an individual person in return for something of his that has been received: this most evidently appears in buying and selling, from which originates the notion of an exchange. There the balance or equalization of a thing is called for, so that a man should repay the other as much as he gains in acquiring the thing which belonged to the other.[142]

Regarding contracts,

> If we look at it first of all as it is in itself, we can say that such a transaction was introduced for the common benefit of both parties, in so far as each one needs something which the other has ... But what is equally useful to both should not involve more of a burden for one than for the other and any contract between two parties should, therefore, be based on an equality of material exchange. But the value of consumer products is measured by the price given, which as Aristotle pointed out, is what coinage was invented for. It follows that the balance of justice is upset if either the price exceeds the value of the goods in question or the thing exceeds the price. To sell for more or to buy for less than a thing is worth is, therefore, unjust and illicit in itself.
>
> The other way in which we can look at a contract of sale is in so far as it happens to bring benefit to one party at the expense of the other, as in the case where one badly needs to get hold of something and the other is put out by not having it. In such a case the estimation of the just price will have to take into account not merely the commodity to be sold but also the loss which the seller incurs in selling it. The commodity can here be sold for more than it is worth in itself though not for more than it is worth to the possessor.[143]

Finally, "It follows that a seller who sells something according to its market price would not seem to be acting unjustly if he fails to disclose a future contingency."[144]

Profit
Acquiring profit in an exchange is not contrary to virtue, so long as the price is just and neither party is placed under an undue burden.

> What men are in business for is the making of exchanges ... there are two sorts of exchange. The first sort is as it were natural and necessary, and consists in the exchange for commodity or of commodity for money, for the maintenance of life.... The other sort of exchange is of money for money, or even of any commodity for money though now for the sake of making a profit, and this is the sort of exchange that belongs to business men in the strict sense.... The former sort of exchange is praiseworthy because it supplies natural needs, whereas the second sort is rightly open to criticism since, just in itself, it feeds the acquisitive urge which knows no limit but tends to increase to infinity.... Nevertheless, profit, which is the point of commerce, while it may not carry the notion of anything right or necessary, does not carry the notion of anything vicious or contrary to virtue either. There is therefore, nothing to stop profit being subordinated to an activity that is necessary, or even right.[145]

Theft

As noted earlier, it is necessary for Man to have title to things as his own. With that ownership comes the responsibility for Man to both care for himself and others from his abundance. In addition, he is required by divine and natural law to do so in a fair and charitable manner. Theft of an individual's property deprives him of the means of fulfilling this requirement and thereby impairs his ability to fulfill his purpose.

> We have already seen that mortal sin consists in cutting oneself off from the charity which is the spiritual life-sap of the soul. But charity consists primarily in loving God, and, secondly, in loving our neighbour which includes wishing him well and acting accordingly. Stealing, however, damages one's neighbour through his property, and human society would perish if everybody started stealing from everybody else. Theft is, therefore, a mortal sin in so far as it is contrary to charity.[146]

> Penalties imposed in this life are corrective rather than retributive, for retribution is reserved to God's judgment which *rightly falls on those who do such things*. A man should, therefore, not be sentenced to death in this life for

any mortal sin, but only for such mortal sins as cause irreparable damage or else as are particularly perverted.[147]

Penalties are to be commensurate with the deed, but should not include death unless irreparable harm has been done or a perversion as defined by divine or natural law is involved.

Fraud
"To practice fraud so as to sell something for more than its just price is an outright sin in so far as one is deceiving one's neighbour to his detriment. This is why Cicero declares, *Contracts are to be free of lies*."[148]

Usury
Thomas states that in general lending money at interest is usury and a sin. It was for the purpose of having equitable exchanges that money was invented.

> Making a charge for lending money is unjust in itself, for one party sells the other something non-existent, and this obviously sets up an inequality which is contrary to justice.[149]

> Now money, however, according to Aristotle, was invented chiefly for exchanges to be made, so that the prime and proper use of money is in use and disbursement in the way of ordinary transactions. It follows that it is in principle wrong to make a charge for money lent, which is what usury consists in.[150]

However, there are some exceptions to this general rule.

1. "A lender is, however, entitled to seek the sort of compensation that cannot be measured in terms of money—things like benevolence and love towards the lender."[151] Non-monetary compensation freely given is not usury.

2. "A person is, however, entitled to accept, and even to ask for, and to expect some service or the expression of some sentiment, provided it is motivated by good will and not by a feeling of obligation, since good will cannot be measured in terms of money."[152]

3. "Somebody, on the other hand, who entrusts his money to a merchant or a craftsman in a sort of partnership does not hand over the ownership, and so it is still at his risk that the merchant trades or the craftsman works. The lender is, therefore, entitled to ask for a part of the profit of the undertaking in so far as it is also his own."[153] Where the lending represents a partnership, a sharing of the profits from the venture is allowed.

4. "It is never right to induce another to lend at interest, although it is permissible to accept a loan from somebody who is prepared to make such a loan and so is already in this business, if the object is the doing of some good in the shape of relieving one's own or another's need."[154] While it is usury to make a loan with interest, it is all right to accept such a loan if the loan is being put to accomplishing good.

5. "Human law, therefore, allows the taking of interest, not because it deems this to be just but because to do otherwise would impose undue restrictions on many people."[155] It is human law which allows interest, contrary to what is right by divine and natural law.

Human Law's Role

Human law ... is made for the people as a whole, which includes many who fall short of being virtuous, and not merely for the virtuous. Human law, cannot, therefore, prohibit whatever is contrary to virtue; it is enough for it to prohibit whatever destroys social intercourse, allowing everything else to be permissible, not in the sense of approving it, but of not attaching a penalty to it ... unless there is either fraud or a gross disparity.... Divine law, on the other hand, leaves nothing contrary to virtue unpunished, so that any failure to keep a due balance in contracts of sale is counted to be contrary to divine law.[156]

Human law attempts to place limits on behaviors which would destroy society. It is up to each individual to behave as though "they are a law unto themselves" as law is intended only for those who by their own nature are unjust. What human law lacks, divine and natural law compensate for as they omit nothing.

Summary

Thomas makes distinctions in the areas of providence, law, and governance. One view of providence agrees with both Clement's and Augustine's. The other view, how providence is executed, is used to make distinctions between divine and human in the areas of law and governance. In regards to free choice, while Man is the master of his choices and deliberations, Thomas believes our Creator provides assistance in the way of moving the soul toward good. This is the nature of grace and is related to free choice as Man is not inherently good. Man must willingly accept this grace to receive its benefits, but in turn he incurs a moral obligation to return love back to the Creator who has shown him love. This love has implications for Man's choices: Man should choose good.

In regards to Law, Thomas states the following:

1. All law is reason oriented toward the common good and is made by the authority of those who have care of the community—with the authority of our Creator first and then Man below Him.

2. Eternal law is the ultimate source of all law, and comes from the Creator.

3. Divine Law looks at ordering Man toward his Creator and the love of Man toward both God and his neighbor. Its purpose is to orient Man both to the fulfillment of his purpose and the common good. Divine law is necessary as Man's end is beyond his natural ability.

4. The new law is called the law of freedom, as it is oriented toward Man's internal thoughts and reason. *It leaves choice to the individual as long as Man's choice is consistent with divine and natural law, and human law where it is consistent with both.*

5. The sharing of eternal law by intelligent creatures—those who use reason—is natural law. Both divine and natural law proceed from divine will and are superior to human law.

6. Natural law is grounded in morality, promoting virtue as it relates to doing what's good.

7. Where human law conflicts with other law, men are called to obey their Creator. Divine and natural law proceed from the divine will and can only be changed by divine authority.

8. Human law's purpose is to bring the people to virtue over time. It is also to be consistent with both divine and natural law.

9. All right law promotes virtue, which is consistent with the Creator's purpose.

10. Laws are intended to apply equally to all, even to the ruler(s) who make them.

To summarize regarding governance, Thomas writes the following:

1. Divine governance is by one ruler, our Creator.

2. Human governance can come from one of several forms, but the form established by divine law combines aspects of a single ruler, who has under him others governing with special endowments. All of these come from the people and are to be elected by the people.

3. Human governance is only concerned with the administration of justice. This is giving to each individual his due by protecting their rights.

4. Law is to be preferred to judges as (1) it is hard to find a large number of men capable of being judges, (2) judges are inconsistent, and (3) law is more oriented to the future instead of the present.

Finally, in regards to virtue,

1. Happiness is the end of all virtue.

2. Faith is required for all virtue, and all virtues end in acts of charity performed out of love.

3. Justice is the only virtue which relates to two or more individuals, which is why it is the highest of the moral virtues—virtue which is necessary for proper human governance. Justice orients Man toward the common

good in a manner similar to the way charity orients Man toward the divine good.[157]

4. All wills are bound by moral rightness to obey our Creator.

The following implications for Man's moral behavior and dominion over creation proceed from the above points.

1. Man exercises stewardship over creation.
2. It is necessary for Man to own things.
3. The accumulation of wealth is okay as long as it is put to its proper use according to divine law: to help care for one's neighbors.
4. Man's fulfillment of his purpose can come only from his own choices as to the distribution of the common goods from his own family, not the decisions of the state. This is the only way Man can acquire virtue, which is necessary to fulfill his purpose.
5. Theft is considered a mortal sin as it is contrary to charity: It deprives another man of his rightful use of a possession. This can harm not only the man, but his family and his neighbor. Theft of one's possessions impairs their ability to fulfill their purpose.
6. One should be honest in all transactions.

The last three chapters have presented the theory for governance based upon biblical principles. It is now time to create the governance model based upon them. That is the subject of this volume's final chapter.

Chapter 6
The Biblical Principles Model

The Two Threads
We've now reviewed some governance related ideas expressed by Clement, Augustine, and Thomas. These ideas have implications for rights, freedom, justice, morality, virtue, and how order is brought to society. America's Founders positions are consistent with these ideas as they were shaped by their English culture and education.

According to Clement, Greek philosophy contained two threads of thought. Both were evident in Plato and Aristotle's writings, among many others. One thread is based upon pagan ideas. The second is based on the Hebrew Tanakh. America's Founders were grounded in biblical principles through this second thread. They attempted to create a governance structure in accordance with the rights, duties, and law outlined by the Tanakh and writers just mentioned. They chose this thread because they saw it presenting the best opportunity for Man, both for living in a way where his rights are recognized and providing the opportunity for fulfilling his purpose.

But what of the pagan thread? This thread is the basis for rule by divine right. It is grounded in Man himself. We'll review the pagan principles underlying the S*tate Religion Society* model, and present that model again. Then we'll build the *Biblical Principles* model, and close with a few implications from the ideas underlying the pagan model. This will serve to both end this volume, and set up the discussions in Volume 2.

Ideas Grounded in Man
From the pagan thread we see the following ideas:

1. Creation has always existed. History is a repetition of cycles.
2. Man makes his god(s). At times, those gods can be made to reside in idols through rituals performed by temple priests.
3. A ruler and/or priest governs society. The governing power is the lowest level in society that matters.
4. Our rights came from that governing power.
5. Only the collective society is relevant. A people exist to see that their society is successful. Individuals matter only to the extent they contribute to society.
6. As we matter in accordance with our ability to contribute, there is no innate equality of nature. We have instead a hierarchy of groups based upon ability as some gifts of nature make others superior. According to Greek philosophy, this is both "expedient and right." Our rights are based upon our perceived abilities and therefore the group(s) we belong to.
7. As all are not equal, the acquisition of knowledge and virtue is only for the elite, only for those who have the ability to properly use them. Citizenship is also not for everyone: It is only for those deemed capable of benefiting from it.
8. Citizens are to be molded to fit the state's needs. As our rights come from the state, those rights can and should be changed by the state to fit its goals and needs.
9. Rule can be by one, the few, or many. However, the power is to be concentrated and absolute. It is only the elite who have the capabilities and gifts to lead.
10. Religious and political power are not the same, but are very closely related. This relationship is emphasized in various ways.
11. Happiness is harmony within society and can achieved by either persuasion or compulsion. Deceit is acceptable

as the ends matter more than the means used to attain them. This last is the idea of the "noble lie."

12. For those who refuse to submit to the ruling authority, war is proper and just.

13. Citizens are the state's herd, to be bred and cultivated for its own ends.

The *State Religion Society* model looks as follows:

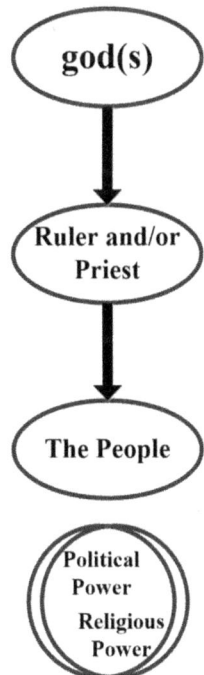

Grounded in Biblical Principles

From the biblical principles thread, we see the following ideas:

1. Our Creator created everything that has ever been created. As Creator, God has the power to create, change, or end anything at any time. His power, authority, and rule are absolute.

2. Our Creator has divine governance and law. These are supreme and can only be changed by Him. All things human lie below His directives and are to be consistent with them.

3. We have rights coming from our Creator. They were His freely given gifts to us. Accepting those gifts creates a moral obligation for Man to return love to God.

4. We have an innate equality of nature. Because we share the same nature, we also all have the same rights before our Creator. This is true equality, an equal standing based upon who and what we are.

5. We were created for the purpose of knowing our Creator. Happiness can only be found in fulfilling this purpose.

6. Each of us chooses whether to believe (faith) and develop knowledge and virtue. These provide the basis for fulfilling our purpose. We are not born with any of those things, but our nature lends itself to acquiring them. We each have the gift of free choice to decide whether we turn toward or away from our purpose.

7. Government is to be molded to fit its people's needs in compliance with our Creator's divine and natural law.

8. Stewardship and dispersion of power are used to reduce the potential for corruption as we are imperfect beings. The greatest prophets, such as Moses, realized the weight being a leader before our Creator carried, and asked that weight be shared among others. Checks and balances prevent some portions of human governance from becoming dominant and reducing or eliminating others' roles.

9. The people are the lowest level of society that matters.

10. Leaders are to come from the people—be elected by the people—to serve the people. By serving the people, leaders in turn serve God.

11. Religious power and political power are separate and distinct. Religious power's purpose is to teach what it means to be God's people. Political power's purpose is to enact justice impartially and even-handedly when someone chooses to do what is not right.

The *Biblical Principles* model can be diagrammed as follows:

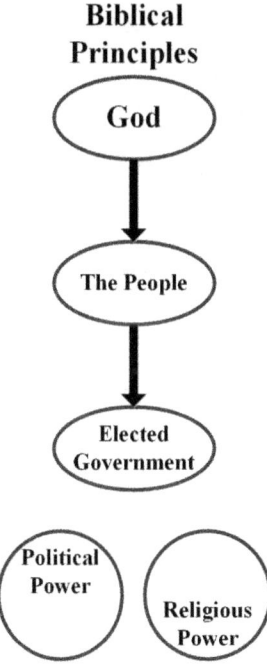

Biblical Principles

It is hard to imagine how these models, or their underlying ideas, could be more different. They are contradictory and incompatible—they cannot coexist. The table below summarizes some of the differences.

	State Religion Model	Biblical Principles Model
Creation	Eternal. God(s) part of creation. Creation about transformation.	God alone is eternal. Creation created by God ex nihilo.
Authority	Man carry's a divine obligation.	God's authority absolute. Man granted creation's stewardship.
Religious and Political Power Relationship	Very closely related. All power is concentrated and absolute.	Separate and distinct. Religious power to educate and political to enact justice.
Man's Nature	Some more equal than others.	Man equal by nature.

	State Religion Model	Biblical Principles Model
People's Place in Society	The people exist to serve the state.	State exists to serve the people.
Type of Rights	Human. Primarily positive.	Natural. Almost exclusively negative.
Source of Rights	Political power—Man.	God and Man. Man's to be consistent with God's.
Social Order	Societal rules brought about by law alone.	Rules created through customs, standards, and practices from individual decision-making. Law only where injustice occurs.
Political Power	Concentrated and absolute. Lawmakers make the rules.	Diffuse and limited. Law makers stewards of society's rules.
Morality	Man's values.	God's values.
Justice	Justice based on law and entitlement.	Negative test. Find and remove injustice.

Where Grounding in Man Leads

There are many implications from the differences in ideas underlying these two threads and the resulting governance models. We will discuss several of them. The following two are philosophical.

The first is the difference in Man's beginning point. In the biblical thread, the beginning point is our Creator, while in the pagan thread, it is Man himself. A second difference is that the biblical thread focuses on our knowledge and actions: how we are to live, both towards our Creator and each other. The same standard applies to each and every one of us. The pagan thread only points to who we are. How we live and behave becomes dependent upon our personal beliefs—that is, relativism. We'll look at some societal differences resulting from the ideas underlying each governance model.

Frances Schaefer discusses the philosophical differences in several of his books. The following diagram appears in his book *Escape from Reason*.[1]

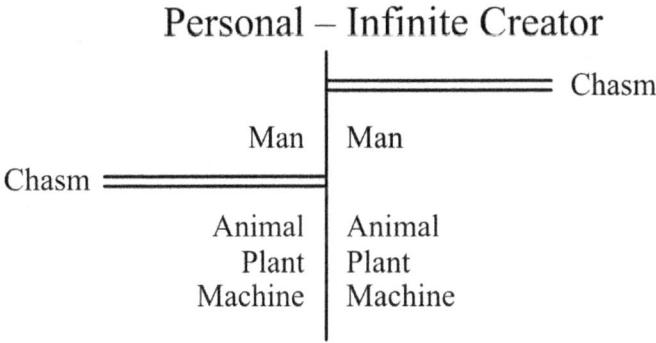

Schaefer asserts that (1) our Creator is not only infinite but also is "personal," and (2) Man has a unique place in all of creation. Both notions are consistent with the writings of Clement, Augustine, and Thomas. Our Creator created everything, including us. He is infinite and all-powerful. He is the first principle from which all other things are derived. He is beyond space and time. In this respect, He is beyond our knowing as we, along with the rest of creation, are finite and complex unities. From this perspective, Man is no different from the rest of creation. This is indicated by the chasm between Creator and His creation on the right side of the diagram.

On the other hand, Man alone was given God's image—an internal image. This both sets Man apart from the rest of creation and allows him to have a personal connection to his Creator. Indeed, this relationship is necessary if we are to fulfill our purpose as a part of His creation. From this perspective, it is possible for Man to have some knowledge of His Creator. It is not full knowledge, but nonetheless is true knowledge. It is also not direct knowledge, but instead is knowledge of Him based on His actions, what He has told us about Himself, and what we observe about His creation. This relationship between Man and Creator is indicated by placing the chasm on the left side of the diagram between Man and the rest of creation.

Man's Beginning Point
Existence, morality, and knowledge are three areas of inquiry within philosophy. The first difference about Man's beginning point has to

do with existence—the right side of the diagram. The second difference regards Man's morality and knowledge—the above diagram's left side.

Clement writes that God is the source of all three areas just mentioned.[2] But when Man turns from His Creator, he is left with a dilemma. The top part of the above diagram (Creator) disappears. Man's intellect becomes autonomous. What can Man use then as a starting point for himself? There is no longer a Creator. There is no longer anything in creation providing a consistent logical starting point for explaining Man's own existence, let alone how he should behave—his morality.

But it goes beyond that. The real problem is why is there any existence at all? Schaefer says,

> This [problem] includes the existence of man, but we must realize that the existence of man is no greater problem as such than is the fact that anything exists at all. No one has said it better than Jean-Paul Sartre, who has said that the basic philosophical question is that something is there rather than that nothing is there.[3]

The biblical thread provides an explanation for all existence. The pagan thread asserts creation has simply always existed: There is no need for a starting point as it has always been. The pagan thread cannot answer the question of existence.

Man's Morality and Knowledge
The second problem can be restated as "How can man be a sufficient integration point for himself?" If man has no starting point for his existence, then what use is there for his intellect, morality, or knowledge? From Schaefer again, "Man is personal and yet he is finite, and so he is not a sufficient integration point for himself. We might remember another profound statement from Sartre that "no finite point has any meaning unless it has an infinite reference point."[4] Without our Creator, there is no infinite reference point.

We can see Man is different from non-Man. Man recording his history supports this notion. From these historical observations, we see that Man is noble. Look daily at the news: People willingly risk their own lives to save someone whom they do not even know, simply because the person is a fellow human being. However, Man is also cruel. Look at the actions of Genghis-Khan, Hitler, Stalin, Che, Mao and many others. No one can reasonably doubt the existence of both.

So within the area of morality, we have two dilemmas that require an explanation. The first is that Man is an insufficient integration point for himself because he is both personal and finite. The second is Man's contradictions between his nobility and cruelty. Some try to resolve the problem by asserting that Man is not personal, using behaviorism or determinism.

Those asserting this idea claim Man is not "intrinsically different from the impersonal."[5] This is nothing more than saying Man is a mere machine. There are two problems with this position. First, it denies all of the historical evidence just mentioned. Second, there is not a single behaviorist or determinist capable of consistently living on the basis of his or her behaviorism or determinism. Even the writings of Francis Crick and B. F. Skinner show this tension.[6] The biblical thread provides an explanation for Man's existence as God is both infinite and personal. As He is the source for all creation and good, God is also the basis for morality. It is Man's choices when he turns from his creator's instruction that lead to cruelty. The pagan thread espouses theories, but at best they are thoughts searching for supporting evidence. *However, the pagan thread takes faith to believe.*

The third philosophical area is that of epistemology: the problem of knowing. Plato understood this area well. It deals with the problem of particulars and universals, of the one and the many discussed in Chapter 3. Particulars are the things we see all around us in the world. It is the universals which provide meaning to the particulars. He provides an example of the use of the word "apple." When we are discussing apples, we do not refer to all of the different kinds of apples that exist each and every time. Instead we put all of these together under the word "apple" to convey meaning.

Greek philosophers looked for a universal which would provide meaning to their existence. They first looked at the *polis* as a possible universal. This word originally meant more than just a mere city-state. It referred to the society within the city-state. They realized this was insufficient. They next turned to their gods to provide a universal, but while their gods were personal, they were not substantial enough to provide a universal. The biblical thread, particularly the writings of Clement, provide an answer to learning, knowing, and faith. The pagan thread attempts to find a universal, the first principle, but is unable to do so in a consistent manner.

Schaeffer calls the universal and particulars *grace* and *nature* respectively. This could also be termed *creator* and *created*. This is the right half of the previous diagram. The creator was the universal and created the particulars making up His creation. By the end of the Renaissance and Enlightenment, through the writings of those such as Kant and Rousseau, the previous relationship between grace and nature had been replaced by the following:

$$\frac{\text{Freedom}}{\text{Nature}}$$

However, nature is now an autonomous one from pagan thought as there is no longer a Creator. This takes us back to the dilemmas just discussed. From a pagan perspective, creation has always existed, so Man must become a mere machine, all springs and strings set into motion by outside forces. Freedom too becomes autonomous because intellect has no infinite reference point:

> The freedom is autonomous in that it has nothing to restrain it. It is freedom without limitations. It is freedom that no longer fits into the rational world. It merely hopes and tries to will that the finite individual man will be free—and all that is left is individual self-expression.[7]

This freedom is simply license to do whatever one wants rather than engage in action directed with purpose—in a word, power. This is not freedom as we've defined it in Chapter 1.

The preceding change represented a significant shift in philosophical thought. Up until this time, all philosophy had three things in common:

1. It was rational. Man began totally with himself, gathered information about particulars, and formulated universals.

2. They all believed in the rational—not rationalism, but instead the notion that the basis of thought was well-founded. They believed in antithesis. Something was either A or not-A.
3. Man hoped to create a unified field of knowledge through philosophy.

This brings us to a final difference, this one about faith. Instead of the relationship between knowledge, reason, and faith described by Clement, we are now presented with a faith requiring an irrational leap as there is no longer knowledge or reason capable of leading us to that same place. A universal morality based upon our Creator and his laws has been replaced by autonomous individualistic self-expression. *Man has faith: Either faith in his Creator or faith in himself.*

Philosophy and religion both deal with the same basic questions, but they do so in different ways. The biblical thread answers these philosophical questions from a religious perspective. Religion is about the relationship between Man and some supreme being, nature, essence, or will. The existence of this supreme entity has implications for the ideology Man chooses to govern his interactions with his Creator and/or fellow Man. The pagan thread answers these same questions from a worldly perspective, which is simply a secular view—or if you prefer, ideology alone. In fact, a definition of secular is *of or pertaining to this world or the present life; temporal; worldly; distinguished from spiritual.* These are two incompatible views, and lead to significant ideological differences.

Societal Implications
These ideological differences influence society. We'll start with the differences in rights. The type of right drives other differences in justice, freedom, virtue, morality, and social order. But it all begins with the idea of rights, specifically the type of rights in question.

<u>Negative and Positive Rights</u>
We mentioned positive and negative rights several times. These should not be thought of as good or bad, but rather as a force or power. Positive attracts you to do something while negative repels you from something. Our natural rights come from our Creator and are almost exclusively negative. As our Creator's nature is good, His

rights repel us from evil. Human rights are almost entirely positive and generally convey information about an acceptable action or entitlement. Negative rights generally underlay the *Biblical Principles* model and positive rights the pagan model.

Negative rights convey the things you are to refrain from doing. Some implications of negative rights are the following:

1. There are relatively few of them.
2. Each individual has a relatively larger range of choices as fewer things are prohibited. Freedom is therefore greater and directed with natural rights.
3. As freedom is greater, morality must be present to ensure just decisions are made.
4. Rules are created by society based upon individual decision-making. Society keeps what is good—what works—and discards what fails. These rules consist of customs, standards of behavior, common practices, etc., in addition to law.
5. Law is created when following the rules creates an unjust outcome, or to punish when someone decides to act unjustly.
6. Law plays a relatively minor role. Lawmakers are stewards of society's rules. They serve society by supporting its rules.

Positive rights convey information about something you are to do, or in our society today, some entitlement you are due. Implications of positive rights include the following:

1. There are usually many of them as each one conveys a single allowable action or entitlement.
2. Freedom comes down to choosing a yes/no proposition with each positive human right. Instead of choosing from all things, you have the choice of selecting only one thing. In short, whether or not to obey.
3. Man's law and commands are to align with his Creator's. If Man chooses another course through the rights he

creates, then Man can be left with the choice of obeying God or Man.

4. Religion is viewed as a two-edged sword. On the one hand, religion instills morality and a moral people is easier to govern. On the other, people may choose to obey God rather than Man. This is seen as a threat to the governing power. Therefore, religion must be controlled by the governing power, and a close relationship must exist between religious power and political power.
5. Society's rules are created through law alone. Law does not exist until it is written by the lawmaker. This profoundly impacts justice (see below).
6. Lawmaking authority becomes concentrated and absolute. Lawmaking becomes a matter of building coalitions to obtain a 51% majority, presenting an opportunity for a tyranny of the majority where a minority may have undue influence on the majority.
7. Freedom becomes a negative state, as Man's nature is to be coerced, unless you are one of the elite. Then freedom becomes license to act—that is, power.

The diagram below shows the differences between negative and positive rights. The areas in white are the thing(s) one is allowed to do. The black areas represent the thing(s) forbidden. Needless to say, the two are incompatible.

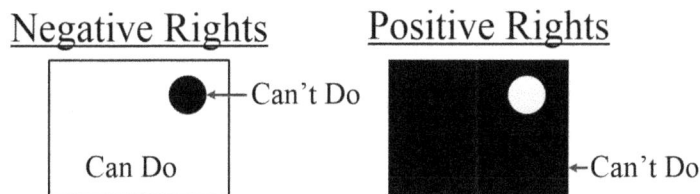

Justice

We have reached the point where we can discuss how both types of rights impact justice. Negative and positive rights create totally different approaches.

With negative rights, all actions are either just or unjust. The rules society creates defines what it accepts as just. Note this is not true justice as society's rules do not always produce a just outcome. This brings up again the importance of society being moral. The relationships are diagrammed below:

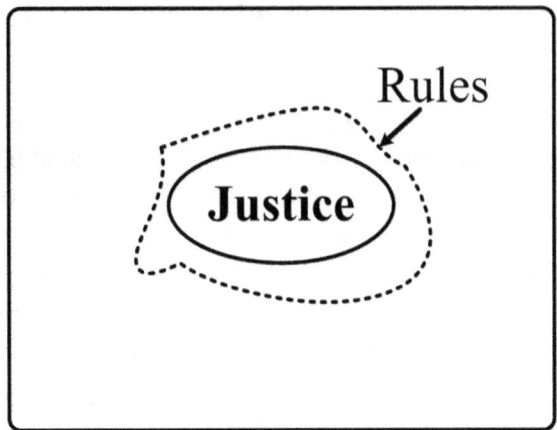

Sometimes these rules come closer to producing justice than others. That is okay. Man is imperfect, so his rules do not produce perfection—including law. *What matters is that society aims to produce just outcomes, outcomes that apply to all because the same rights apply to all.* It is the law's role to identify instances where the rules produce an unjust outcome and remove it from that instance—a negative test.

This may come about from the lawmaker, but more generally happens through the courts and the justice system itself. Human law only applies to the specific instance or situations that are substantially identical to it. Over time, society's rules change as society itself changes by adapting to new circumstances.

Now for positive rights. Remember that positive rights define either something you are to do or are entitled to receive. Society no longer creates the rules. Instead rules come about solely through law, and law defines the criteria for receiving a positive right. In other words, you need to belong to the correct category (group) to receive a positive right. Positive rights themselves define what is just. Therefore, there can be no test for justice as existed with negative rights. Instead law defines justice, and it matters simply whether you belong to the group(s) possessing the correct criteria. The relationships for justice under positive human rights are diagrammed below.

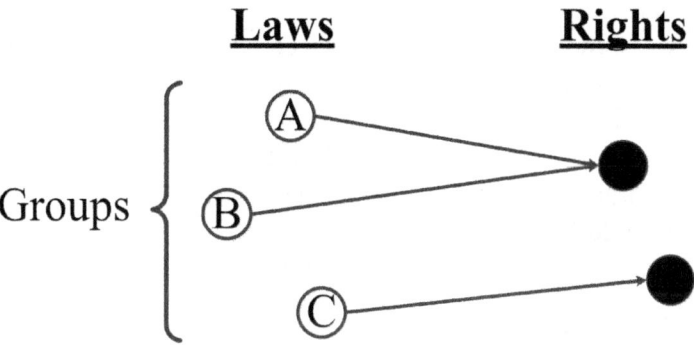

I mentioned earlier that Man is imperfect. That is also born out through society's rules creating instances of unjust outcomes. It is no different with law. Positive rights criteria leave out some who are due a right and grant it to others who do not need it. Think of welfare programs and food stamps as modern relevant examples of government policy defined by law. All this doesn't even consider what occurs when two positive rights contradict one another. Man is imperfect. Justice as we've defined it cannot exist in a society built upon positive human rights. *A positive human rights society becomes driven by emotions, by what Man wants.* Desire rises above reason. Our Creator's image becomes diminished.

Virtue

This leaves us with virtue and morality before we close. Morality has to do with righteousness, which is virtue. So when talking about morality and virtue, we are really discussing different perspectives of the same thing: what it means to be and do good.

Just as with rights and justice, there is a profound difference in virtue.[8] Pagan thought regarded virtue as a mixing of good and bad, a blending of white and black into gray. Something just needed to be a little more white or a little less black to become "virtuous." Virtue is relative, based on Man's ideas and the underlying dilemmas mentioned earlier.

Judeo-Christian principles stand this notion on its head. There is no mixing, no blending. There is only white and black. There is only good and bad. God being the source of all good is the source of all morality. Man's fulfilling his purpose voluntarily uses his freedom to choose to become good. He chooses building virtue. Virtue comes from both education and practice, from knowing and doing.

This pagan view of virtue underlies its governance model and is one reason we sometimes hear we are faced with a choice of a "greater good" or a "lesser evil." Nothing could be further from the truth. There is only good and only evil. Both are fully present. Both are fully active at the same time. Our choices make the difference. This principle underlies the *Biblical Principles* governance model. Nothing could be more different. *Man's actions may fall short, but the principles are timeless as God stands outside time.*

Final Thoughts
We have traced the biblical thread through the writings of Clement, Augustine, and Thomas.[9] In the next volume, we'll examine how this thread played out through history and two pagan responses to the *Biblical Principles* model. We'll begin with Rome's fall, advance through the Middle Ages and feudalism, review some European documents written during the Middle Ages and after, and end by examining America's Declaration and Constitution.

And the pagan thread? A few years after the American Revolutionary War, the French Revolution occurred. Initially, some of America's Founders were sympathetic toward what they perceived to be the cause of liberty in France. However, within a short period of time, only a few of America's Founders any longer supported the French Revolution. The one notable exception was Thomas Paine, who was not a signer of either document or a representative to the Continental Congress. Why did this change of heart occur among America's Founders? What was so different about the French Revolution that they could not support it?

We will look at the French Revolution's founding document, The Declaration of the Rights of Man (Rights of Man). This document played a similar role as a catalyst for the ideas of that revolution as the Declaration did within America. Material from Edmund Burke's *Reflections on the Revolution in France* is used to identify these differences and their implications for society. We will see that the Rights of Man, and the subsequent French Revolution, reflect the pagan thread. And this thread had its basis in philosophical writing from the Renaissance and Enlightenment.

The second pagan response is Islam, which grew out of seventh-century Bedouin culture and represents its marriage with monotheism. While it is often presented as a religion, many of its principle thought leaders assert that it is much more than a religion. I agree.

Let me return briefly to the very beginning of this book. Not only do words matter, so does their meaning. We'll see that Islam is simply ideology with a religious facet. Volume 2 examines Islam from a governance perspective as well as the societal implications of its ideology. For those interested in a fuller discussion of Islam, I would refer you to *A War for God*.[10]

Man needs something outside of himself to keep him on track. God's direction provides that. But direction alone is insufficient. There must be a relationship between Man and God for this to work—that is, religion must be present. Religion provides the basis for an ideology supporting Man and his efforts—if Man chooses to commit himself to God. This is always our choice, regardless of our circumstances, and we can make that choice at any time.

Appendix A - Timeline of Events and People

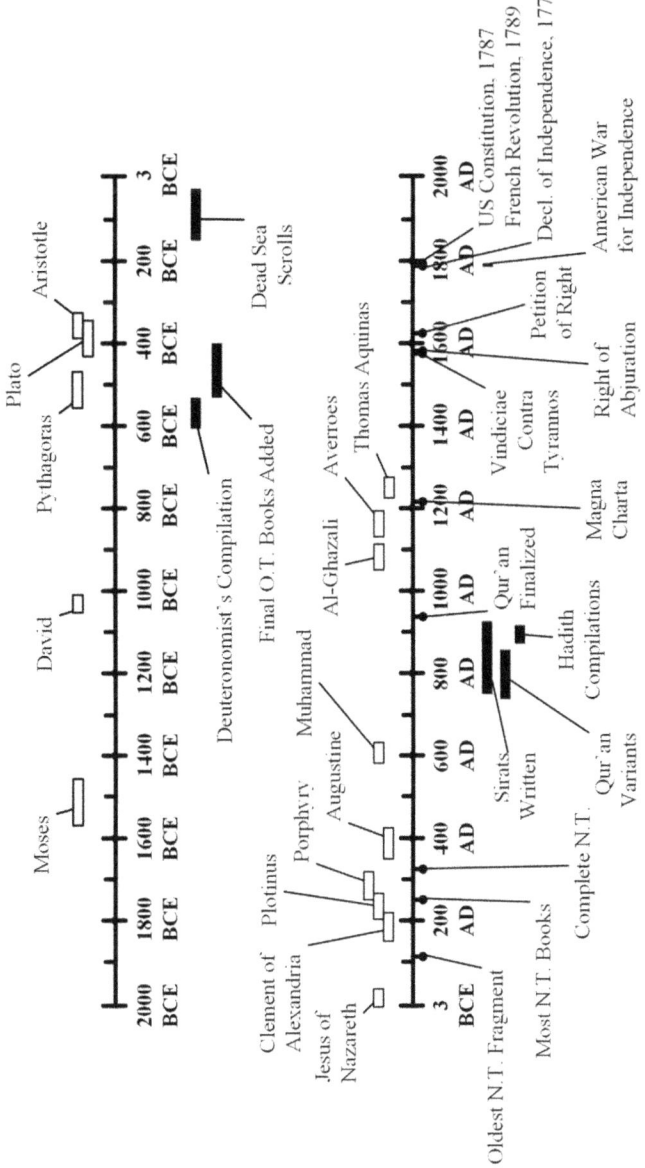

Notes:

INTRODUCTION

CHAPTER 1

[1] Evans, M. Stanton, *The Theme is Freedom: Religion, Politics, and the American Tradition*, p. 23, Regency Publishing, 1994.

[2] A fuller explanation of this relationship is also provided in Wolf, Dan, *A Handbook of Natural Rights*, Living Rightly Publications, 2018.

[3] Aquinas, St. Thomas, *Summa Theologicae,* Vol. 5, p. 89, McGraw-Hill Book Company, 1964. Part 1a, Question 22. Further references to this work will also include the part and question number along with the volume and page number.

[4] Stark, Rodney, *Discovering God*, p. 46, Harper-Collins, 2007.

[5] Ibid, p. 46.

[6] Ibid.

[7] Ibid, p. 47.

[8] Stark, Rodney, *The Victory of Reason,* p. 5, Random House, 2005.

[9] Stark, Rodney, *Discovering God*, pp 21-63, Harper-Collins, 2007. A list of additional literature is included at the end of this chapter for someone who is interested in finding out more about this topic.

[10] Ibid, p. 9.

[11] Ibid, p. 45.

[12] Ibid.

[13] Ibid, p. 10.

[14] Ibid.

[15] Ibid, pp. 10-11.

[16] Ibid, p. 55.

[17] Ibid, p. 56.

[18] Ibid, p. 58.

[19] Ibid, p. 96.

[20] Ibid, p. 97.

[21] Baly, Denis, *The Geography of Monotheism,* as cited in Stark, Rodney, *Discovering God*, p. 97, Harper-Collins, 2007.

[22] Stark, Rodney, *Discovering God*, p. 97, Harper-Collins, 2007.

[23] Ibid.

[24] Frankfort, Henri, *Kingship and the Gods* as cited in Stark, Rodney, *Discovering God*, p. 102, Harper-Collins, 2007.

[25] Aristotle, *On the Heavens*, http://classics.mit.edu/Aristotle/heavens.html.

[26] Barnes, Jonathan, Ed., *The Complete Works of Aristotle: The Revised Oxford Translation, Vol. II*, p. 2110, Princeton University Press, 1995. *Politics*, Book VII, Part X. Further references to this work will include *Politics* followed by the book and chapter.

[27] Stark, Rodney, *The Victory of Reason*, p. 19, Random House, 2005.

[28] Barnes, Jonathan, Ed., *The Complete Works of Aristotle: The Revised Oxford Translation, Vol. II*, p. 2044, Princeton University Press, 1995. *Politics*, III, XVII.

[29] Ibid, p. 1990, *Politics*, I, V.

[30] Ibid, p. 1991, *Politics*, I, VI.

[31] Ibid, p. 1992, *Politics*, I, VII.

[32] Ibid, p. 2028, *Politics*, III, V.

[33] Ibid, p. 2101, *Politics*, VII, II.

[34] Ibid, p. 2121, *Politics*, VIII, I.

[35] Ibid, p. 1997, *Politics,* I, X.

[36] Cooper, John M., Ed., *Plato: Complete Works,* p. 1137, Hackett Publishing Company, Inc. 1997. *Republic*, Book VII, 520. Further references to this work will include *Republic* followed by the Book and verse.

[37] Ibid, p. 1155, *Republic*, VII, 543.

[38] Ibid, p. 1086, *Republic,* V, 458(d).

[39] Ibid, p. 1087, *Republic,* V, 459(e) – 460.

[40] Ibid, p. 1086, *Republic,* V, 458(e).

[41] Stark, Rodney, *The Rise of Christianity,* pp. 118-122, HarperCollins Publishing, 1997. This chapter contains further discussion of infanticide, abortion, and birth control in both the Greek and Roman Republics.

CHAPTER 2

[1] Stark, Rodney, *Discovering God*, p. 7, Harper-Collins, 2007.

[2] Augustine, St., *Confessions,* p. 320, Doubleday, 1960. Book XII, Chapter 18.

[3] Stark, Rodney, *Discovering God*, p. 156, Harper-Collins, 2007.

[4] Ibid, p. 180.

[5] Ibid.

[6] Ibid, p. 181.

7. Rev. Alexander Roberts and James Donaldson, *The Ante-Nicene Fathers, Fathers of the Second Century: Hermas, Tatian, Athenagora, Theophilus, and Clement of Alexandria (Entire)*, Vol. 2, p. 309, Wm. B Eerdmans Publishing Co., 1989. *Strom,* I, VIII.
8. Ibid, p. 321, *Strom,* I, XIX.
9. Ibid, p. 351, *Strom,* II, IV.
10. Ibid, p. 376, *Strom,* II, XXII.
11. Ibid, pp. 367-368, *Strom,* II, XVIII.
12. Ibid, p. 323, *Strom,* I, XX.
13. Walsh, Gerald G. et al, *City of God,* pp. 145-146, Doubleday Publishing, 1958. Book VIII, Chapter 2. All future references to this work will include the book and chapter.
14. Ibid, pp. 146-147, VIII, 3.
15. Ibid, p. 147, VIII, 3.
16. Ibid, p. 148, VIII, 4.
17. Ibid, p. 148-149, VIII, 4.
18. Ibid, p. 149, VIII, 4.
19. Ibid, pp. 149-150, VIII, 4.
20. Rev. Alexander Roberts and James Donaldson, *The Ante-Nicene Fathers, Fathers of the Second Century: Hermas, Tatian, Athenagora, Theophilus, and Clement of Alexandria (Entire)*, Vol. 2, p. 347, Wm. B Eerdmans Publishing Co., 1989. *Strom,* II, I. Further references to this work will include *Strom,* followed by the book and chapter.
21. Ibid, p. 347, *Strom,* II, I.
22. Ibid, pp. 334-335, *Strom,* I, XXII.
23. Ibid, p. 334, *Strom,* I, XXII.
24. Ibid.
25. Ibid.
26. Ibid.
27. Ibid, p. 324, *Strom,* I, XXI. This part of his case is laid out in *Strom* I, Chapters XXI, XXII, and XXIII.
28. Ibid, pp. 449-457, *Strom,* V, Chapters IV, V, VII and VIII.
29. Ibid, p. 315, *Strom,* I, XV.
30. Ibid, p. 316, *Strom,* I, XV.
31. Ibid.
32. Ibid, p. 338, *Strom,* I, XXV.
33. Ibid, p. 365, *Strom,* II, XVII.

[34] Ibid, p. 464, *Strom*, V, XIII.
[35] Ibid.
[36] Ibid, p. 466, *Strom*, V, XIV.
[37] Ibid, p. 469, *Strom*, V, XIV.
[38] Ibid, pp. 466-467, *Strom*, V, XIV.
[39] Ibid, p. 467, *Strom*, V, XIV.
[40] Ibid, p. 320, *Strom*, I, XVII.
[41] Ibid, p. 313, *Strom*, I, XIII.
[42] Ibid, p. 308, *Strom*, I, VII.
[43] Ibid.
[44] Ibid, p. 305, *Strom*, I, V.
[45] Ibid, pp. 319-320, *Strom*, I, XVII.
[46] Ibid, p. 491, *Strom*, VI, VI.
[47] Ibid, p. 37.
[48] Ibid.
[49] Ibid, p. 54.
[50] Ibid, p. 85.
[51] Ibid, p. 86.
[52] Ibid, p. 178.
[53] Ibid, p. 179.
[54] Ibid, p. 178. Emphasis added.
[55] Rev. Alexander Roberts and James Donaldson, *The Ante-Nicene Fathers, Fathers of the Second Century: Hermas, Tatian, Athenagora, Theophilus, and Clement of Alexandria (Entire)*, Vol. 2, p. 307, Wm. B Eerdmans Publishing Co., 1989. Clement of Alexandria, *The Stromata*, Book I, Chapter V.
[56] Ibid, p. 304, *Strom.*, I, II.
[57] Richard, Carl J., *The Founders and the Classics*, p. 171, Harvard University Press, 1994.
[58] Ibid.
[59] Cooper, John M. (Ed.), *Plato: Complete Works*, p. 877, Hackett Publishing Company, Inc. 1997.
[60] Richard, Carl J., *The Founders and the Classics*, p. 170, Harvard University Press, 1994.
[61] Ibid, p. 171.
[62] Aquinas, St. Thomas, *Summa Theologicae*, Vol. 28, p. 162, McGraw-Hill Book Co., 1964. Part Ia2ae, 91.
[63] Ibid, p. 163.

⁶⁴ Ibid.

⁶⁵ Ibid.

⁶⁶ Evans, M. Stanton, *The Theme is Freedom,* p. 79, Regnery Publishing, Inc. 1994.

⁶⁷ Richard, Carl J., *The Founders and the Classics,* p. 20, Harvard University Press, 1994.

⁶⁸ Ibid, p. 13.

⁶⁹ Ibid, p. 18.

⁷⁰ Ibid, p. 12.

⁷¹ Ibid, p. 305, *Strom*, I, IV.

⁷² Ibid, p. 307, *Strom*, I, VI.

⁷³ Ibid.

⁷⁴ Ibid, p. 444, *Strom*, V, I.

CHAPTER 3

¹ Hastings, Adrian, Ed., *A World History of Christianity,* 28-29, Wm. B. Eerdmans Publishing Co., 1999.

² Rev. Alexander Roberts and James Donaldson, *The Ante-Nicene Fathers*, Vol. 2, p. 409, Wm. B Eerdmans Publishing Co., 1989. *Strom,* IV, II.

³ Osborn, E.F., *The Philosophy of Clement of Alexandria,* pp. 17-24, Cambridge University Press. 1957.

⁴ Cooper, John M., Ed., *Plato Complete Works,* pp. 372-387, Hackett Publishing Company. 1997. This and the other quotes in this section come from *Parmenides*.

⁵ Osborn, E.F., *The Philosophy of Clement of Alexandria,* p. 18, Cambridge University Press. 1957.

⁶ Rev. Alexander Roberts and James Donaldson, *The Ante-Nicene Fathers, Fathers of the Second Century: Hermas, Tatian, Athenagora, Theophilus, and Clement of Alexandria (Entire),* Vol. 2, p. 348, Wm. B Eerdmans Publishing Co., 1989. *Strom,* II, II.

⁷ Rev. Alexander Roberts and James Donaldson, *The Ante-Nicene Fathers, Fathers of the Second Century: Hermas, Tatian, Athenagora, Theophilus, and Clement of Alexandria (Entire),* Vol. 2, p. 192, Wm. B Eerdmans Publishing Co., 1989. *Protrepticus,* Chapter VI. Further references to this work with use *Prot* followed by the Chapter.

⁸ Ibid, p. 449, *Strom,* V, IV. "All then, in a word, who have spoken of divine things, both Barbarian and Greeks, have veiled the first principles of things,

and delivered the truth in enigmas, and symbols, and allegories, and metaphors, and such like tropes."

[9] Ibid, p. 460, *Strom,* V, XI. "But the most of men, clothed with what is perishable, like cockles, and rolled all round in a ball in their excesses, like hedgehogs, entertain the same ideas of the blessed and incorruptible God as themselves. But it has escaped their notice, though they be near us, that God has bestowed on us ten thousand things in which he does not share: birth, being Himself unborn; food, He wanting nothing; and growth, He being always equal; and long life and immortality, He being immortal and incapable of growing old. Wherefore let no one imagine that hands, and feet, and mouth, and eyes, and going in and coming out, and resentments and threats, are said by the Hebrews to be attributes of God. By no means; but that certain of these appellations are used more sacredly in an allegorical sense."

[10] Ibid, p. 461, *Strom,* V, XI. "We shall understand the mode of purification by confession, and that of contemplation by analysis, advancing by analysis to the first notion, beginning with the properties underlying it; abstracting from the body its physical properties, taking away the dimension of depth, then that of breadth, and then that of length. For the point which remains is a unit, so to speak, having position; from which if we abstract position, there is the conception of unity.

"If, then, abstracting all that belongs to bodies and things called incorporeal, we cast ourselves into the greatness of Christ, and thence advance into immensity by holiness, we may reach somehow to the conception for the Almighty, knowing not what He is but what He is not. And form and motion, or standing, or a throne, or place, or right hand or left, are not at all to be conceived as belonging to the Father of the universe, although it is so written."

[11] Ibid, p. 461, *Strom,* V, XI.

[12] Ibid, p. 462, *Strom,* V, XI. "In reasoning, it is possible to divine respecting God, if one attempt without any of the senses, by reason, to reach what is individual; and do not quit the sphere of existences, till, rising up to the things which transcend it, he apprehends by the intellect itself that which is good, moving in the very confines of the world of thought."

[13] Ibid, p. 350, *Strom,* II, IV.

[14] Ibid, p. 461, *Strom,* V, XI.

[15] Ibid, p. 463-464, *Strom,* V, XII. "This discourse respecting God is most difficult to handle. For since the first principle of everything is difficult to find out, the absolutely first and oldest principle, which is the cause of all other things being and having been, is difficult to exhibit. For how can that be expressed which is neither genus, nor difference, nor species, nor individual, nor number; nay more, is neither an event, nor that to which an event happens? No one can rightly express Him wholly. For on account of His greatness he is ranked as the All, and is the Father of the universe. Nor are any parts to be predicated of Him.

"For the One is indivisible; wherefore also it is infinite, not considered with reference to inscrutability, but with reference to its being without dimensions, and not having a limit. And therefore it is without form and name."

[16] Ibid, p. 464, *Strom*, V, XII. "And if we name it, we do not do so properly, terming it either the One, or the Good, or Mind, or Absolute Being, or Father, or God, or Creator, or Lord. We speak not as supplying His name; but for want, we use good names, in order that the mind may have these as points of support, so as not to err in other respects. For each one by itself does not express God; but all together are indicative of the power of the Omnipotent. For predicates are expressed either from what belongs to things themselves, or from their mutual relation. But none of these are admissible in reference to God. Nor any more is He apprehended by the science of demonstration. For it depends on primary and better known principles. But there is nothing antecedent to the Unbegotten."

[17] Ibid, p. 460, *Strom*, V, X.

[18] Ibid, p. 462, *Strom*, V, XI. "He set up no image in the temple to be worshipped; showing that God was invisible, and incapable of being circumscribed; and somehow leading the Hebrews to the conception of God by the honour for His name in the temple."

[19] Ibid. "'For it was not from need that God made the world; that He might reap honours from men and the other gods and demons, winning a kind of revenue from creation, and from us, fumes, and from the gods and demons, their proper ministries,' says Plato... Zeno says in this book of the Republic, 'that we ought to make neither temples nor images; for that no work is worthy of the gods.'"

[20] Ibid, p. 462, *Strom*, V, XI.

[21] Ibid, p. 462, *Strom*, V, XII. "'For both it is a difficult task to discover the Father and Maker of this universe; and having found Him, it is impossible to declare Him to all. For this is by no means capable of expression, like the other subjects of instruction,' says Plato."

[22] Rev. Alexander Roberts and James Donaldson, *The Ante-Nicene Fathers, Fathers of the Second Century: Hermas, Tatian, Athenagora, Theophilus, and Clement of Alexandria (Entire)*, Vol. 2, p. 190, Wm. B Eerdmans Publishing Co., 1989. *Prot*, IV. "How great is the power of God! His bare volition was the creation of the universe. For God alone made it, because He alone is truly God. By the bare exercise of volition he creates; His mere willing was followed by the springing into being of what He willed."

[23] Rev. Alexander Roberts and James Donaldson, *The Ante-Nicene Fathers, Fathers of the Second Century: Hermas, Tatian, Athenagora, Theophilus, and Clement of Alexandria (Entire)*, Vol. 2, p. 215, Wm. B Eerdmans Publishing Co., 1989. *Paedagogus*, Book I, Chapter VI. Further references to this work with include *Paed* followed by the book and chapter.

[24] Ibid, p. 211, *Paed*, I, III.

[25] Osborn, E.F., *The Philosophy of Clement of Alexandria*, p. 31, Cambridge University Press. 1957.

[26] Rev. Alexander Roberts and James Donaldson, *The Ante-Nicene Fathers, Fathers of the Second Century: Hermas, Tatian, Athenagora, Theophilus, and Clement of Alexandria (Entire)*, Vol. 2, p. 215, Wm. B Eerdmans Publishing Co., 1989. *Paed*, I, V.

[27] Ibid, pp. 209-210, *Paed*, I, II.

[28] Ibid, p. 225, *Paed*, I, VIII.

[29] Ibid, p. 232, *Paed*, I, IX.

[30] Ibid, p. 257, *Paed*, II, VIII.

[31] Ibid, p. 438, *Strom*, IV, XXV.

[32] Ibid, p. 524, *Strom*, VII, II.

[33] Ibid, p. 525, *Strom*, VII, II.

[34] Ibid, p. 453, *Strom*, V, VI.

[35] Ibid, p. 493, *Strom*, VI, VII.

[36] Ibid, p. 354, *Strom*, II, VI.

[37] Ibid, p. 174, *Prot*, I.

[38] Barnes, Jonathan, Ed., *The Complete Works of Aristotle: The Revised Oxford Translation, Vol. II*, p. 1600, Princeton University Press, 1995. *Metaphysics*, Book 5, 1013a.

[39] Rev. Alexander Roberts and James Donaldson, *The Ante-Nicene Fathers, Fathers of the Second Century: Hermas, Tatian, Athenagora, Theophilus, and Clement of Alexandria (Entire)*, Vol. 2, p. 438, Wm. B Eerdmans Publishing Co., 1989. *Strom*, IV, XXV.

[40] Ibid, p. 523, *Strom*, VII, I.

[41] Ibid, p. 438, *Strom*, IV, XXV.

[42] Ibid, p. 511, *Strom*, VI, XVI.

[43] Ibid, pp. 516-517, *Strom*, VI, XVII.

[44] Ibid, p. 541, *Strom*, VII, XI.

[45] Ibid, p. 190, *Prot*, IV. "For if the heavenly bodies are not the works of men, they were certainly created for man. Let none of you worship the sun, but set his desires on the Maker of the sun; nor deify the universe, but seek after the Creator of the universe."

[46] Ibid, p. 440, *Strom*, IV, XXVI. "For all things are of one God. And no one is a stranger to the world by nature, their essence being one, and God one. But the elect man dwells as a sojourner, knowing all things to be possessed and disposed of . . . having care of the things of the world . . . but leaving his dwelling place and property without excessive emotion . . . and blessing [God] for his departure, embracing the mansion that is in heaven."

[47] Ibid, pp. 210-211, *Paed,* I, III. "The other works of creation He made by the word of command alone, but man He framed by Himself, by His own hand, and breathed into him what was peculiar to Himself. What, then was fashioned by Him, and after He likeness, either was created by God Himself as being desirable on its own account, or was formed as being desirable on account of something else."

[48] Ibid, p. 527, *Strom,* VII, III. "He is the true Only-begotten, the express image of the glory of the universal King and Almighty Father, who impresses on the Gnostic the seal of the perfect contemplation, according to His own image; so that there is now a third divine image, made as far as possible like the Second Cause, the Essential Life."

[49] Ibid, p. 370, *Strom,* II, XIX.

[50] Ibid, p. 199, *Prot,* X. "For the image of God is His Word, the genuine Son of Mind, the Divine Word, the archetypal light of light; the image of the Word is the true man, the mind which is in man, who is therefore said to have been made 'in the image and likeness of God.'"

[51] Ibid, p. 495, *Strom,* VI, VIII.

[52] Ibid, p. 271, *Paed,* III, I.

[53] Ibid.

[54] Wolf, Dan, *A Handbook of Natural Rights*, pp. 55-91, Living Rightly Publications, 2018.

[55] Rev. Alexander Roberts and James Donaldson, *The Ante-Nicene Fathers, Fathers of the Second Century: Hermas, Tatian, Athenagora, Theophilus, and Clement of Alexandria (Entire)*, Vol. 2, p. 506, Wm. B Eerdmans Publishing Co., 1989. *Strom,* VI, XIV.

[56] Ibid, p. 534, *Strom,* VII, VII. "Prayer is, then, to speak more boldly, converse with God. Though whispering, consequently, and not opening the lips, we speak in silence, yet we cry inwardly. For God hears continually all the inward converse."

[57] Ibid, p. 515, *Strom,* VI, XVII.

[58] Ibid, p. 203, *Prot,* XI.

[59] Ibid, p. 491, *Strom,* VI, VI. "One righteous man, then differs not, as righteous, from another righteous man, whether he be of the Law or Greek. For God is not only Lord of the Jews, but of all men."

[60] Ibid, p. 211, *Paed,* I, IV.

[61] Ibid, p. 420, *Strom,* IV, VIII. "We do not say that woman's nature is the same as man's as she is woman. For undoubtedly it stands to reason that some difference should exist between each of them, in virtue of which one is male and the other female. . . As then there is sameness, as far as respects the soul, she will attain to the same virtue (as man)."

[62] Ibid, p. 524, *Strom,* VII, II.

63 Ibid, p. 460, *Strom,* V, XI.

64 Ibid.

65 Ibid, p. 461, *Strom,* V, XI.

66 Ibid.

67 Ibid, p. 445, *Strom,* V, I. "He who communicated to us being and life, has communicated to us also reason, wishing us to live rationally and rightly. For the Word of the Father of the universe is not the uttered word, but the wisdom and the most manifest kindness of God, and His power too . . . but since some are unbelieving, and some are disputations, all do not attain to the perfection of the good. For neither is it possible to attain it [faith] without the exercise of free choice."

68 Ibid, p. 525, *Strom,* VII, II.

69 Ibid, p. 321, *Strom,* I, XVIII.

70 Ibid, p. 353, *Strom,* II, VI.

71 Ibid, p. 363, *Strom,* II, XV.

72 Ibid, p. 364, *Strom,* II, XVI.

73 Ibid, p. 437, *Strom,* IV, XXIII.

74 Ibid, p. 413, *Strom,* IV, V.

75 Ibid, p. 361, *Strom,* II, XIV.

76 Ibid, p. 195, *Prot,* IX.

77 Ibid, p. 418, *Strom,* IV, VII.

78 Ibid, p. 338, *Strom,* I, XXV.

79 Ibid, p. 341, *Strom,* I, XXVIII.

80 Ibid, p. 235, *Paed,* I, XIII.

81 Ibid, p. 341, *Strom,* I, XXIX.

82 Ibid, p. 340, *Strom,* I, XXVIII.

83 Wolf, Dan, *Collectivism and Charity*, pp. 7-17, Living Rightly Publications, 2016.

84 Wolf, Dan, *A Handbook of Natural Rights*, pp. 4-7, Living Rightly Publications, 2018.

85 Rev. Alexander Roberts and James Donaldson, *The Ante-Nicene Fathers, Fathers of the Second Century: Hermas, Tatian, Athenagora, Theophilus, and Clement of Alexandria (Entire)*, Vol. 2, p. 465, Wm. B Eerdmans Publishing Co. *Strom,* V, XIII.

86 Ibid, p. 375, *Strom,* II, XXII.

87 Ibid, p. 225, *Paed,* I, VIII.

88 Ibid, p. 459, *Strom,* V, X.

89 Ibid, p. 232, *Strom,* I, IX.

[90] Ibid, p. 516, *Strom,* VI, XVII.

[91] Ibid, p. 305, *Strom,* I, V.

[92] Ibid, p. 535, *Strom,* VII, VII.

[93] Ibid, p. 445, *Strom,* V, I.

[94] Ibid, p. 320, *Strom,* I, XVII.

[95] Ibid, p. 526, *Strom,* VII, II.

[96] Ibid, p. 355, *Strom,* II, VII.

[97] Ibid, p. 303, *Strom,* I, I.

[98] Ibid, p. 494, *Strom,* VI, VII.

[99] Ibid, p. 496, *Strom,* VI, IX.

[100] Ibid, p. 410, *Strom,* IV, III.

[101] Ibid, p. 465, *Strom,* V, XIII.

[102] Ibid, p. 362, *Strom,* II, XV.

[103] Ibid, pp. 354-355, *Strom,* II, VII.

[104] Ibid, p. 553, *Strom,* VII, XVI.

[105] Ibid.

[106] Ibid, p. 423, *Strom,* IV, XI.

[107] Ibid, p. 438, *Strom,* IV, XXIV. "Therefore the good God corrects for these three causes: First, that he who is corrected may become better than his former self; then that those who are capable of being saved by examples may be driven back, being admonished; and thirdly, that he who is injured may not be readily despised, and be apt to receive injury. And there are two methods of correction – the instructive and the punitive, which we have called the disciplinary."

[108] Ibid, p. 226, *Paed,* I, VIII. "For God does not inflict punishment from wrath, but for the ends of justice; since it is not expedient that justice should be neglected on our account. Each one of us, who sins, with his own free-will chooses punishment, and the blame lies with him who chooses. God is without blame."

[109] Ibid, p. 411, *Strom,* IV, III.

[110] Ibid, p. 308, *Strom,* I, VII.

[111] Ibid, p. 305, *Strom,* I, V.

[112] Ibid, pp. 349-350, *Strom,* II, IV.

[113] Ibid, p. 223, *Paed,* I, VII.

[114] Ibid, p. 323, *Strom,* I, XX.

[115] Ibid, p. 350, *Strom,* II, IV.

[116] Ibid, p. 323, *Strom,* I, XX.

[117] Ibid, p. 502, *Strom,* VI, XI.

[118] Ibid, p. 323, *Strom*, I, XX.

[119] Ibid, p. 550, *Strom*, VII, XV.

[120] Ibid, p. 502, *Strom*, VI, XI.

[121] Ibid, p. 420, *Strom*, IV, VIII.

[122] Ibid, p. 369, *Strom*, II, XIX.

[123] Ibid, pp. 356-357, *Strom*, II, IX.

[124] Ibid, pp. 369-370, *Strom*, II, XIX. "We are taught that there are three kinds of friendship: and that of these the first and the best is that which results from virtue, for the love that is founded on reason is firm; that the second and intermediates is by way of recompense, and is social, liberal, and useful for life; for the friendship which is the result of favour is mutual. And the third and last we assert to be that which is founded on intimacy... And Hippodamus the Pythagorean seems to me to describe friendships most admirably: 'That founded on knowledge of the gods, that founded on the gifts of men, and that on the pleasures of animals.'"

[125] Ibid, p. 354, *Strom*, II, VI.

[126] Ibid, p. 348, *Strom*, II, II.

[127] Ibid, p. 349, *Strom*, II, II.

[128] Ibid, pp. 446-447, *Strom*, V, I.

[129] Ibid, p. 354, *Strom*, II, VI.

[130] Ibid, p. 352, *Strom*, II, V.

[131] Ibid, p. 349, *Strom*, II, II.

[132] Ibid, p. 307, *Strom*, I, VI.

[133] Ibid, p. 310, *Strom*, I, IX.

[134] Ibid, p. 306, *Strom*, I, V.

[135] Ibid, p. 307, *Strom*, I, V.

[136] Ibid, p. 307, *Strom*, I, VI.

[137] Ibid.

[138] Ibid, p. 302, *Strom*, I, I.

[139] Ibid, p. 492, *Strom*, VI, VII.

[140] Ibid, p. 494, *Strom*, VI, VII.

[141] Ibid, p. 350, *Strom*, II, IV.

[142] Ibid, p. 538, *Strom*, VII, IX.

[143] Ibid, p. 350, *Strom*, II, IV.

[144] Ibid, p. 352, *Strom*, II, V.

[145] Ibid, p. 364, *Strom*, II, XVII.

[146] Ibid, p. 441, *Strom*, IV, XXVI.

[147] Ibid, p. 515, *Strom,* VI, XVII.
[148] Ibid, p. 499, *Strom,* VI, X.
[149] Ibid, p. 308, *Strom,* I, VII.
[150] Ibid, p. 420, *Strom,* IV, VIII.

CHAPTER 4

[1] Walsh, Gerald G. et al, *City of God,* p. 300, Doubleday Publishing, 1958. Book XIV, Chapter 4. Future references will also cite the book and chapter.
[2] Schaff, Philip, *Nicene and Post-Nicene Fathers, Vol. 2, Augustin: City of God, Christian Doctrine,* pp. 210-211, Wm. B. Eerdmans Publishing Company, 1989. Book XI, Chapter 10. Future references will include the book and chapter.
[3] Ibid, pp. 218-219. Book XI, Chapter 24.
[4] Ibid, p. 227. Book XII, Chapter 2.
[5] Walsh, Gerald G. et al, *City of God,* pp. 104-105, Doubleday Publishing, 1958. Book V, Chapter 9.
[6] Ibid, pp. 105-107, V, 9.
[7] Ibid, pp. 107-108, V, 9.
[8] Schaff, Philip, *Nicene and Post-Nicene Fathers, Vol. 2, Augustin: City of God, Christian Doctrine,* p. 247, Wm. B. Eerdmans Publishing Company, 1989. XIII, 5.
[9] Ibid, p. 215, XI, 19.
[10] St. Augustine, *Confessions,* p. 320, Doubleday Dell Publishing Group, Inc., 1960. Book 12, Chapter18.
[11] Walsh, Gerald G. et al, *City of God,* pp. 235-236, Doubleday Publishing, 1958. XI, 26.
[12] Schaff, Philip, *Nicene and Post-Nicene Fathers, Vol. 2, Augustin: City of God, Christian Doctrine,* p. 206, Wm. B. Eerdmans Publishing Company, 1989. XI, 2.
[13] Ibid, p. 262, XIV, 1.
[14] Walsh, Gerald G. et al, *City of God,* p. 235, Doubleday Publishing, 1958. XI, 25.
[15] Schaff, Philip, *Nicene and Post-Nicene Fathers, Vol. 2, Augustin: City of God, Christian Doctrine,* pp. 502-503, Wm. B. Eerdmans Publishing Company, 1989. XXII, 24.
[16] Ibid, p. 271, XIV, 11.
[17] Ibid, p. 266, XIV, 6.

[18] Ibid.

[19] Ibid, p. 229, XII, 6.

[20] Ibid, p. 230, XII, 7.

[21] Ibid, p. 256, XIII, 21.

[22] Ibid, pp. 92-93, V, 10.

[23] Ibid, p. 66, IV, 3.

[24] Walsh, Gerald G. et al, *City of God,* p. 224, Doubleday Publishing, 1958. XI, 16.

[25] Ibid, pp. 468-469, XIX, 21.

[26] Schaff, Philip, *Nicene and Post-Nicene Fathers, Vol. 2, Augustin: City of God, Christian Doctrine*, p. 35, Wm. B. Eerdmans Publishing Company, 1989. II, 21.

[27] Ibid, p. 36, II, 21.

[28] Ibid, p. 66, IV, 4.

[29] Ibid, p. 98, V, 17.

[30] Ibid, p. 418, XIX, 23.

[31] Wolf, Dan, *A Handbook of Natural Rights*, pp. 22-3, Living Rightly Publications, 2018.

[32] Schaff, Philip, *Nicene and Post-Nicene Fathers, Vol. 2, Augustin: City of God, Christian Doctrine*, p. 403, Wm. B. Eerdmans Publishing Company, 1989, XIX, 7.

[33] Ibid, pp. 226-227, XII, 1.

[34] Ibid, p. 286, XV, 4.

[35] Walsh, Gerald G. et al, *City of God,* p. 235, Doubleday Publishing, 1958. XII, 1.

[36] Schaff, Philip, *Nicene and Post-Nicene Fathers, Vol. 2, Augustin: City of God, Christian Doctrine*, p. 397, Wm. B. Eerdmans Publishing Company, 1989. XIX, 1.

[37] Ibid, p. 400, XIX, 3.

[38] Ibid, p. 413, XIX, 19.

[39] Ibid, pp. 263-264, XIV, 3.

[40] Ibid, p. 273, XIV, 13.

[41] Ibid, p. 251, XIII, 14.

[42] Ibid, p. 102, V, 20.

[43] Ibid, p. 419, XIX, 27.

[44] Ibid, p. 384, XVIII, 41.

[45] Ibid, pp. 406-407, XIX, 10.

[46] Ibid, p. 409, XIX, 13.
[47] Ibid, p. 288, XV, 7.
[48] Ibid, p. 286, XV, 4.
[49] Ibid, pp. 35-36, II, 21.
[50] Ibid, p. 418, XIX, 24.
[51] Ibid, p. 97, V, 15.
[52] Walsh, Gerald G. et al, *City of God,* p. 114, Doubleday Publishing, 1958. V, 17.
[53] Ibid, p. 97, V, 14.
[54] Schaff, Philip, *Nicene and Post-Nicene Fathers, Vol. 2, Augustin: City of God, Christian Doctrine*, p. 385, Wm. B. Eerdmans Publishing Company, 1989. XVIII, 41.
[55] Ibid, pp. 361-362, XVIII, 2.
[56] Ibid, p. 34, II, 20.
[57] Ibid, p. 101, V, 19.
[58] Ibid, p. 82, IV, 32.
[59] Ibid, p. 78, IV, 27.
[60] Ibid, p. 405, XIX, 7.
[61] Ibid, pp. 407-408, XIX, 12.
[62] Ibid, pp. 282-283, XIV, 28.
[63] Plotinus, Translated by Armstrong, A.H., *Enneads*, Vol. II, p. 221, Harvard University Press, 1984. Introductory Notes to II, 9. Future references to this work will include the volume, book, and chapter number.
[64] Ibid, Vol. II, pp.221-222.
[65] Ibid, Vol. II, p. 225, II, 9, 1.
[66] ibid, Vol. VI, p. 139, VI, 2, 9.
[67] Ibid, Vol. V, p. 119, V, 3, 13.
[68] Ibid, Vol. V, p.145-149 , V, 4,2.
[69] Ibid, Vol. V, p. 213-217, V, 6,6.
[70] Ibid, Vol. V, p. 117, V, 3,13.
[71] Ibid, Vol. VII, p. 313-315, VI, 9,3.
[72] Ibid, Vol. VII, p. 317, VI, 9,4.
[73] Ibid, Vol. V, p. 179, V, 5,8.
[74] Ibid, Vol. V, p. 123-127, V, 3,15-16.
[75] Ibid, Vol. VII, p. 317, VI, 9,4.
[76] Ibid, Vol. VII, p. 321, VI, 9,5.
[77] Ibid, Vol. VII, p. 311-313, VI, 9,3.

[78] Ibid, Vol. IV, p. 405-407, IV, 8, 3.
[79] Ibid, Vol. II, p. 229, II, 9,1.
[80] Ibid, Vol. V, p. 21-23, V, 1,4.
[81] Ibid, Vol. V, p. 23-25.
[82] Ibid, Vol. V, p. 59, V, 2, 1.
[83] Ibid, Vol. V, p. 179, V, 5, 8.
[84] Ibid, Vol. VII, p. 319, VI, 9, 5.
[85] Ibid, Vol. IV, p. 407, IV, 8,3.
[86] Ibid, Vol. IV, p. 405, IV, 8, 2.
[87] Ibid, Vol. VII, p. 319, VI, 9, 5.
[88] Ibid, Vol. VII, p. 229, VI, 8, 1.
[89] Ibid.
[90] Ibid.
[91] Ibid, Vol. VII, p.233, VI, 8, 2.
[92] Ibid, Vol. VII, p. 235, VI, 8, 3.
[93] Ibid, Vol. VII, pp.235-237, VI, 8, 3.
[94] Ibid, Vol. VII, pp. 237-239, VI, 8,4.
[95] Ibid, VI, p. 289, VI, 8, 18.
[96] Ibid. Vol. VII, p. 239.
[97] Ibid, Vol. VII, p.241-243, VI, 8, 5.
[98] Ibid, Vol. VII, p. 243-247, VI, 8, 6.
[99] Ibid, Vol. VII, p. 247, VI, 8, 7.
[100] Ibid, Vol. VII, p. 251, VI, 8, 8.
[101] Ibid, Vol. VII, p. 279, VI, 8, 15.
[102] Ibid, VI, p. 281.
[103] Ibid, VI, p. 283-285, VI, 8, 17.
[104] Osborn, E.F., *The Philosophy of Clement of Alexandria,* pp. 35-37, Cambridge University Press, 1957.

CHAPTER 5

[1] Aquinas, St. Thomas, *Summa Theologicae,* Vol. 5, p. 99, McGraw-Hill Publishing Co., 1970. Part 1a, Chapter 22, Article 3. Future references to this work will include the part, question, and article numbers.

[2] Aquinas, St. Thomas, *Summa Contra Gentiles, Book Three: Providence Part II*, pp. 53-57, University of Notre Dame Press, 1975. Chapter 94. Further references to this work will include the chapter number.

[3] Wolf, Dan, *A Handbook of Natural Rights*, pp. 1-23, Living Rightly Publications, 2018.

[4] Aquinas, St. Thomas, *Summa Theologicae,* Vol. 30, pp. 109-111, McGraw-Hill Publishing Co., 1970. 1a2ae, 110, 1.

[5] Ibid, Vol. 30, p. 145, 1a2ae, 112, 1.

[6] Ibid, Vol. 30, p. 77, 1a2ae, 109, 2.

[7] Ibid, Vol. 30, p. 149, 1a2ae, 112, 2.

[8] Ibid, Vol. 30, p. 153, 1a2ae, 112, 3.

[9] Ibid, Vol. 17, p. 125, 1a2ae, 13, 1.

[10] Ibid, Vol. 17, p. 131, 1a2ae, 13, 3.

[11] Ibid, Vol. 17, p. 135, 1a2ae, 13, 5.

[12] Ibid, Vol. 17, p. 139, 1a2ae, 13, 6.

[13] Ibid, Vol. 11, p. 239, 1a, 83, 1.

[14] Ibid, Vol. 13, p. 51, 1a, 93, 1.

[15] Ibid, Vol. 13, p. 55, 1a, 93, 2.

[16] Ibid, Vol. 13, pp. 59-61, 1a, 93, 4.

[17] Wolf, Dan, *A Handbook of Natural Rights*, Living Rightly Publications, 2018.

[18] Aquinas, St. Thomas, *Summa Theologicae,* Vol. 28, p. 17, McGraw-Hill Publishing Co., 1970. 1a2ae, 90, 4.

[19] Ibid, Vol. 28, pp. 19-21, 1a2ae, 91, 1.

[20] Ibid, Vol. 28, p. 59, 1a2ae, 93, 3.

[21] Ibid, Vol. 28, p. 149, 1a2ae, 97, 3.

[22] Ibid, Vol. 28, pp. 29-31, 1a2ae, 91, 4.

[23] Aquinas, St. Thomas, *Summa Contra Gentiles, Book Three: Providence Part II*, p. 124, University of Notre Dame Press, 1975. Chap. 115.

[24] Ibid, p. 125, Chap. 116.

[25] Ibid, p. 127, Chap. 117.

[26] Ibid, pp. 160-161, Chap. 128.

[27] Ibid, pp. 141-142, Chap. 121.

[28] Ibid, pp. 161-162, Chap. 128.

[29] Ibid, p. 162. Chap. 128.

[30] Aquinas, St. Thomas, *Summa Theologicae,* Vol. 29, p. 83, McGraw-Hill Publishing Co., 1970. 1a2ae, 100, 6.

[31] Ibid, p. 23, Vol. 30, 1a2ae, 107, 1.

[32] Ibid, Vol. 30, p. 25.
[33] Ibid, Vol. 30, pp. 43-45, 1a2ae, 108, 1.
[34] Ibid, Vol. 30, p. 45.
[35] Ibid, Vol. 28, p. 23, 1a2ae, 91, 2.
[36] Ibid, Vol. 28, p. 151, 1a2ae, 97, 3.
[37] Ibid, Vol. 29, p. 43, 1a2ae, 99, 4.
[38] Ibid, Vol. 29, p. 255, 1a2ae, 104, 1.
[39] Ibid, Vol. 29, p. 45, 1a2ae, 99, 4.
[40] Ibid, Vol. 28, p. 85, 1a2ae, 94, 3.
[41] Ibid, Vol. 28, p. 87, 1a2ae, 94, 4.
[42] Ibid, Vol. 28, p. 81, 1a2ae, 94, 2.
[43] Ibid, Vol. 28, pp. 89-91, 1a2ae, 94, 4.
[44] Ibid, Vol. 28, p. 95, 1a2ae, 94, 5.
[45] Ibid, Vol. 28, p. 93, 1a2ae, 94, 5.
[46] Ibid, Vol. 28, p. 97, 1a2ae, 94, 6.
[47] Ibid, Vol. 28, p. 109, 1a2ae, 95, 3.
[48] Ibid, Vol. 28, p. 125, 1a2ae, 96, 2.
[49] Ibid, Vol. 28, pp. 127-129, 1a2ae, 96, 3.
[50] Ibid, Vol. 28, pp. 115-117, 1a2ae, 95, 4.
[51] Ibid, Vol. 28, p. 131, 1a2ae, 96, 4.
[52] Ibid, Vol. 28, pp. 131.
[53] Ibid, Vol. 28, p. 131-133.
[54] Ibid, Vol. 28, p. 133-135, 1a2ae, 96, 5.
[55] Ibid, Vol. 28, pp. 105-107, 1a2ae, 95, 2.
[56] Ibid, Vol. 28, pp. 123-125, 1a2ae, 96, 2.
[57] Ibid, Vol. 28, p. 137, 1a2ae, 96, 5.
[58] Ibid, Vol. 28, p. 145, 1a2ae, 97, 1.
[59] Ibid.
[60] Ibid.
[61] Ibid.
[62] Ibid, Vol. 28, p. 147, 1a2ae, 97, 2.
[63] Ibid, Vol. 28, pp. 153-155, 1a2ae, 97, 4.
[64] Ibid, Vol. 14, pp. 5-7, 1a, 103, 1.
[65] Ibid, Vol. 14, p. 11, 1a, 103, 2.
[66] Ibid, Vol. 29, p. 299, 1a2ae, 105, 3.

[67] Ibid, Vol. 14, pp. 7-9, 1a, 103, 1.
[68] Ibid, Vol. 14, pp. 15-17, 1a, 103, 3.
[69] Ibid, Vol. 14, p. 19, 1a, 103, 4.
[70] Ibid, Vol. 14, p.21 , 1a, 103, 5.
[71] Ibid, Vol. 29, p. 63, 1a2ae, 100, 2.
[72] Ibid, Vol. 29, p. 75, 1a2ae, 100, 5.
[73] Ibid, Vol. 28, pp. 13-15, 1a2ae, 90, 3.
[74] Ibid, Vol. 29, p. 63, 1a2ae, 100, 2.
[75] Ibid, Vol. 28, pp. 115-117, 1a2ae, 95, 4.
[76] Ibid, Vol. 29, p. 269, 1a2ae, 105, 1.
[77] Ibid, Vol. 28, p. 151, 1a2ae, 97, 3.
[78] Ibid, Vol. 29, p. 279, 1a2ae, 105, 2.
[79] Ibid, Vol. 29, pp. 263-265, 1a2ae, 104, 4.
[80] Ibid, Vol. 29, pp. 261, 1a2ae, 104, 3.
[81] Ibid, Vol. 29, p. 103, 1a2ae, 95, 1.
[82] Ibid, Vol. 29, p. 75, 1a2ae, 100, 5.
[83] Ibid, Vol. 29, p. 273, 1a2ae, 105, 1.
[84] Ibid, Vol. 16, pp. 31-35, 1a2ae, 2, 1.
[85] Ibid, Vol. 16, pp. 35-37, 1a2ae, 2, 2.
[86] Ibid, Vol. 16, pp. 37-39, 1a2ae, 2, 3.
[87] Ibid, Vol. 16, pp. 39-43, 1a2ae, 2, 4.
[88] Ibid, Vol. 16, pp. 43-47, 1a2ae, 2, 5.
[89] Ibid, Vol. 16, pp. 47-51, 1a2ae, 2, 6.
[90] Ibid, Vol. 16, pp. 51-55, 1a2ae, 2, 7.
[91] Ibid, Vol. 16, pp. 55-57, 1a2ae, 2, 8.
[92] Ibid, Vol. 16, p.55.
[93] Ibid, Vol. 16, pp. 117-199, 1a2ae, 5, 1.
[94] Ibid, Vol. 16, p. 131, 1a2ae, 5, 5.
[95] Ibid, Vol. 16, pp. 131-133.
[96] Ibid, Vol. 26, p. 63, 1a2ae, 84, 1.
[97] Ibid, Vol. 26, p. 65, 1a2ae, 84, 2.
[98] Ibid, Vol. 37, p. 21, 2a2ae, 58, 1.
[99] Ibid, Vol. 26, pp. 81-83, 1a2ae, 85, 1.
[100] Ibid, Vol. 23, p. 141, 1a2ae, 62, 2.
[101] Ibid, Vol. 23, p. 41, 1a2ae, 57, 1.

[102] Ibid, Vol. 23, p. 67, 1a2ae, 58, 2.

[103] Wolf, Dan, *Collectivism and Charity*, pp. 11-5, Living Rightly Publications, 2016.

[104] Augustine, *Treatise on Grace and Free Will, Nicene and Post-Nicene Fathers*, p. 1239, Vol. V, Wm. B. Eerdmans Publishing Co., 1970. Ch. 13.

[105] Aquinas, St. Thomas, *Summa Theologicae*, Vol. 31, p. 165-7, McGraw-Hill Publishing Co. 1970. 2a2ae, 6, 1.

[106] Ibid, Vol. 31, p. 133, 2a2ae, 4, 5.

[107] Ibid, Vol. 31, p. 139, 2a2ae, 4, 7.

[108] Ibid, Vol. 33, p. 5, 2a2ae, 17, 1.

[109] Ibid, Vol. 34, p. 25, 2a2ae, 23, 6.

[110] Ibid, Vol. 31, p. 125, 2a2ae, 4, 3.

[111] Ibid, Vol. 34, p. 121, 2a2ae, 26, 1.

[112] Wolf, Dan, *A Handbook of Natural Rights*, pp. 111-8, Living Rightly Publications, 2018.

[113] Aquinas, St. Thomas, *Summa Theologicae*, Vol. 37, p. 5, McGraw-Hill Publishing Co. 1970. 2a2ae, 57, 1.

[114] Ibid, Vol. 37, p. 21, 2a2ae, 58, 1.

[115] Ibid.

[116] Ibid, Vol. 37, p. 29, 2a2ae, 58, 4.

[117] Ibid, Vol. 37, p. 5, 2a2ae, 57, 1.

[118] Ibid, Vol. 37, p. 9, 2a2ae, 57, 2.

[119] Ibid.

[120] Ibid, Vol. 37, pp. 9-11.

[121] Ibid, Vol. 37, p. 11.

[122] Ibid, Vol. 37, pp. 11-13, 2a2ae, 57, 3.

[123] Ibid, Vol. 37, pp. 35-37, 2a2ae, 58, 6.

[124] Ibid, Vol. 37, p. 41, 2a2ae, 58, 8.

[125] Ibid, Vol. 37, p. 69, 2a2ae, 60, 1.

[126] Ibid, Vol. 41, p. 49, 2a2ae, 104, 1.

[127] Ibid.

[128] Ibid, Vol. 41, p. 59, 2a2ae, 104, 3.

[129] Ibid, Vol. 41, pp. 63-65, 2a2ae, 104, 4.

[130] Ibid, Vol. 41, pp. 67-69, 2a2ae, 104, 5.

[131] Ibid, Vol. 41, p 71.

[132] Ibid, Vol. 41, p. 135, 2a2ae, 109, 1.

[133] Ibid, Vol. 41, p. 141, 2a2ae, 109, 3.
[134] Ibid, Vol. 41, pp. 141-143.
[135] Ibid, Vol. 38, p. 65, 2a2ae, 66, 1.
[136] Ibid.
[137] Ibid, Vol. 38, pp. 67-69, 2a2ae, 66, 2.
[138] Ibid, Vol. 38, p. 69.
[139] Ibid, Vol. 37, pp. 89-91, 2a2ae, 61, 1.
[140] Ibid, Vol. 38, p. 81, 2a2ae, 66, 7.
[141] Ibid, Vol. 38, p. 85, 2a2ae, 66, 8.
[142] Ibid, Vol. 37, p. 93, 2a2ae, 61, 2.
[143] Ibid, Vol. 38, p. 215, 2a2ae, 77, 1.
[144] Ibid, Vol. 38, p. 225, 2a2ae, 77, 3.
[145] Ibid, Vol. 38, pp. 227-229, 2a2ae, 77, 4.
[146] Ibid, Vol. 38, p. 79, 2a2ae, 66, 6.
[147] Ibid.
[148] Ibid, Vol. 38, p. 215, 2a2ae, 77, 1.
[149] Ibid, Vol. 38, p. 235, 2a2ae, 78, 1.
[150] Ibid.
[151] Ibid, Vol. 38, p. 243, 2a2ae, 78, 1.
[152] Ibid, Vol. 38, p. 245.
[153] Ibid.
[154] Ibid, Vol. 38, p. 251, 2a2ae, 78, 4.
[155] Ibid, Vol. 38, p. 237, 2a2ae, 78, 1.
[156] Ibid, Vol. 38, p. 217, 2a2ae, 77, 1.
[157] For more, see Wolf, Dan, *Collectivism and Charity*, pp. 11-7, Living Rightly Publications, 2016.

CHAPTER 6

[1] Schaefer, Francis A., *Escape from Reason*, p. 26, InterVarsity Press, 1968.
[2] Rev. Alexander Roberts and James Donaldson, *The Ante-Nicene Fathers, Fathers of the Second Century: Hermas, Tatian, Athenagora, Theophilus, and Clement of Alexandria (Entire)*, Vol. 2, p. 438, Wm. B Eerdmans Publishing Co., 1989. *Strom*, IV, XXV.
[3] Ibid, p. 1.
[4] Ibid, p. 1.

[5] Ibid, p. 2.

[6] Ibid, p. 2.

[7] Schaefer, Francis A., *Escape from Reason,* p. 34, InterVarsity Press, 1968.

[8] Wolf, Dan, pp. 122-3, *A Handbook of Natural Rights*, Living Rightly Publications, 2018.

[9] The biblical basis for these rights and duties is discussed in Wolf, Dan, *A Handbook of Natural Rights*, Living Rightly Publications, 2018.

[10] Wolf, Dan, *A War for God*, Living Rightly Publications, 2017.

www.ingramcontent.com/pod-product-compliance
Lightning Source LLC
Chambersburg PA
CBHW060822050426
42453CB00008B/542